Applying Lean in Health and Social Care Services

Improving Quality and the Patient Experience at NHS Highland

Applying Lean in Health and Social Care Services

Improving Quality and the Patient Experience at NHS Highland

By
Cameron Stark and Gavin Hookway

Routledge
Taylor & Francis Group

LONDON AND NEW YORK

Cover image: The County Community Hospital Invergordon.

First published 2019 by Routledge/Productivity Press

2 Park Square, Milton Park, Abingdon, Oxon OX14 4RN
605 Third Avenue, New York, NY 10017

Routledge is an imprint of the Taylor & Francis Group, an informa business

First issued in paperback 2021

Publisher's Note

The publisher has gone to great lengths to ensure the quality of this reprint
but points out that some imperfections in the original copies may be apparent.

ISBN-13: 978-0-367-00189-6 (hbk)
ISBN-13: 978-1-03-217841-7 (pbk)
DOI: 10.4324/9780429400865

Cameron Stark: Thanks to Marilyn, Katherine, Alasdair and Rhona for their support and patience. I hope you like the book.

Gavin Hookway: To Helen. Thank you for your love and support.

Contents

Foreword

Health and social care services have been tremendously successful. Public health approaches of immunisation, prevention, screening and early intervention, combined with better interventions have led to markedly improved health outcomes and to increased life expectancy. Public expectations are high: services have delivered enormous improvements in health and well-being, and people expect this to continue.

Pressures on services have changed. Increasing numbers of people with major health problems survive into adult life. Conditions that were often missed, such as some types of neurodevelopmental disorders in children, are identified more often, with significant increase in demand.

Treatments for many conditions, including cancer, have improved, resulting in people living with long-term conditions. Interventions become available for previously untreatable conditions, such as macular degeneration or dementia that, while not always curative, produce valuable benefits while incurring considerable costs and organisational pressures.

As people live longer, frail older people may need a great deal of support from multiple services. Gaps between services, and flow from one service to another, become very important, particularly when delays can leave people stranded in hospitals. Moreover, people often fall while in hospital, sometimes resulting in death. Services need to be person-centred and responsive but organised in such a way that they can act rapidly and effectively, at scale. Health and social care services are no longer a cottage industry, if they ever were such.

High-technology care produces its own risks and benefits. Treatment with some antibiotics increases the risks of other diseases. With restrictions on public finance, increasing numbers of people living into old age, new and expensive technologies, harm resulting from care and high public expectations of service quality, services are in the spotlight.

The traditional response to problems in quality is to spend more money. This often layers systems on systems, and sometimes teams upon teams, all trying to resolve an underlying problem. In the current cash-constrained environment and changing demographics, increased spending is often not an available option, and even if it was, it would be part of the solution rather than the whole answer.

Investing in quality is one response – perhaps the only acceptable response – to these challenges. Quality improvement can be regarded as the responsibility of clinical staff alone, or as a function of investment in services. To produce an organisation-wide approach to quality improvement, organisations have to decide that improvement is the responsibility of the whole organisation.

To prevent this meaning 'everyone's responsibility but no one's problem,' certain conditions are required:

- Commitment to quality from the organisation's Board members and Executive Team.
- Investment in training and supporting structures, including specialist staff who can mentor and support.
- Alignment of methods and approaches throughout the organisation to use information, to identify problems and to encourage structured problem-solving.
- A management system that helps to maintain standard work, promote improvement and support transformational change.

There are no miracles here. Change demands focus, consistency and commitment over time. Some of the ideas in quality improvement, particularly respecting and trusting front-line staff to make improvements in their own services, are at odds with ideas of command and control. Today's health and social care services are complex organisms, with functions often spread across multiple providers, and investing in staff and creating mechanisms to support improvement are preferable to the illusion of managerial control.

This does not mean that staff are unaccountable. In Lean systems, every employee has two tasks – to do their job and to improve their job by continuous improvement. Managers support this by creating the conditions for change and by working with staff to identify areas where larger, transformational, changes are required.

Our experience is that systems of stabilisation of processes, development of Standard Work, use of daily management methods and targeted larger scale improvement work can reap benefits even in times of financial constraint.

This handbook includes teaching that we find to be of value to our staff. It is based on the work of people who have forged ahead, in industry and in health and social care organisations. In care organisations, we have learnt from the Virginia Mason Institute, Thedacare, Intermountain, Tees, Esk and Wear Valley NHS Trust and many others. In recent years, people from other parts of the UK, and from outside the UK have visited us. These visitors from Europe, North America and South East Asia have all taught us more than they learnt from us, and we are grateful to them for their time and wisdom.

I hope this handbook will provide others with a chance to join us on our exciting quality improvement journey.

Professor Elaine Mead
Chief Executive, NHS Highland

Acknowledgements

Thanks to our coaches, including Diane Miller and Celeste Derheimer from the Virginia Mason Institute; Maureen Raine, Keith Appleby and Steven Bartley from Tees, Esk and Wear Valley NHS Foundation Trust. Iain Smith of NETS, and now at the Sustainable Improvement Team in NHS England, developed our understanding of the application of industrial processes in health and social care.

Within NHS Highland, Anne Gent, Linda Kirkland and Gill McVicar introduced the application of Lean methods and were responsible for the development of the required infrastructure. Dr Hugo van Woerden, Director of Public Health, was generous in allowing Cameron Stark time to collaborate in the development of teaching materials. Alex Medcalf provided meticulous proofreading and advice.

Elaine Mead, Chief Executive of NHS Highland, and Gary Coutts and David Alston, successive Chairs of NHS Highland Board, provided Board level support, and personal leadership.

In the wider NHS, Ruth Glassborow and Heather Shearer generously supported the development of materials and provided valuable links to other organisations. Lesley-Anne Smith had an important role in the introduction of Lean in NHS Highland and has provided advice and support in her later posts. Paul Arbuckle of NHS Tayside and Andy Crawford of NHS Greater Glasgow and Clyde are sources of unfailing advice and have been generous in sharing their expertise.

Externally, the podcasts and blog posts by Mark Graban and others played an important role in letting us understand what is possible.

Carrie Milligan of NHS Greater Glasgow and Clyde kindly allowed use of examples from her MSc dissertation, and Brian James of the University of Stirling permitted use of his PDSA cycle version.

Thanks to all staff at NHS Highland for their enthusiasm and interest. Many people led work described in this book, including Dr Adrian Baker, Dr Michelle Beattie, Suzy Calder, Murdina Campbell, Gill Cooksley, Kay Cordiner, Dr Paul Davidson, Yvonne Dent, Mr Jim Docherty, Colin Farman, Alison Finlay, Chrishan Folan, Mairi Fraser, Sarah Harwood, Jane Howe, Dr Jacqui Howes, Laurie Johnston, Lisa Kenley, Mr David Knight, Mandy Leslie, Emma Lowe, Rachel Mann, Sue Menzies, Charlie Mulraney, Jean McCulloch, Cora MacLeod, Christian Nicolson, Amy Noble, Neil Pellow, Mr Andrew Pyott, Jocelyn Reid, Kirstin Robertson, Neil Stewart, Shona Urquhart and Wendy van Riet.

Chapter 1

Introduction

The principles of QI can be taught and demonstrated, but typically the work of QI, if pursued at all, is simply layered onto the work of service delivery. For local health systems to be strengthened by QI, it must ultimately be built into existing policies and infrastructure; it must become part of the fabric of care itself, not separated as a "program".

Leatherman et al. (2010)

1.1 Introduction

Quality Improvement (QI) has its greatest impact when it is at the heart of an organisation's activity. Based on views from a consensus conference, Leatherman et al. (2010) identify characteristics that they regard as core to making QI work in practice:

- Systematic examination of processes used in service delivery, operations research, teamwork assessment and improvement
- Optimal use of measurement and statistics in daily work, benchmarking and participative management techniques
- Methods focused on patients and their families
- Enabling both front-line providers of care and organisations within which they work to learn continually and to change the processes of care delivery with the goal of improved health outcomes

This combination of purpose, information, focus on services to patients and their families, and active engagement of staff to make changes to the services in which they work are likely to have the greatest impact on quality (Mead et al. 2017).

This book sets Lean in the context of Health and Social Care services. Much of the material relates to health care, but the approach is equally as applicable to social care services, and examples are included of application in this setting.

1.2 Quality

Examples of quality definitions are shown in Table 1.1. The definitions shown generally agree on the service or product meeting a need and being manufactured or delivered in such a way as to contain no errors or deficiencies. This is very similar to the definition of 'Value' discussed in Chapter 2.

Definitions of quality in caring services build on these wider definitions (Table 1.2). The definitions have a lot in common. Most see quality as having

Table 1.1   Examples of General Definitions of Quality

Source	Definition
Juran (1988)	Quality is fitness for use.
Deming (1994)	A product or service possesses quality if it helps somebody and enjoys a good and sustainable market.
Juran and Godfrey (1999)	1. Quality means those features of products which meet customer needs and thereby provide customer satisfaction. 2. Quality means freedom from deficiencies – freedom from errors that require doing work over again (rework) or that results in field failures, customer dissatisfaction, customer claims and so on.
ISO 2005	(The) degree to which a set of inherent characteristics fulfils requirements.
American Society for Quality (undated)	A subjective term for which each person or sector has its own definition. In technical usage, quality can have two meanings: (1) the characteristics of a product or service that bear on its ability to satisfy stated or implied needs; (2) a product or service free of deficiencies. According to Joseph Juran, quality means 'fitness for use;' according to Philip Crosby, it means 'conformance to requirements.'

Table 1.2   Definitions of Quality in Health and Social Care

Source	Definition
Institute of Medicine 1990	The degree to which health care services for individuals and populations increase the likelihood of desired health outcomes and are consistent with current professional knowledge.
Institute of Medicine 2001	Quality care is safe, effective, patient-centred, timely, efficient and equitable.
US Agency for Healthcare Research and Quality (undated)	Doing the right thing, at the right time, in the right way, for the right person – and having the best possible results.
World Health Organisation (2006)	A health system should seek to make improvements in six areas or dimensions of quality, which are named and described subsequently. These dimensions require that health care be: effective … efficient …accessible … acceptable/ patient-centred …equitable (and) safe.
Department of Health (2008)	Care which is clinically effective, personal and safe.
Royal College of Nursing (2009)	Nursing has a major role to play in the quality of care experienced by patients and users. This includes the provision of person-centred care … Effective care (and) Systems of care.
Think Local Act Personal (undated)	The quality of services starts from what matters most to those people using them. A quality service also pays close attention to areas which may be invisible to users, such as medicines management or workforce development. Achieving quality should balance the three 'core components' • The individual experience of people receiving care and support and their personal expectations and outcomes. • Services which keep people safe through recognised standards, safeguards and the adoption of good practice. • The recognised processes that ensure the effectiveness of services including their value for money.

(Continued)

Table 1.2 (Continued) Definitions of Quality in Health and Social Care

Source	Definition
The Scottish Government (2010)	(The definition of quality is) based on the internationally recognised six dimensions of health care quality (Institute of Medicine): person-centred, safe, effective, efficient, equitable and timely. Three Quality Ambitions – Safe, Patient-Centred, Effective.
HM Government (2012)	A high-quality care and support service must consist of the following core components: safety, effectiveness and a positive experience of care.
National Quality Board (2013)	(There are) three dimensions of quality, all three of which must be present to provide a high-quality service. (These are) clinical effectiveness … safety … (and) patient experience.
Health Foundation (2013)	The Health Foundation regards quality as the degree of excellence in health care. This excellence is multidimensional. For example, it is widely accepted that health care should be safe, effective, person-centred, timely, efficient and equitable.

several dimensions. Some reflect Juran's quality trilogy of Quality Planning, Quality Control and Quality Improvement (Juran 1988), while the Institute of Medicine's 2001 definition influences most later descriptions. There is wide agreement that safety, effectiveness and patient-centred are core attributes of care quality, with others adding equity, efficiency and timeliness. The Royal College of Nursing paper (2009) is unusual in making specific reference to underlying systems that influence care.

Berwick and colleagues (1990) expand on the idea of the importance of processes in the influential text 'Curing Health Care,' commenting that 'productive work is accomplished through processes.' This idea, that improving outcomes requires the improvement of processes, is considered in more detail later in the handbook.

1.3 Quality in Health and Social Care

Disease and disability are understood better than ever before. Effective treatments are available for many conditions that were previously untreatable. Despite this, the pressures on services are larger than ever. In developed countries, this is partly because of advances in public health and overall affluence, which have combined to extend lives. People may now live long enough to develop diseases linked to lifestyle, or to become frail and often dependent on others. To this extent, increased service demand is a success story.

While demand has increased, and treatments and interventions have improved, the methods of delivery of care have not kept up. There are resource and capacity constraints that contribute to this, but even with greater investment in health and social care, there will be an upper limit to the level of investment with which any society is comfortable. No matter the level of income, it makes sense for any health and social care system to make the best possible use of its available resources by focusing on value, and by decreasing waste.

The three constants in the definitions of quality reviewed in Section 1.2 were effectiveness, safety and person-centred care. Several national surveys provide information on experience of services. Overall, people are usually positive about their care experience, but there are still significant challenges and some evidence of adverse trends.

1.3.1 *Primary Care*

The national Primary Care Survey (Scottish Government 2016a) found that 87% of people were positive about primary care. People particularly valued time spent with doctors and nurses, and rated many aspects of care from nurses and doctors in primary care very highly.

Some responses were less positive and some have worsened.

- In 2009/10 81% of people had positive views about 'arrangements for getting to see a doctor' in primary care in Scotland. This had decreased to 71% by 2015/16, part of a general downwards trend.
- 23% of people referred onwards reported arrangements for referral to other professionals as fair, poor or very poor.
- 7% of people believed that a mistake had been made in their treatment or care by the practice in the previous year, and of these, 54% were not satisfied in how the practice had then dealt with the mistake.

On outcomes, for people seeking help with pain or discomfort, 51% reported an improvement in their pain or discomfort following treatment.

1.3.2 Secondary Care

The corresponding inpatient experience survey (Scottish Government 2016b). Again, care was scored highly overall, with staff receiving highly positive ratings. Less positive issues raised were

- 27% did not know which nurse was in charge of their care.
- 40% reported being delayed on the day they left hospital, with medication delays accounting for 56% of these delays.
- 17% waited in hospital longer than expected for care to be organised.
- 20% reported experiencing harm or injury from their inpatient care.
- 8% of people reported a clinical error in their care – of these, 41% were not satisfied with how staff dealt with the error.

While overall scores are high, there is scope to improve services further.

1.4 Development of Quality Improvement in Health and Social Care

Definitions of QI in health and social care are shown in Table 1.3. Again, the precise words vary, but they generally describe a systematic approach to

Table 1.3 Definitions of Quality Improvement in Care Services

Source	Definition
Batalden and Davidoff (2007)	The combined and unceasing efforts of everyone – health care professionals, patients and their families, researchers, payers, planners and educators – to make the changes that will lead to better patient outcomes (health), better system performance (care) and better professional development.
Leatherman et al. (2010)	A philosophy (the pursuit of continuous performance improvement) and a family of discrete technical and managerial methods.
Health Foundation (2013)	A number of definitions describe it as a systematic approach that uses specific techniques to improve quality. One important ingredient in successful and sustained improvement is the way in which the change is introduced and implemented.

service improvement, using agreed methods which include attention to the maintenance of successful changes.

QI has a long history in health and social care. Sheingold and Hahn (2014) join others in identifying Florence Nightingale as an early proponent of QI in care settings. They note her focus on information, graphical representations of results and working to engage others in improvement efforts. Other pioneers include Semmelweiss, Osler and Codman (Merry and Crago 2001; Marjoua and Bozic 2012). More recently, the Health Foundation notes the work of Juran, Deming, Feigenbaum and Ishikawa as having a general influence on approaches to QI, with Berwick having an important influence on care services (Health Foundation 2013: pp 18–22).

While details of different systems vary, there are general principles that are present in most approaches to care quality. The Health Foundation, probably with an eye on system level change, summarises these as follows (2013: p 11):

∎ Understanding the problem, with a particular emphasis on what the data tell you
∎ Understanding the processes and systems within the organisation – particularly the patient pathway – and whether these can be simplified
∎ Analysing the demand, capacity and flow of the service
∎ Choosing the tools to bring about change, including leadership and clinical engagement, skills development, and staff and patient participation
∎ Evaluating and measuring the impact of a change

They also argue for paying attention to leadership for change; spread of innovation; improvement methodology; rigorous delivery; transparent measurement; system drivers and engagement to mobilise (Health Foundation 2013: p 12).

1.5 The Importance of Context

Peter H Rossi, an American sociologist and evaluator, described 'laws' based on his long experience of evaluation. The best known is his 'Iron Law' (Rossii 1987):

'The expected value of any net impact assessment of any social programme is zero. This means that our best a priori estimate of a net impact assessment of a program is that it will have no effect. It also means that the average of net impact assessments of a large set of social programs will crawl asymptomatically towards zero.'

Rossi accompanied this by other statements, including that the better the evaluation, the less the effect that will be found, and that more successful programmes are less likely to be evaluated in the first place. Rossi clarified his position in a later address (Rossi 2003) commenting that:

'I did not undertake anything that might be remotely called empirical research,' going on, 'there are quite a large number of well conducted impact assessments that yield statistically and substantively significant effect sizes.' 'I believe that we are learning how properly to design and implement interventions that are effective.'

This relates at least in part to debates on the design and purpose of programme evaluation (Rossi et al. 2004). Despite Rossi's later re-statement of his position, interesting insights have come from his work, or at least from interpretations of his original meaning. The commonest reflection is that programmes that work in a pilot, and even in some supported extension sites, often do not have the expected impact when extended to whole systems (Parry 2014).

There are several reasons why this can happen (Perla et al. 2015). These include lack of attention to context, and application of the outward appearance of the intervention without understanding the less visible elements of change that allowed the intervention to be effective. Mary Dixon-Woods described this as 'cargo-cult quality improvement' in a reference to mistaking the appearance of an intervention for its active ingredients (Dixon-Woods et al. 2011).

Perla et al. (2015) suggest that organisations should,

'Encourage a pragmatic approach to model expansion that starts with a focus on the concepts and theories underpinning the innovative model. The aim should be to provide methods and tools for people to assess whether or not the model can be adapted to their setting — including the detailed tasks and pre-conditions required to do this locally.'

Powell et al. (2009: p 7) came to very similar conclusions, commenting, 'the success or otherwise of implementation depends crucially on the interaction between the local context and the approach as it is applied.'

The relevance to Lean is that conveying ideas and giving people the ability to adapt methods to their own settings, is likely to be more effective than requiring people to blindly follow strict rules. This does not remove accountability, but it does increase ownership.

1.6 Effectiveness of Quality Improvement in Organisations

The Health Foundation report that only around two-thirds of health care improvements 'go on to result in sustainable change that achieves the planned objective' (Health Foundation 2013: p 12).

Powell et al. (2009), from the Universities of Dundee and St Andrews, undertook a review for NHS Quality Improvement Scotland. They argue that, because organisational context, method of implementation and the QI methods used interact, traditional Randomised Controlled Trials are not a practical, or even appropriate, design for evaluation. They comment that, 'quality improvement initiatives or programmes like Total Quality Management (TQM) or rapid cycle change are best understood as complex interventions that are introduced into complex and diverse 'social worlds' (Powell et al. 2009: p 18).

After reviewing a range of QI methods transferred from industry to health and social care, Powell et al. (2009: p 71) concluded:

'What is clear from this review and from the broader literature on organisational change is that there is no one "right" quality improvement method. Instead, successful implementation may be more about the interaction between any given programme and its implementation in the local context.'

Powell et al. (2009) also suggested that there are 'core conditions' that have to be met for the successful application of QI. They were speaking in the context of health care, but their messages are likely to be applicable to both health and social care (Powell et al. 2009: p 70):

- Apply methods consistently over a sufficiently long timescale with demonstrated, sustained organisational commitment and support.
- Involve doctors and other health professionals in a wide team effort while providing adequate training and development.
- Seek active involvement of middle and senior managers, the board (including nonexecutive directors) and, most obviously and visibly, the Chief Executive.
- Integrate quality improvement into the organisation's other activities (so that it is part of the organisation's strategic plans and priorities, targets etc.).
- Tailor the selected methods to local circumstances
- Create robust IT systems that enable the measurement of processes and impacts, iteratively refining the approaches used.
- Acknowledge – and ameliorate as far as possible – the impact of competing activities/changes.

NHS Highland has sought to follow these recommendations as far as possible.

1.7 Applying a Method

As Powell et al. observe, the NHS is a complex system, with existing initiatives and approaches. The NHS already uses audit (Stark 2017), and Clinical Networks and Collaborative Improvement Programmes (Institute for Healthcare Improvement 2003; Nadeem et al. 2013). The Scottish Patient Safety Programme, based on the methods of the Institute of Healthcare Improvement, is very well known, and has been successful (Healthcare Improvement Scotland 2016).

NHS Scotland identifies key aspects of improvement work as (NHS Scotland 2017):

1. Identify and Diagnose
2. Improve
3. Evaluate

They set this in the wider context of human factors, safety management, change management and leadership, and emphasise the role of Juran's Quality Trilogy, described previously.

The NHS Scotland 2020 document (NHS Scotland 2017: p 33) notes:

> The focus in Lean on establishing what value means to those who we provide services to brings an excellent focus to our aim to be person-centred and collaborative in our redesign and improvement work. These approaches are also gaining ground across the wider public sector with many organisations keen to apply systems thinking supported by some key tools to focus their improvement efforts.

Lean is a quality management system with a long track record in industry (Shah and Ward 2003; Bhamu and Sangwan 2014). Originally developed in Japan (Hines et al. 2018), based on earlier international methods with links to Deming and Juran, the approach was popularised in Western countries.

Lean focuses on value to users of the service and seeks to maximise value and reduce waste. Table 1.4 shows aspects of Lean commonly mentioned in the published literature in health and social care. These are discussed in detail later in the volume.

Table 1.4   Lean Components and Characteristics

Components of Lean	*Sources*
Aims	
Focus on value to service users	Young et al. (2004), Jimmerson et al. (2005), Kim et al. (2006), Joosten et al. (2009), Poksinska (2010), Hawthorne and Masterson (2013)and Toussaint and Berry (2013)
Aim to remove 'waste'	Young et al. (2004), Kim et al. (2006), Joosten et al. (2009), Poksinska (2010) and Dahlgaard et al. (2011)
Approach	
Respect for staff	Jimmerson et al. (2005), Kim et al. (2006), Toussaint and Berry (2013) and Hawthorne and Masterson (2013)
Critical of processes, rather than people	Hawthorne and Masterson (2013)
Improvements led by the people who deliver the service	Jimmerson et al. (2005), Dahlgaard et al. (2011) and Hawthorne and Masterson (2013)
Supports continuous improvement	Jimmerson et al. (2005), Hawthorne and Masterson (2013)
Incorporates a management system	Mazzocato et al. (2010) and Dahlgaard et al. (2011)
Methods	
Processes directly observed	Kim et al. (2006)
Root cause analysis	Poksinska (2010), Dahlgaard et al. (2011)
Use of value stream maps to visualise problems	Jimmerson et al. (2005), Kim et al. (2006), Joosten et al. (2009), Poksinska (2010), Toussaint and Berry (2013) and Hawthorne and Masterson (2013)
Improvement of flow	Young et al. (2004), Jimmerson et al. (2005), Kim et al. (2006), Joosten et al. (2009), Mazzocato et al. (2010) and Poksinska (2010)
Use of improvement (PDSA) cycles	Jimmerson et al. (2005), Kim et al. (2006) and Poksinska (2010)
Improvement 'events' used when required	Kim et al. (2006) and Toussaint and Berry (2013)
Development of 'Standard' processes	Mazzocato et al. (2010) and Dahlgaard et al. (2011)

(Continued)

Table 1.4 (Continued)   Lean Components and Characteristics

Components of Lean	Sources
5S	Joosten et al. (2009), Mazzocato et al. (2010), and Poksinska (2010)
Error proofing	Mazzocato et al. (2010) and Poksinska (2010)
Visual controls	Mazzocato et al. (2010), Mazzocato et al. (2010) and Toussaint and Berry (2013)
Kanban	Joosten et al. (2009)

In relation to hospitals, Dahlgaard et al. (2011: p 677) summarise the use of Lean as:

> Lean health care is a management philosophy to develop a hospital culture characterised by increased patient and other stakeholder satisfaction through continuous improvements, in which all employees (managers, physicians, nurses, laboratory people, technicians, office people etc.) actively participate in identifying and reducing non-value-adding activities (waste).

Joosten et al. (2009: p 343) offer a more technical definition:

> An integrated operational and sociotechnical approach of a value system, whose main objectives are to maximize value and thus eliminate waste, by creating cumulative capabilities.

Toussaint and Berry (2015: p 75) offer the definition:

> An organization's cultural commitment to applying the scientific method to designing, performing, and continuously improving the work delivered by teams of people, leading to measurably better value for patients and other stakeholders.

1.8 Challenges in Applying Lean in Health and Social Care

While several organisations have reported success with the use of Lean in health care (Mannon 2014; D'Andreamatteo et al. 2015; Leggat et al. 2015;

Ronge 2015; Kovacevic et al. 2016; Costa et al. 2017), there are also numerous challenges reported in its application (Moraros et al. 2016; Lindsay 2016). Table 1.5 summarises some of the commonly reported issues in health care.

These relate to many of the points made by Powell et al. (2009) in their recommendations for successful change programmes at scale. Most are not

Table 1.5　Challenges in Implementing Lean in Health Care

Challenges	Sources
Strategy and Management	
Consistency of management and leadership	Furman and Caplan (2007) and Dickson et al. (2009)
Lack of strategic perspective	Hines et al. (2004) and Ballé and Régnier (2007)
Accountability routes	Leggat et al. (2015)
Clear statements of staff and management roles	Leggat et al. (2015) and Costa et al. (2017)
Competing professional interests	Lindsay (2016)
Lack of attention to equity of access	Radnor and Osborne (2011)
Introduction and Training	
Education	Poksinska (2010) and Leggat et al. (2015)
Methods to support active staff participation	Poksinska (2010), D'Andreamatteo et al. (2015), Leggat et al. (2015) and Lindsay (2016)
Over-reliance on specialist improvement staff	Radnor (2011) and Lindsay (2016)
Reliance on external support	Radnor et al. (2006) and Costa et al. (2017)
Sustainability	Burgess and Radnor (2013), D'Andreamatteo et al. (2015) and Lindsay (2016)
Technical Aspects	
Application of a narrow range of Lean tools	Joosten et al. (2009) and Lindsay (2016)
Variation in Lean technical skills	Herron and Hicks (2008) and Lindsay (2016)
Inadequate attention to core principles	Dahlgaard et al. (2011) and McCann et al. (2015)
Lean approaches applied mechanistically with limited attention to human factors	Hines et al. (2004)

unique to Lean implementations, but all need to be addressed to maintain staff confidence, and to increase the likelihood of success. Linday (2016: p 226) recommends:

> A clearly mapped process articulating intentions, approach and expected outcomes which is applied by those responsible for Lean improvement, (that) provides consistency of approach in the implementation of Lean.

1.9 Conclusions

This handbook provides information on Lean methods, but the wider organisational aspects of Lean, and of QI in general, are also important.

Toussaint and Berry (2015: p 76) state:

> Lean is not a program; it is not a set of quality improvement tools; it is not a quick fix; it is not a responsibility that can be delegated. Rather, Lean is a cultural transformation that changes how an organization works; no one stays on the sidelines in the quest to discover how to improve the daily work. It requires new habits, new skills, and often a new attitude throughout the organization from senior management to front-line service providers. Lean is a journey, not a destination.

This volume deals with the methods and management system involved in Lean. It describes their application in health and social care and gives examples of use in practice. As with all methods of QI, applying the techniques in local settings provides the greatest learning. Use of the approach with a team, and reflection on success using improvement cycles, increases learning and allows rapid progress.

Chapter 2

Value and Waste

Search for the waste that usually escapes notice because it has
become accepted as a natural part of everyday work.

Shigeo Shingo (2005: p 76)

2.1 Aims of the Chapter

The aims of the chapter are

1. To be able to define value and waste
2. To know the types of waste and be able to describe them
3. To understand approaches to identifying waste

2.2 Examples of Value and Waste

Examples given in this book are sometimes composite examples, taken from
a variety of teams, hospitals, settings and organisations.

- A community service coordinator was told to return referrals if they
  were not sent electronically. When the referrals arrived as e-mail attach-
  ments, the coordinator printed them out, typed their content in to
  a database, and put them in a folder. They then sent an e-mail to a
  person in a coordinating centre. This second person printed out the

referral, typed them in to a second database, and then stored them in a folder in their office. An audit found that, in just over one record in ten, at least one mistake had been made when the data was re-entered.

■ A doctor discovered that an urgent blood sample, which needed to be analysed quickly after it had been taken, had been put in the wrong sample tube. The patient lived in a distant location and had returned home. The doctor spent their lunch hour arranging to have a second blood sample taken locally and brought to the hospital for analysis by special transport. This was the third time in a year that the doctor knew of this mistake being made.

■ Nurses in a busy ward spent considerable time looking for the colleague who had the keys to the drug trolley, leaving the patient they were with to go to look for the keys, and so be able to administer the required treatment.

The staff in these examples were busy and often harassed. They worked hard to follow the procedures as they understood them and to overcome problems when they occurred, in order to do their best for patients. All of these examples include waste, however, and concepts of value and waste are discussed in the next section.

2.3 Value Definition

In Lean, value is defined from the perspective of the customer or patient (Eaton 2013). Activities that add value are activities that get a customer or patient closer to their goal. This will usually involve goals such as receiving a diagnosis, having treatment to cure or ameliorate their condition, having pain or discomfort alleviated, receiving social support, advice to prevent a problem recurring and so on.

To add value, an action must

■ Meet the needs of a patient or service user
■ Be done correctly the first time
■ Change the product or service in some way

Meet a patient or service user need: It is easy to assume that most actions by health and social care staff benefit patients or service users. Mark Graban notes that we 'need to learn to separate motion (the things we do) from value (the things that help the patient)' (Graban 2012: p 31; see also Shingo 2005: p 67; Hirano and Furuya 2006: pp 48–9).

For an action to be of value, it must meet a patient or service user need or contribute to meeting a need. If the service is for an internal customer, rather than directly for a patient or service user, such as a housekeeping service or other support service, then the actions should still, in some way, contribute to meeting client needs. In some instances, such as child protection procedures or support for people with a mental illness that affects their insight, the need may not always be immediately apparent to the person using the service, but the value to the user should still be identifiable.

Be done correctly the first time: No one is satisfied if errors have to be corrected. If the action results in a defect, then it cannot be of value. The subsequent actions to correct the defect are required to fix the problem, but they should not have been needed, and therefore duplicate effort (Ohno 1988).

Change the product or service in some way: If a referral, an invoice or a patient or service user is simply passed from one place to another or one queue to another with no intervention, then there is no added value from the activity. It may be currently required because of the system being used, but there is no added value to the patient or service user (Shingo 2005: p 76).

2.4 Waste Definition

Non-value added activities, or waste, are defined as activities that do not add value to the patient, customer or service user (Shingo 2005). These activities use time or resources.

There are two main divisions of waste – absolute waste that is of no value at all, and non-value added activities that are currently required because of the existing system (known as 'Necessary Non-Value Added Activities' – NNVA). The intention of Lean is to eliminate absolute waste and to reduce other non-value added activities as far as possible (Ohno 1988: pp 57–9).

Accepting that a Necessary Non-Value Added activity is currently required because of the process should not be an end to the matter – the service should review this type of waste periodically and decide if there is any action that can be taken to reduce or eliminate it.

It can be useful to distinguish between waste that happens the first time a process is undertaken and waste that is a result of an earlier failure, often termed 're-work.' This relates to John Bicheno's distinction between Value

Demand – first time demand – and Failure Demand – demand that results from an earlier failure in the process (Bicheno 2008).

For example, work rescheduling appointments because a clinic is cancelled is necessary, but it is waste because the appointments have already been made once. Decreasing the time to make these revised appointments will save time, but the greatest saving is by working out ways of preventing the clinic being cancelled in the first place.

2.4.1 Jargon Buster: Waste

In books and articles on Lean, the Japanese term *muda* is often used for waste. This is sometimes expanded to use *muri* for waste from overwork or overburdening of people or equipment, and *mura* for waste related to variations in processes or workloads (Eaton 2013).

Other authors talk about Type I and Type II waste. Type I waste is Necessary Non-Value Added Activities, and Type II waste is absolute waste.

2.5 Types of Waste

There are seven types of waste (Figure 2.1) (Ohno 1988, Japanese Management Association 1989):

- Waiting
- Over-processing
- Defects
- Transportation
- Motion
- Overproduction
- Inventory

Many other types of waste have been identified, and they may be important in specific settings or areas of work:

- Producing goods or services that do not meet the needs of users (Womack and Jones 2003)
- Untapped human potential (Bicheno 2008; Graban and Swartz 2012) – for example, not making use of improvement ideas from staff because of their grade
- Wasted energy, water and natural resources (Bicheno 2008)

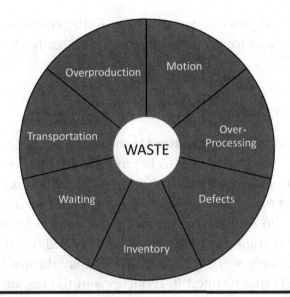

Figure 2.1 Waste wheel.

2.5.1 *Waiting*

Waiting is often the most readily identifiable waste, when people, information, equipment or supplies are not ready for the next stage of a process. Service users and patients wait for referrals to be processed, wait for appointments to be allocated, wait at clinics or offices to be seen, wait for test results, wait for discharge arrangements, wait for medications and so on.

Health and social care staff wait for patients, laboratory results, assessments or the correct materials to arrive. They may wait for colleagues to arrive to begin to see patients or for managers to make a decision on a prioritisation request. This lost time is never recovered.

For an individual who is using the service, most of their time in a service is usually spent waiting for something to happen. When the whole time that a person is in contact with a service is considered, the 'value added' time is often well under 1%. For example, if a person is referred for an outpatient appointment and waits 12 weeks for a half hour appointment, then even including administrative time, they are likely to have no more than 45 minutes of value in a 12 week period, which is less than 0.04% of the total time elapsed from the time of referral.

A useful distinction in thinking of waits is to distinguish between delays in the process and delays related to batches (Shingo 1986). Process delays occur in the course of an activity. Batch delays occur when items, or patients, are waiting for an entire batch to be completed before they are moved to the next process. For example, in the course of a discharge, an ambulance may wait for a second person to be ready, delaying the first individual.

2.5.1.1 Waiting Examples

■ A surgical team waited in theatre for the next patient to arrive for 48 minutes after they were ready to begin. Theatre time costs around £21 a minute (2010 UK costs, CIPFA 2010), so this represented over £800 of lost time. In total, the surgical team spent over 80 minutes waiting in one theatre, in one morning, at a cost of around £1600. Meanwhile, patients were being scheduled for surgery on additional weekend sessions because there were no available weekday theatre slots, resulting in additional costs that resulted in reductions in the resources available for other services. The service developed a visual control system (Chapter 8 – Visual Control) that made it easier for wards to know when people were to be transferred, and markedly reduced delays between patients.

■ Patients attended an outpatient clinic at which they usually saw several different staff members, who all undertook relevant procedures. Many of the patients were elderly and frail. The average time spent at the clinic was 103 minutes. Of this time, on average, 38 minutes was spent with staff – the other 65 minutes (63% of the time) was spent waiting to be seen by one person or another. By developing Standard Work (Chapter 9 – Standard Work), making sure a number of staff could undertake each process, and changing appointment times to make the flow through the clinic more even, the staff reduced waits by 43%.

■ Service users were assessed by social care staff. If care packages over a specified weekly cost were required, an area panel considered them and allocated the funds. In over 40%, further information was requested, resulting in delays of up to three weeks. Very few requests were refused once all the information was gathered. The service clarified what information was needed in Standard Work and provided training on this The service also delegated the level of decision-making authority for most packages. This reduced the number reviewed at area level, and in those that were still considered, reduced the proportion in which the decision had to be deferred.

■ Community Occupational Therapists (OTs) visited clients at home to teach them how to use pieces of equipment, such as a bath board. The OTs took the equipment with them for the demonstration. After showing the person how to use the equipment, the OT returned the equipment to their team base. A piece of equipment for the person was delivered to their home three or four days later. The service resolved the problem by improving the stock system, and taking the specific item for the client out to be demonstrated and then left with the client, avoiding a second journey. This also allowed the client to practice the skills they had been taught immediately.

2.5.2 Over-Processing

Over-processing refers to unnecessary steps that add no value from the patient or service user's perspective. This can include

- Asking a person to give the same information several times
- Collecting information on forms that is not then used
- Entry of the same data into different information systems
- Continuing to produce multiple drafts of a document when the content is already acceptable

2.5.2.1 Over-Processing Examples

- Forms: The administrator who received a referral for a community social care service carefully entered over 30 pieces of information into a spreadsheet. Only twelve of the information items were ever used by the service. The staff reviewed the process, and removed the unused items. In the longer term, they planned to integrate the referral with another information system, avoiding the need to enter much of the information at all.
- Duplicate Data Entry: Referrals for a community nursing service were logged on a database that was used to manage the allocation of staff to perform an assessment. If a referral to the Occupational Therapy (OT) service was then required, a new form was completed electronically which was then sent to the second service, who entered the person's information on to a second database. The same information on name, address, date of birth, general practitioner and so on. had been entered by the original referrer, the administrator of the community nursing service, and finally by the OT service administrator. There was no added value to the service user, but the services did this because they could not share information electronically.

■ Computer Recording: A group of obstetric ultrasound machines had internal computer memory, and stored 'clips' of scans. These were planned to upload to a server each day. The link between the individual machines and the server did not work, and the reason could not be identified, despite involvement of the manufacturers of both the ultrasound machines, and the server. As the ultrasound machines had a limited internal memory, each week a staff member had to go to each machine and copy that week's scans on to a DVD, and file the DVDs in case the scans needed later review.

2.5.2.2 Over-Processing: History Note

In industrial literature, processing waste was often used to refer to waste in the processing work itself, such as a malfunctioning machine (Japan Management Association 1989: pp 19–20). Suzaki (1987: pp 15–16) extended this meaning to workarounds to overcome processing problems. In other settings, the meaning has gradually altered to refer to excess processing, rather than problems with processing itself.

2.5.3 Defects

Defects include both work that contains errors, and the effort of 'rework' – of correcting the errors, or undertaking further work that is then required because of the consequences of an error. This also includes work where something necessary is omitted – for example, a blood test that is omitted, with the consequence that the patient then has to return for that test. A defect can also disrupt the flow of a process, because staff have to take time to correct the error, which then results in delays for other patients.

Examples include medication errors, wrong patient or wrong procedure errors and rescheduling of procedures or appointments.

2.5.3.1 Defects Examples

Administration: Community staff completed a form to request equipment for people's homes. Boxes were in free text, and different staff members used different names for the same item of equipment. When stores staff checked the names against the stock list, they often believed the item was not in stock, because it had a different catalogue description, and returned the request. Changing the form to have a forced choice for equipment problems, prevented the defect (Chapter 7 – Error Proofing).

System Connections: A service sent outpatient appointments by mail. When the person received their appointment, if they needed patient transport, they called the ambulance service to book an appointment. In some cases, no ambulance was then available, and the appointment had to be cancelled. The service resolved the problem by asking if patient transport was required, and if it was, booking the transport at the same time as the appointment was made.

Treatment: An outpatient service had very busy clinics. Patients often waited for some time. As it was difficult to find a chair, patients sat in any available part of the waiting area. Many of the patients were elderly and some had poor sight and hearing. A nurse called for a patient to come for a procedure. A person responded from the other side of the waiting room and was taken in for the treatment after again appearing to confirm their name. It was the wrong person. The person had no adverse effects, but the incident caused the clinic to review its processes. They improved flow by identifying specific seating areas in the clinic for different procedures, rearranging appointment times to produce less people waiting at any one time, and reinforced the process for identification of identity.

2.5.4 Transportation

Transportation waste is the movement of materials or equipment – of forms, records, supplies, blood samples and so on – that does not add value (Suzaki 1987). It can also be used for the electronic transfer of information, if relevant.

Improvements in transportation are often considered to be more rapid ways of moving materials or equipment to allow more material to be moved at once. Using Lean principles, it is first necessary to decide whether the transportation is necessary at all. Shingo (1988: p 29) comments, 'improving transport means reducing or even eliminating it.'

In some cases, some transportation is needed, but it is still possible to reduce it. For example, stock may be transferred from a central store to a ward store, and then to a bedside or bed bay store. It may be possible to move stock directly to a bedside store, and so free up the space used for a ward store.

2.5.4.1 Transportation Examples

Stock: A care home needed weekly stock deliveries. A delivery lorry passed the driveway of the care home each day, moving stock between sites. As the driveway of the care home had difficult access, stock for the care home was delivered to a depot 40 miles away, and it was then transported back to the care home by van, adding a further 80 miles to the journey for the supplies. Using smaller vehicles with a more frequent delivery schedule avoided the additional mileage.

Prescriptions: Patients attended a clinic where blood was taken, the results reviewed and, if necessary, a treatment was prescribed to be administered that day. When the doctor decided that a treatment was needed, the staff e-mailed a notification to the hospital pharmacy. The patient was also asked to carry a note of the prescription to the pharmacy, in case other systems failed. This was also an example of motion waste for the patient. The service introduced an electronic alert system with online tracking and confirmation which removed the waste.

Case Notes: A service needed to consult case notes before beginning treatments. It was common for the case notes to be out of storage, with no tracer card completed. Often these notes were eventually located in a doctor's office, waiting for dictation to be completed. The notes would have to be located, moved to the required location and then returned to the pile in the doctor's office to await completion of a letter. Improving flow at the clinic and introducing an electronic dictation and checking system reduced the need for doctors to have notes in their room.

Referrals: A hospital service received referrals from community services. They stored the referrals each day, and then transported them to a ward where they were reviewed overnight by ward nurses, to ensure that the referrals were in keeping with referral policies. An audit of actions found that, in a three-week period, no referrals were reclassified. This was both an example of transportation and over-processing. This step was removed altogether, with no adverse effects.

2.5.5 Motion

Motion is the unnecessary or excessive movement of human beings (Eaton 2013). Motion waste can result from supplies or equipment not being organised well, and this is one of the challenges that 5S can help to tackle. Unnecessary motion can also result from delays in flow. If staff have an interruption to their schedule, for example because the next patient is not ready, then they will often move off to find something to do. This is more difficult to spot, as staff are doing something –but not the activity they intended to be doing at that time. This can make disruptions to flow more difficult to identify.

Reducing unnecessary motion is worthwhile, but it is important to think through unintended consequences of decreasing motion. For example, reducing motion by batching items will often not be a useful trade off.

2.5.5.1 Motion Examples

■ A cardiac catheter laboratory was added to an existing hospital. The journey from the Accident and Emergency Department to the catheter laboratory was around 200 metres of corridors. This journey added no value to the patient – it was the treatment in the Cath lab that added value – but the journey was unavoidable because of the layout of the hospital.
■ A new high volume photocopier was situated in a different corridor from a community service, so that it could be used by several groups. The copier was 165 feet from the administrator's work area. In the course of a day, he had to make seven trips to the copier. This amounted to 2,310 feet a day, which equates to over 600,000 feet (113 miles) in a 52-week year. Apart from the fitness of the administrator, there was no added value to this travel. The service decided to use smaller multi-purpose scanning and printing devices in more locations. The location of these devices was designed to minimise motion, and so reduce delays.

2.5.6 Overproduction

Overproduction is producing more than is needed, or faster than is needed. Overproduction causes difficulties because it can, in turn, cause other types of waste, and because it can conceal problems elsewhere in the system. Taiichi Ohno, one of the originators of the Lean system, commented:

> Overproduction creates a countless number of wastes, such as over-staffing, pre-emptive use of materials and energy costs, advance payment to workers, interest charges on mechanical devices and products, storage areas needed to accommodate the excess products and the cost of transporting them.

> **(Japan Management Association 1989: p 20)**

Overproduction can produce a buffer of stock, which is then used when there are problems elsewhere in the system. This makes pragmatic sense, but has the disadvantage that it can then conceal the other system problem, which means that the underlying problem may not be identified and resolved (Suzaki 1987; Ohno 1988).

Shingo (2005) distinguishes between two types of overproduction:

1. Producing more than is needed
2. Producing earlier than is needed

Overproduction can also be a response to producing items with defects (Shingo 2005). If the service knows that some items will have problems – for example, sterile theatre sets with missing or incorrect items – then it may produce extra to allow for replacements for incorrect sets. Hirano (1988: p 24) describes these as 'surface improvements': the service or unit seems to be working on improvement, but it is not tackling the underlying problems. The better response is to resolve the problems that cause the errors in the first place.

If items are produced more quickly than needed, then this produces a 'push' system, and is liable to result in delays later in the process. They also require storage, inventory systems and maintenance. Waste which results from another waste is sometimes termed 'secondary waste' (Ohno 1988).

2.5.6.1 Overproduction Examples

■ Medical physicists routinely maintain machines used for treatment. Each radiotherapy machine needs careful weekly calibration and is on a replacement schedule. During an improvement event, staff in a radiotherapy department realised that two machines were very rarely used, because newer equipment had been purchased. One machine was never used, and the other was uncommonly used. Each machine took over 50 hours of medical physicist time per year to maintain. The machines were still maintained and had remained on the replacement schedule. One was sold, and the other moved to a schedule linked to use. A specialist concrete-lined room was also freed to be reused.
■ An integrated community service had an average of 80 new clients a month. They kept a stock of 400 blank case notes, made up and ready to use, the equivalent of five-months' average activity. A storage rack covering an entire wall was used to store these blank case notes.

Working out the takt time (see Chapter 5 - Continuous Flow) allowed the service to understand the demand for the service and adjust their stock accordingly.

■ When patients were being readied for surgery, the assessing nurses routinely requested a particular investigation as part of the suite of blood tests. The test was part of a standard list of investigations, provided to the team some years previously. If these results came back as outside the usual range, the person was referred to an anaesthetist. This result was not relevant to the anaesthetist as it did not affect their decision on an anaesthetic, or affect their intra-operative management. If this was the only abnormality, the anaesthetists invariably went ahead with the anaesthetic. After discussion between nursing and medical staff, the test was removed from the standard suite of tests.

■ Patients were moved between wards as 'boarders' or 'off service patients',' to allow new admissions to a particular ward. It was common for meals to be taken to the ward for patients who had now moved. Altering times of moves between wards allowed information to be more easily conveyed, and so avoid meals being transported to the wrong ward.

2.5.7 *Inventory*

Having more stock than is needed results in additional costs and storage space, and it can conceal problems in systems. Equally, not having equipment or supplies available when needed results in delays for patients and staff, and it may require wasted motion as staff have to go to look for the required materials. As Graban and Swartz point out (2012: p 300), 'the key is to have the right amount of inventory, not just the lowest levels possible.'

2.5.7.1 *Inventory Examples*

■ A community service had cupboards filled with information leaflets and forms. When the team looked at the material, they discovered forms relating to previous versions of relevant legal requirements, and outdated information leaflets with now incorrect information on benefits and services. The service applied 5S (see Chapter 3 – 5S) and consulted patients on what information was needed, and the best format in which to provide them, and reduced stock accordingly, combined with a kanban system (Chapter 8 – Visual Control). This reduced both stock, and times when no stock was available.

■ A room visited in the course of improvement work was crammed with stock. When asked about the room, the staff explained that it was a treatment room, A staff member explained that it was necessary to keep at least a week's supply. When asked if this was a week's supply, they looked surprised and replied 'no, it's much more than that.' Despite this, there were no minimum levels set for requirements, and some items ran out regularly. The staff applied 5S and Visual Control. Both safety and staff morale improved.

■ An estates department wanted to work on their stores. When they sorted out their materials, they discovered that they had six staff but nine identical spades. Some stock was re-cycled to other areas.

■ A mental health service used blood specimen tubes, but in small quantities. The ordering system required them to order in quantities designed for general hospital wards. Tubes regularly went out of date and had to be returned to be destroyed. Discussion with procurement colleagues revealed that the procurement staff had not known about the problem. They altered their systems to supply smaller quantities to low use wards, resolving the problem.

2.5.8 Practice Tip

Groups may want to spend time discussing exactly what type of waste they have identified. Some wastes can be classified in one of several groups, and the distinction is often unimportant. Lean Leaders sometimes have to move the group on to action. If there is general agreement that something is waste, it does not matter in what category it is recorded: the important thing is to move on to try to eliminate or reduce the identified waste.

2.6 Working with Teams

When introducing the idea of waste to a new team, it can be useful to suggest that they use a waste observation form. In groups from multiple settings, they may wish to pair up and visit one another's work area. It can be instructive to see a work area through another person's eyes.

When working with a wider team, a Waste Wheel mounted on a wall is a good way of encouraging visibility and sharing (Figure 2.2). Waste Wheels can be drawn on a flip-chart or be a laminated, reusable version. Members

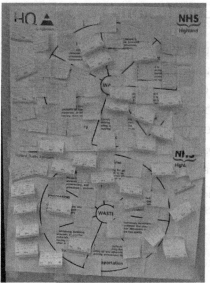

Figure 2.2   Waste wheels in use.

of the team can be encouraged to fix sticky notes to the wheel, in the category of waste that they feel appropriate. The advantages to the service are that everyone can see what other people perceive to be waste. This can prompt valuable conversations, and often reveals parts of a process of which some team members were unaware, and problems that may have escaped their attention.

Teams sometimes feel that they are not encouraged to identify problems. Visible acknowledgement of the issues that concern them can have a powerful effect, particularly when they see that all comments are left on the waste wheel.

The key coaching point with teams is to promote a positive view of waste elimination. Shingo comments (2005: p 80):

> As long as we affirm the present condition by saying there is no other way, we will miss opportunities for improvement. We cannot find the waste if we are not looking for it.

It is easy to identify reasons why the current state cannot be changed. Part of the work is promoting a spirit of inquiry and supporting the intrinsic motivation the staff has to improve the service, and the experience for people who use their service.

2.7 Conclusions

Value and waste are key concepts in Lean. Helping people to think through what value their service provides, and what aspects of their work and processes do not add value, is an important step in the improvement process. Staff and service users can become inured to problems, to such an extent that they are barely acknowledged. In other cases, they are seen as inevitable parts of a system, rather than as consequences of a process which can be altered.

Helping people to look at their systems in this way, and encouraging active sharing of problems with no intention of blame, are valuable building blocks in quality improvement efforts.

Further Reading

Full references are included in the bibliography.

Lean Hospitals (Graban 2016) has a good chapter on value and waste in health care. Mark Eaton's book, *The Lean Practitioner's Handbook* (2013) also includes a useful discussion of waste.

Chapter 3

5S

3.1 Aims of the Chapter

The aims of the chapter are

1. To understand the purpose of 5S
2. To know the terms used
3. To be able to describe the stages of the process
4. To be aware of the need to sustain the process over time

3.2 Introduction

3.2.1 Waste Examples

- A nurse is admitting a patient to a ward. They look in the duty room drawers for the correct forms, but they discover that some of them have run out. They walk to another ward to find a copy.
- A social worker wants a computer projector to take to a group that they run in a community centre. They are sure it is in their equipment store. It is not immediately obvious where it is, and they move various other pieces of equipment trying to find it. They eventually locate it, put the other equipment and stores back and take it to their group.

Once there, they find that the projector is not in working order, and their group is disrupted.

◾ A junior doctor wants to check a blood pressure. The sphygmoma-nometer cuff is the wrong size for the person's arm. The doctor looks around the ward but cannot find the size they want. They take the measurement with the cuff they have.

Does any of this sound familiar? These are common stories from the front line of health and social care. In the previous examples, all of the actions caused delay, and at least one of them had some risk to patient safety, and in none of them was the underlying problem corrected. The process of 5S is an important step in reducing these problems by separating the necessary from the unnecessary, putting things in their place, and developing a system to keep things the way you want them.

5S is a key component of Lean. It is easy to think of 5S as good house-keeping, but it involves more than tidying up (Gapp et al. 2008). 5S contributes to quality and flow by helping to have the right equipment in the right place at the right time. It also reduces waste by decreasing rework, travel time, unnecessary stock and time spent looking for supplies. In care settings, 5S increases safety by making it more apparent when equipment or supplies are missing, and it can decrease the risk of out-of-date guidance information.

Undertaking 5S also makes it easier to see problems in the system. When a system feels chaotic, it can be very difficult to work out what is happening: as a system begins to flow more easily, any disruptions become more apparent.

3.3 Reasons to Undertake 5S

Clutter and unnecessary stock

◾ Can affect support and treatment
◾ Makes it harder to find needed items, which takes up time and decreases the time available for valuable tasks
◾ Ties up money that could be used to improve care
◾ Takes up space that could be used for something else
◾ Items can go out of date, resulting in them having to be discarded

- Old guidelines and information may be out of date, leading to delay and frustration, or even to safety hazards
- Makes it difficult to see what has been used up or is missing
- Can conceal problems in processes

3.4 Stages of 5S

The five Japanese terms, and their approximate translations, are (Shinbun 1995; Hirano 2009b):

Seiri – Sort
Seton – Set in order
Seisi – Sweep (termed 'Shine' by some authors)
Seiketsu – Standardise
Shitsuke – Sustain or self-discipline

5S is key to Lean because it is the foundation of so many other Lean activities. In Japanese, the five terms are sometimes grouped into smaller categories of 'orderliness' (Sort and Set in Order), 'cleanliness' (Sweep and Standardise) and 'discipline' (Sustain) (Osada 1991). Table 3.1 shows a comparison of the terms used. A sixth 'S' – Safety – is sometimes added (Gabb et al. 2008), but this may be better considered as an issue to be considered at each step, rather than a stand-alone consideration.

Several authors have noted that the apparent simplicity of 5S is a challenge to its implementation. Western translations, particularly in earlier years, often described 5S as 'housekeeping' (Gapp et al. 2008). This translation carries the risk of losing the visual control (Shimbun 1995) and continuous improvement elements of 5S (Young 2014), and its integral part in Lean as a whole.

Table 3.1   Comparison of Terms Used in 5S

Stage	Category	Japanese
Sort	Orderliness	*Seiri*
Set in order		*Seton*
Sweep (or Shine)	Cleanliness	*Seisi*
Standardise		*Seiketsu*
Sustain	Discipline	Shitsuke

3.4.1 History Note

History Note: 5S dates back many years. An academic study found references to 5S in the Japanese literature from the early 1970s onwards, building on earlier work. Takashi Osada is often credited with describing the whole approach in the early 1980s (Ho et al. 1995). Hiroyuki Hirano's book, *5 Pillars of the Visual Workplace*, published in Japan in 1990 and translated in to English in 1995, helped to make the approach accessible outside Japan. Gapp et al. (2008) provide a useful review of the 5S literature as a whole, and Black and Miller (2008) and Young (2014) give examples of its development and use in health care.

3.5 Getting Started

You cannot 'do 5S' to people – active involvement is essential. This does not mean that it is impossible to start until everyone agrees, but it does mean that local staff need to be involved.

Methods to involve staff vary. Larger organisations sometimes use a formal structure with

- Sponsor – the person sponsoring the project, usually a service manager.
- Process owner – a person in charge of the day-to-day working of the clinical area or team.
- Project lead – the person who leads the work in the area. This can be the process owner, but in some cases, it is another person. This can be a good development role.

In other settings, this may be too formal – services and teams should know what works best for them. In wards or care homes, and in offices or equipment stores used by several teams, it is important to think about how to involve people from all the relevant teams or shifts. Even if the formal process with allocation of detailed duties mentioned previously is not used, meetings are going to be needed, and a way of communicating to relevant staff is essential. In a ward, the night shift needs to be engaged as well, and keeping everyone involved will take some thought.

Challenges in engaging staff can include a view that it is 'not their problem,' that they are too busy, or that this is a domestic matter that does not apply to professional staff. It is best to tackle this head on, by helping people to see that the point of the work is not tidiness for its own sake, but rather to ensure that they can spend more time with patients, and less time battling with missing, broken or incorrect items.

Tip:

When working across shifts, a device such as a '5S book' can be valuable in sharing ideas and information.

3.6 Sort

Purpose: Identify what is needed.

In the Sort stage, necessary items are separated from unnecessary items (Hirano and Furuya 2006). Items can include

- Office clutter
- Supplies (e.g. forms, materials for clients, blood tubes, bed sheets, standard test forms, information sheets for patients, service users and relatives)
- Furniture
- Posters and memos on the wall
- Guidelines and information
- Equipment (e.g. ophthalmoscopes, sphygmomanometers)

Three things are important:

1. Is this item needed?
2. If so, is it located in the best place?
3. What quantity of it is required?

The process of identifying potentially unnecessary equipment, or equipment that is present in the wrong quantity or is located in the wrong place, is known as 'red tagging' (Hirano 2009b). This refers to the industrial practice of attaching red tags to surplus, worn or damaged equipment for later removal. In health care, red tags are not always used, but the term has stuck. An example of a Red Tag is shown in Figure 3.1.

The stages of Sort are

1. Agree the physical area to be covered. Is it all parts of a ward or a team office, for example? Are store rooms included? Are patient information displays included, for example?

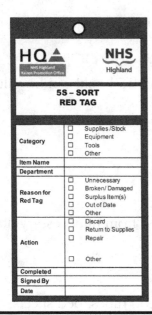

Figure 3.1   5S red tag and red tag in use.

2. Take photos of the current condition so that you know your starting position. Photos make a good record of 5S work and can be a great motivator.

3. Agree the criteria for 'necessary items.' Items needed daily may be needed in the workplace, items needed weekly may be needed nearby, but not necessarily in the workplace. Some items needed very urgently may need to be in the immediate workplace even if they are not used often (e.g. resuscitation trolleys, adrenaline). If you do need the item, do you need it in its current quantity? Taking some time to think through these points can save time later in the process.

4. Set up a 'red tag' area. This is an area of a room or storeroom in which items that may be unnecessary are placed. Mark the area by a prominent sign, so that everyone knows where it is, and what it is (see Figure 3.2). Giving people the chance to leave things in place before they are removed can help to encourage people to red tag items: if it's a once-only decision, people may be less willing to make the decision.

5. Leave items in the red tag area for an agreed period – for example a fortnight. If it has not been needed in that time, people are usually willing to agree that it can be removed. Record items removed on a Red Tag Log (Figure 3.3).

Figure 3.2   5S sort area sign.

5S RED TAG LOG

NHS Highland
Kaizen Promotion Office

Department: _____   Sheet ___ of ___

Tag No	Date of Tag	Item Name	Asset Number	Reason for Red Tag	Action	Item Cost

Completed By : _____   Date: _____

Figure 3.3   Red tag log.

6. When red tagging, it is good practice to go round and physically touch every single item in an area. It is easy for your eyes to skim over items that have been there a long time. Make a decision about everything.
7. For larger items, tag them in place, for example by putting a sticker or a label on them.
8. When you have identified the red tagged items, sort them into items that can be returned to central stores, items that are broken, out

of date or no longer of value and which should be discarded, and items that you need, but which can be stored outside the immediate patient area.

9. In planning work on 5S, it is very useful to talk to people from other service areas that have been through the same process. Having someone come along to a team meeting to talk about their own experience is worthwhile, if you can arrange it.

3.6.1 Sort Tips

- Encourage staff to be brave when red tagging. Don't let' Just in Time' become 'Just in Case.'
- If you are putting a red tag on a box of mixed items, or a shelf of items, be clear whether you are 'red tagging' all of them: it's usually best to red tag each individual item.
- Don't let staff red tag each other. To some people it's a joke, but it is often a joke with a malicious undercurrent, and it leaves people upset. Include this in your ground rules. In Lean, the problem is the system, not the people who have to work in it.
- Red tag excess items, as well as unnecessary items. For example, you may need an item, but have more than you need: red tag the extra items.

3.7 Set in Order

> In the early days it was a 'Lining Things Up Competition.' But this was not good since the first item received was buried at the bottom and they have to move everything on top of it out of the way when they needed to use it. This was not setting in order at all.
>
> **Taiichi Ohno (2013: p 112)**

Purpose: Give everything a place that makes work as easy as possible.

Once you have worked out what you need, it then has to be Set in Order. This is sometimes described as 'Simplifying.' This underestimates the process, which involves making sure that equipment is in the right place for it to be used when needed. The previous quotation makes the point that this is not about neatness: it is intended to make the function as straightforward as possible.

A common example is a professional kitchen. In a home kitchen, pots and pans, knives and ingredients are usually put away neatly in cupboards. In a professional kitchen, these items are still stored in an orderly way, but their location is designed to make the chef's task easier, rather than designed with an eye to neatness. 5S in health care settings is similar: the point is to make the processes as efficient as possible. Orderliness is normally a result, but the purpose is to make care easier to deliver, not to produce neatness. If staff confuse the two ideas, then it is possible to produce a neat, orderly area that is no more efficient than it was in the first place. Focus on quality.

The Sort process will help to identify what can be removed altogether or can be stored further away from the work area. For the remaining equipment, the staff making use of it should be involved in working out how best to store it.

Ask:

■ Who uses which equipment/supplies?
■ Where is it used?
■ In what order is it used?
■ Which equipment is used most frequently?
■ Are there equipment or supplies that are often used together?

For some tasks, using a Process Worksheet – also known as a spaghetti diagram – may help to work out what equipment is best grouped together, and where it should go (Figure 3.4). For example, if some supplies are retrieved from a distant store cupboard many times a day, then it may make sense to move in different parts of a ward, or even in each room, although this is less likely in mental health settings than in general hospitals.

Supplies and equipment can be grouped by type – for example, all forms in one place – or by function – for example, all the equipment and forms needed for a first assessment, or for an admission in one place. In some cases, clinical areas settle on a combination of the two. Admission documents may be made up into a pack together, and placed near to a sphygmomanometer, while other documents may be kept separately because the processes in which they are used are unpredictable. Social care and other community teams may keep packs of assessment forms and informational materials related to similar issues together. There is no absolutely right answer. The main factor in deciding how to do it is that it should make sense to the staff or team who work there.

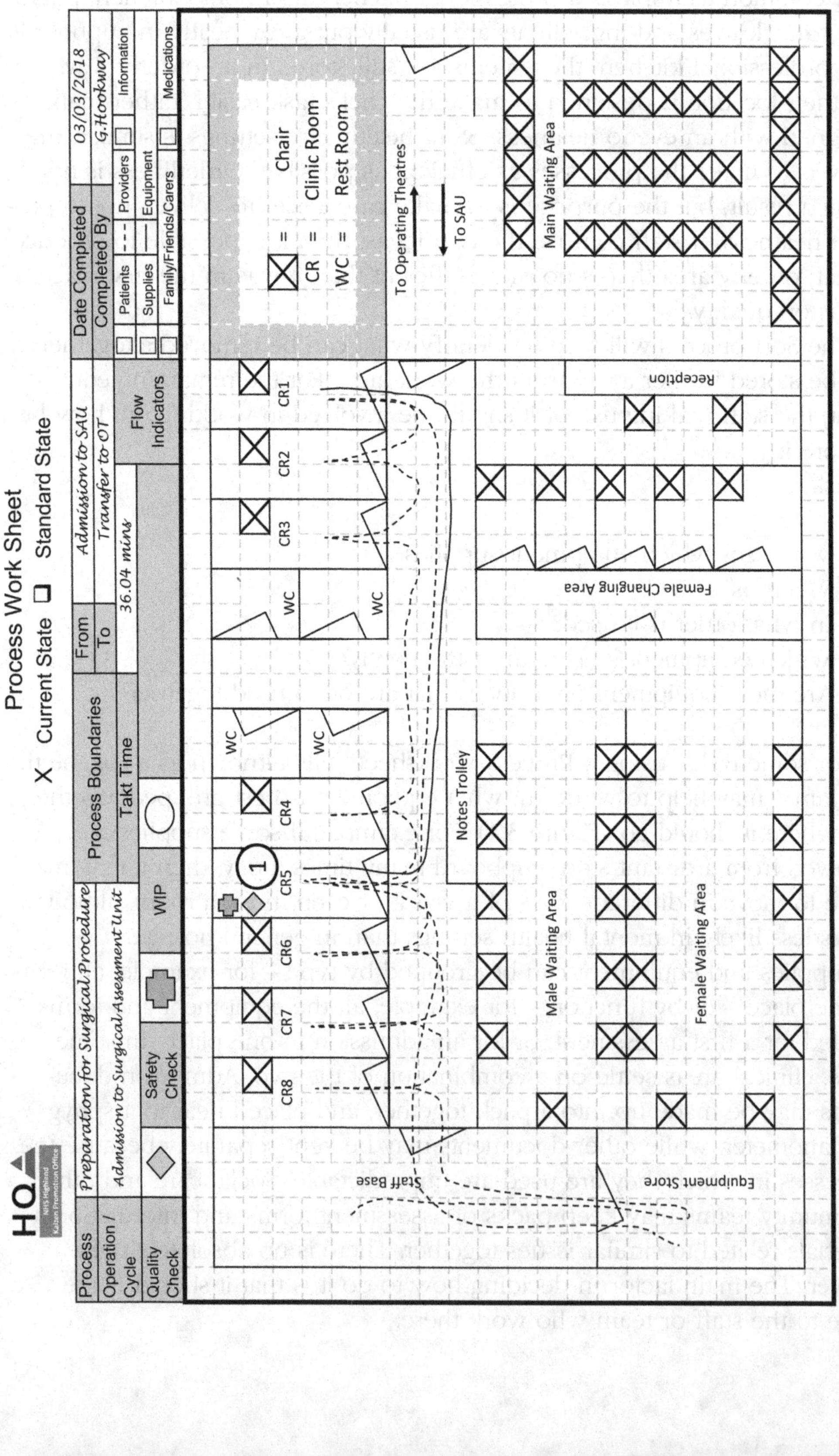

Figure 3.4 Process worksheet showing movement to access item in a clinical area.

Consider using visual controls as part of the arrangements. Kanban and visual controls are discussed in more detail in the Visual Controls chapter, but they are a good fit with 5S. For example, when you identify a place for particular supplies, you can also decide on the quantity needed, and put in cues that show the maximum and minimum supplies needed. If you do this, make it clear who is to reorder, and how this should be done.

Showing how things should be done is often effective. Standard work is discussed next, but placing a photograph on the wall beside an area showing how items should be stored can be a useful reminder for staff of the planned arrangements (Figure 3.5). This is sometimes known as a '5S Map.'

Storage areas can easily deteriorate. Marking out areas is useful, for example by using tape on shelves to show an area. A labelling machine can be used to show what goes where, or a photograph can show locations (Figure 3.6). Do not make storage areas for items too tight: if people cannot fit something back in to a space easily, they often lay it on top, or nearby, making it easy to lose it.

Shadow boards are used in some industrial and clinical environments (Figure 3.7). These have a cut out of the shape of the tool or instrument that shows where it should go. They can be fiddly to make, but most office supply stockists make self-adhesive sheets from which they can be cut out. The advantage of shadow boards is that they make it particularly easy to see what is missing, as well as what is in the right place. An example is shown in the Visual Controls chapter.

In care settings, there can be particular rules about the use of tape and labels, as they can be difficult to clean to the required standards. It is important to check with the relevant control of infection staff to find out local rules. Sometimes tape can be used in the short-term, and then the markings

Shelf A	Shelf B	Shelf C
Small Plasters	Small Bandages	Small Stockinette
Medium Plasters	Medium Bandages	Medium Stockinette
Large Plasters	Large Bandages	Large Stockinette
Extra Large Plasters	Extra Large Bandages	Extra Large Stockinette

Figure 3.5   Example of a 5S map.

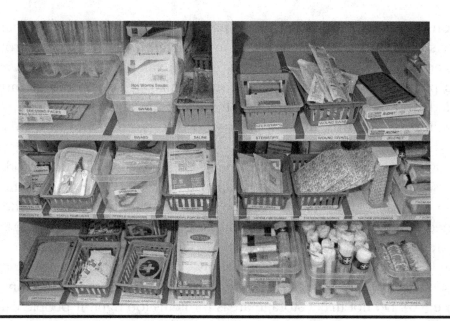

Figure 3.6 Example of a store cupboard with marked locations.

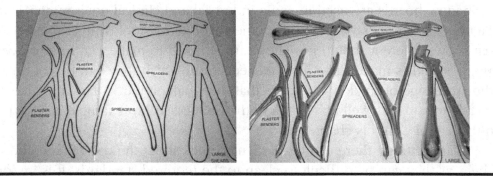

Figure 3.7 Example of a shadow board in use.

can be painted in later. In some other areas this may not matter, and tape and labels may be acceptable for long-term use.

3.7.1 Set in Order Tips

When arranging equipment or supplies:

■ Put the most frequently used equipment in the most accessible places.
■ Avoid placing commonly used supplies in places where lifting or bending is bound to be required.

■ Make a decision on what equipment is best stored together – you can always change it if it doesn't quite work, or you later decide on a better method.

■ Consider colour coding labels or markers for equipment that is often used together, to make it easier to locate related items.

■ Build in visual controls where possible – mark out areas, put a photo nearby that shows how the area should look, and consider including visual cues that show when stock should be re-ordered.

3.8 Sweep

Purpose: Check and maintain the workplace.

The third stage of 5S is Sweep (or Shine as it is called in some workplaces) (Hirano 2009b). This stage involves visually checking and maintaining the workplace.

The work done in the 'Set in Order' stage is an essential prerequisite of this stage. The photographs and diagrams produced in that work provide the standard against which the Sweep stage is conducted.

Sweep involves three processes:

1. Reducing the mess that is made in the first place
2. Taking responsibility for cleaning and replacing as work is done
3. Establishing regular mechanisms for checking

Prevention is better than cure. If staff members understand the standard required, and the reasons for it, then they are much more likely to stick to it. Photographs help with this, as they show the standard to which they aspire. John Grout (2006) comments, 'this involves creating "automatic recoil" a system of location and item labelling that makes returning items to their designated place obvious and easy.'

When problems are found, it is important that staff step back and think about why they have happened, particularly if they are potentially serious problems, or if they have occurred before. Hyland et al. (2000) describe 5S as a 'problem-solving tool.'

There will often be a reason why a problem recurs. It may be that the stock level is inadequate, that there is a problem with maintenance of an item, or in some cases there is a particular staff member who does not

HQ
NHS Highland
Kaizen Promotion Office

NHS Highland - 5S Sweep Rota

NHS Highland

Department / Area		Clinic Area 1			Date	Month	Aug-18	Review	End August 18	
						W/C	06/08/2018			
Assigned Area → Person Responsible		Room 1	Room 2	Room 3	Room 4	Room 5	Room 6	StoreRoom 1	Equipment Room	Store Room 2	
Pugh		✓	✓								
Pugh				✓	✓						
McGrew						✓	✓				
Cuthbert								✓			
Dibble									✓		
Grubb										✓	

Figure 3.8   Example of a sweep rota.

understand the process or does not follow it. The Sweep stage should be seen as part of work on prevention, as well as maintenance.

As well as the roles of all staff, Sweep can include agreed duties. Some services find it useful to have a rota that shows who should check which area each day (Figure 3.8).

This is combined with standard work, as the checking staff need a good understanding of what the area should look like. This can involve producing a checklist, or it may be as simple as having a photograph to which they can compare (Figure 3.9).

Staff have to understand what to do when they find a problem. Often this can be readily resolved, for example by putting something back in place. In other cases, for example if a piece of equipment is broken, then it has to be clear how to deal with this. Guidance can be included in the Standardisation stage, discussed subsequently.

3.8.1 Sweep Tip

If an end-of-day or once-a-week Sweep identifies many problems time after time – equipment out of place, supplies that have run out – then there is probably an underlying issue that needs to be resolved. Don't just fix the immediate issue – look for the root cause and correct that.

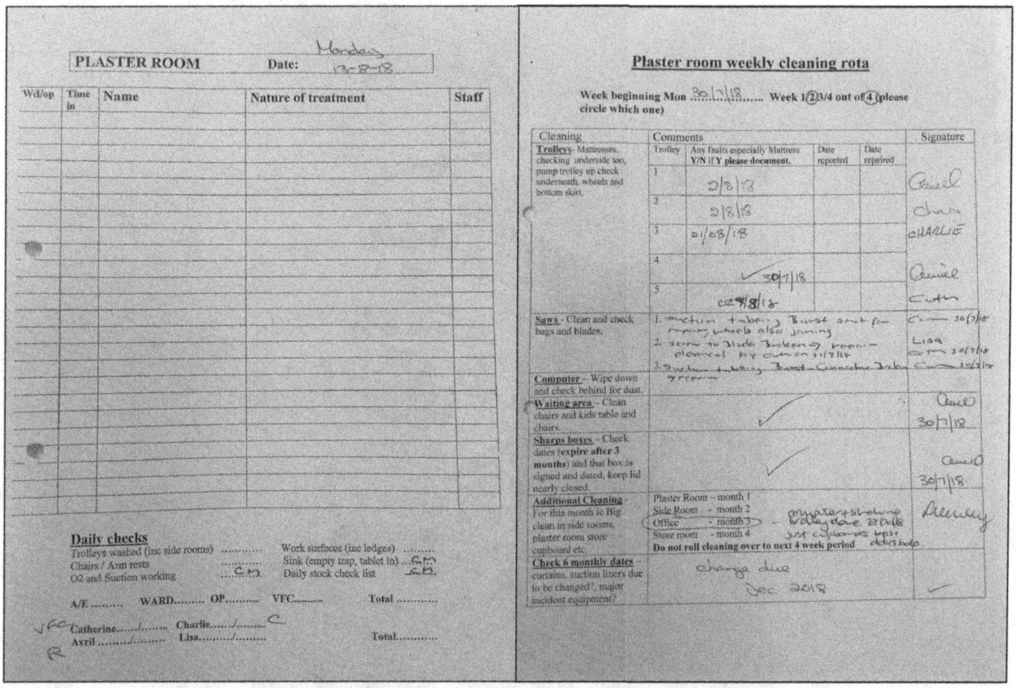

Figure 3.9 Examples of checklist and sweep rota.

3.9 Standardise

Purpose: Develop a consistent process.

Much of this may have been done in the previous stages, but consider

- Clear documentation of the agreed standards, including the use of photographs and diagrams where appropriate (Figure 3.10).
- Make sure staff understand what is expected of them: define the roles of everyone involved – for example, the role of a person undertaking a particular process or of a person responsible for a daily sweep.
- This can include standard expectations – for example, if you use it, replace it, if you spill it, clean it up and so on.
- Eliminate the need to check the manual if at all possible – use visual controls – photographs, shadow boards, marks showing stock levels and so on.
- Communicate the requirements across shifts/teams – make this a priority. Consider using a 5S Book to share information.
- Use checklists where necessary and make them easily understandable.

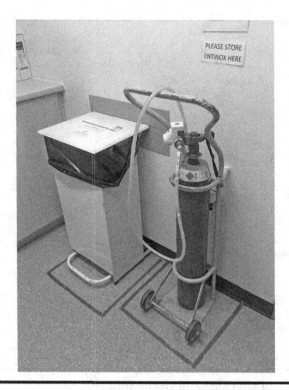

Figure 3.10 Photograph illustrating locations for equipment.

3.10 Sustain

Purpose: Maintain and improve.

Keeping the work going requires the development of continuous action to ensure that processes are maintained. This will not happen by chance. It requires management involvement to permit time to undertake the tasks, and to make the importance of the work clear.

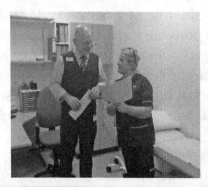

Figure 3.11 Examples of a *Gemba* walk.

Many managers find that a weekly walk through the area makes a big difference (Figure 3.11). If they do this with a staff member, there is a good opportunity for mutual learning. This fits well with the general Lean tenet of 'going to the *Gemba*,' the place the work is undertaken. It gives both people an insight into the working of the team.

It is easy for staff who work in an area every day to overlook things – they become so commonplace that they are not noticed at all. Walking round with another person gives an excellent opportunity to look at things afresh. For the manager, it provides a chance to convey ideas about Lean – or to learn them, if the team member has led the project, and it also helps them to learn about the day-to-day detail of the work, which is easy to overlook.

In some cases, a team leader might conduct a walk round with a staff member, who then undertakes a later walk round with a second staff member. They then report back to the Team Leader. This has the advantage of both spreading learning and understanding and increasing the number of staff involved.

Incorporating the work in appropriate processes is important, as it helps to demonstrate the importance of the work and to embed it in existing activities. For example, responsibilities can be included in objectives, job plans and weekly rotas. This also assists in making accountability clear.

Sustaining change also requires a good understanding that 5S is not an inoculation, but rather part of a continuous process. If arrangements do not work out in some way – for example, a piece of equipment proves to be needed more commonly than had been thought, or some paperwork proves consistently difficult to locate – then it is important not to be afraid to change the processes. Standard work should only remain fixed until the service thinks of something better. Lean aims at continuous improvement, and 5S can be a good example of this.

5S status can be audited, for example using a standard form (Hirano 2009f).

3.10.1 Sustain Tip

It is easy to take things for granted. Some teams or wards find it helpful to swap with other services, with each attending a walk round in one another's departments.

Involving customers of the department or team can be useful. For example, could a Community Mental Health Team member come into a ward? This can have several advantages: it helps to spread the method, it increases the knowledge of the partner services of one another's work, and it demonstrates a respect for their opinions and input.

'Five Minute 5S' can be used in two ways. Once you have your system in place, you can allocate staff to spend five minutes each day, or each shift, on the 'Shine' phase. Five minutes in a seven-day week is 35 minutes a week, or over 30 hours a year. If each staff member does this each day, or each shift, then the time adds up quickly.

Five Minute 5S can also be used to review 5S as a whole, rather than focusing on the 'Shine' phase. So, for example, each staff member were asked to spend five minutes once a week looking at the 5S arrangements in an area in which they work, and to identify any further improvements that can be made – and then to make them.

3.11 Practice Example

A general hospital outpatient department supported clinics from many hospital specialties, and over 90 Consultants. There were over 30,000 attendances a year in the department. The nurse in charge found it challenging to keep rooms stocked and ready for multiple specialties. Different doctors had different room requirements, and some doctors had become used to using the same room, and expected it always to be available to them, causing problems with room allocation.

The service identified a model cell – one room – and developed a standard layout using Process Mapping, 5S and kanban. Medical staff took part in the discussions. Once a standard room layout and stock was identified, a wider kanban system was introduced to the department to supply and manage stock. The system was gradually extended to 23 outpatient rooms.

Separate supplies for specific clinics that were needed in addition to routine stock were identified, and put in the rooms in advance of the clinic. Despite initial concerns from staff who were used to the old system, the advantages – materials always available, able to find things in every room, smoother running clinics – the system was accepted rapidly and doctors ceased to require specific rooms, making room scheduling and balancing of work across clinic areas easier.

3.12 Conclusions

5S is a key component of Lean. It aims to improve quality, rather than promote tidiness, although through the application of 5S, workplaces usually do become tidy. Gabb et al. (2008) examined how 5S concepts were applied in organisations in Japan, the country with the longest track record of the use of 5S. While service organisations tended to be at an earlier stage of development than manufacturing organisations, they found four key features grouped together repeatedly:

- Management
- Activity
- Training
- Improvement

  The meanings are discussed in detail by Gadd et al., but the main ideas – a managed system, involving active intervention, supported by training and leading to improvements in quality – are the reason for, and the focus of, the application of 5S.

Further Reading

There are some excellent books on 5S. Full references are included in the
   bibliography.

5S for Operators: 5 Pillars of the Visual Workplace, by the Productivity Press
   Development Team (2006), is a summary of a longer book by Hirano. It has
   good illustrations, frequent summaries and flows well.
5S for Healthcare by Thomas L Jackson (2009), published by CRC press, has numerous examples specifically from health care.
Two out-of-print books, *JIT Factory Revolution* by Hiroyuki Hirano (1988) and *JIT Is Flow* by Hirano and Makoto Furuya (2006) are good introductions, both written for an industrial audience.

Chapter 4

Improvement Cycles

To make improvements we must be clear about what we are trying to accomplish, how we will know that a change has led to improvement, and what change we can make that will result in an improvement.

Don Berwick (1996: 619)

4.1 Aims of the Chapter

The aims of the chapter are

1. To understand the concept of cycles of improvement
2. To be able to describe the stages of an improvement cycle
3. To understand the need to scope a problem
4. To be familiar with forms that can be used in improvement cycles

4.2 Introduction

Poor results are always due to problems in the process. And so, we do something about the process.

Yoji Akao (Akao 2004: p 161)

People have good ideas for improving their service. Often, staff members try to make a positive change. In some cases this is effective, but in other instances, the work just drifts. Someone has a good idea and tries it out, and believes it is an improvement. Other staff may not agree that there was a problem in the first place, or if they do, they may not agree whether the change was successful.

Improvement cycles are used because they provide a standard way of structuring improvement work. The commonest improvement cycle used in health care settings is Plan – Do – Study – Act (PDSA). The model is useful partly because it can be used for small projects involving changes to one process on one ward or in one team, but it can also be applied to larger change projects. They use 'inductive learning – the growth of knowledge through making changes and then reflecting on the consequences of those changes' (Berwick 1996: p 62).

The advantage of PDSA cycles, according to the NHS Scotland Quality Improvement Hub (undated), is that it provides

1. A structured approach for making small incremental changes to systems
2. A full cycle for planning, implementing, testing and identifying further changes
3. A practical tool for bringing about change as it can reduce anxiety about the impact of the change as people can see outcomes quickly
4. A reduction in the time invested into change projects which may not work, as this is known before full scale implementation is attempted.

The core approach in this process is to

■ Have a clear understanding of the nature of a problem
■ Generate possible responses
■ Decide what will constitute improvement
■ Select an improvement to try
■ Undertake the change
■ Compare the new process against the measure of success
■ Decide if the change is an improvement and whether further changes are required
■ Learn from any unsuccessful changes and embed successful changes

4.3 Deciding on the Work to Prioritise

People who say, "Unless they buy us that machine there is no point in kaizen" will not be able to do kaizen no matter what kind of machine you give them.

Taiichi Ohno (2013: p 118)

Often, the best way to tackle improvement is to start by working on the manual processes, and later to tackle the overall service process and equipment. One of the hazards of improvement work is focusing on solutions that involve only equipment or electronic information systems: there are almost always improvements that can be made in the work itself. This also means that it is then easier to know precisely what type of equipment or information system is required, and less chance that a series of revisions to the information system, or alterations to equipment, will be needed.

4.4 Identifying the Need for a PDSA Cycle

There are several ways of identifying the need for PDSA cycles, and of preparing for the work, such as the Model for Improvement (Langley et al. 1994, Langley et al. 2009) and the FOCUS model (Batalden 1992). The Model for Improvement is widely used and has been adopted by the Institute for Healthcare Improvement.

There are differences between approaches, but the questions to consider include (Langley et al. 2009, World Health Organisation 2012)

1. What are we trying to accomplish?
2. How will we know that a change is an improvement?
3. What changes can we make that will result in improvement?

4.5 Preparation

4.5.1 What Are We Trying to Accomplish?

4.5.1.1 What Is the Nature of the Problem?

Understanding the nature of the problem is important. It is common for a team to have different understandings of the problem, so stating it clearly is essential, or people may expect different outcomes and can have trouble understanding why some solutions are being proposed.

For example, a care home service had repeated complaints about the time taken to deliver meals to service users in one area. Most staff had heard about this, but few had seen the written complaints. Most had heard about the complaints second hand. When the team decided to look at this, it quickly emerged that some staff had interpreted the complaints as being about users waiting while meals were served in a dining room, while others had taken it to refer to the time it took to deliver meals to the serving area before they were handed out.

When staff asked service users, it became clear that the main concern was about food being cold by the time they were ready to eat.

An example of how understanding of a problem can change after talking to colleagues is shown in Figures 4.1 and 4.2 (Milligan 2015). This work was undertaken by an Occupational Therapist, seeking to improve discharge arrangements for patients. Figure 4.1 sets out the initial understanding of the nature of communication on a mental health ward at the time of discharge, while Figure 4.2 describes an increased understanding after discussion with colleagues.

This richer understanding of the process in the current state is more complex, but basing work on the actual situation rather than the assumed situation is more likely to be successful in producing lasting change. The diagrams also allow easier sharing and communication compared to a long-written document.

4.5.1.2 What Are the Possible Causes of the Problem?

It is easy to jump to a conclusion about possible causes. Sometimes these reflect previous experience, and at other times draw on the expectations of

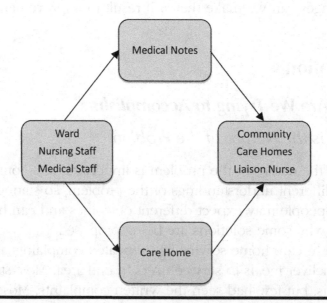

Figure 4.1   Initial view of process of formal written communication on patient discharge.

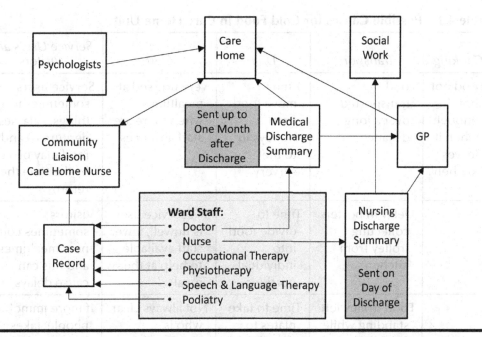

Figure 4.2 Formal communication on patient discharge pathways: understanding after discussion with stakeholders.

members of the staff group. The PDSA process involves consideration of the range of possible causes, before deciding which potential cause to tackle.

Some improvement processes include a 'Define' phase, and this is very similar: the person or team should take time to consider causes.

In the previously mentioned cold food example, the clinical team brain-stormed potential reasons for the problem at a meeting. The system used was that food came in large trays from a distant kitchen, and was served on to plates by staff, and taken to tables in a dining area.

The staff came up with a number of possible causes for cold food, including problems in the cooking, delays in transport, transport over long distances, inadequate insulation, delay in distributing it after it arrives at the serving area, time to distribute the food to the tables, service users who were not ready to eat, or who were not able to get to the table promptly due to other care activities or difficulty in moving the person. The team thought that it could be difficult to help people with immobility problems to the tables because there were staffing pressures on some shifts, and if someone else was unwell and needed attention, it was difficult to do everything at the same time.

The team then looked at the causes they had identified and grouped them up into categories of related issues (Table 4.1).

Table 4.1 Possible Causes for Cold Food in Care Home Unit

Cooking	Transport	Unit	Staff	Service Users and Visitors
Food not hot enough when it leaves kitchen	Food transported over a long distance	Time to move food from trolleys in to the servery	Very pressed at mealtimes when there are staff absences	Service users sometimes forget things – glasses, dentures – and food may be cold by the time they return
	Delay in porters collecting trolley from kitchen	Time to divide food into individual portions	If a service user is unwell, fewer staff available to help at the meal	Visitors sometimes come near mealtimes, and this can cause delays
	Food trolley left standing while food delivered to other areas	Time to take plates to the tables	Not always clear who is supposed to undertake what task, so sometimes delays	If more immobile people, takes longer to help them to the tables
	Poor insulation of the food trays/trolley			

These can be displayed graphically, using Cause and Effect diagrams (also referred to as Ishikawa or Fishbone diagrams). The use of Cause and Effect diagrams is discussed in more detail in Chapter 7, Error Proofing. It is common to find that there are several different factors that seem to contribute to the problem.

4.5.1.3 What Is Our Aim?

Being clear on the aim of the work is very important. This needs to be explicit. For example, if a physiotherapy service has a long waiting list and wants to decrease it, 'improving patient experience' is too vague as an aim of the work. 'Decreasing waiting times' is better but does not spell out how much of an improvement is wanted, or by when. 'Decreasing waiting times for a first clinic appointment to no more than six weeks by September this year' is more precise and explains what change is sought, in what service, and in what timescale.

In the previously mentioned mental health discharge example, the aim was

> '100% of patients discharged from the assessment ward, have the new standardised discharge form completed by end of January 2015' (Milligan 2015). This has a numeric standard and a timescale for meeting that standard.

4.5.2 How Will We Know That a Change Is an Improvement?

> Measure little and often: measurement for improvement does not require large datasets. It is better to start with one measure, and add more, than to be ambitious about the number of measures to be collected and feel defeated by the scale of it.

> **King's Fund (2016)**

Knowing if change is an improvement is linked to the description of the problem. If you find that it is difficult to describe what an improvement will be like, then it may be that more work is needed on defining the problem. Often the nature of the expected improvement will be obvious – less waiting, fewer defects, and so on – but in other cases it needs more thought to identify precisely what measures you expect to have improved.

Measurement is a key part of the improvement cycle process: the process tries to move from assumption to evidence. The work undertaken to define the problem is very useful at this stage, and in the PDSA cycle itself, as you will usually have measured the problem. Many health care staff are used to the type of measurements undertaken in research projects. There are distinct differences between measurement undertaken in research and measurement for improvement (Table 4.2).

There are three common types of measure used in improvement work (Clarke et al. 2009):

- Outcome measures – these monitor an expected improvement in outcome and are usually the expected end result of your work, such as a shorter length of stay for a patient.
- Process measures – this refers to measures that are intended to produce the outcome, such as the percentage of discharge plans commenced within two days of admission.

Table 4.2 Measurement for Improvement and for Research

	Measurement for Research	Measurement for Learning and Process Development
Purpose	To discover new knowledge	To bring new knowledge into daily practice
Tests	Often one large, 'blind' test	Many sequential, observable tests
Biases	Control for as many biases as possible, in the design or analysis	Stabilise the biases from test to test
Data	Large amounts of data gathered	Gather 'just enough' data to learn and complete another cycle
Duration	Can take long periods of time to obtain results	'Small tests of change' approach accelerates the rate of development

Source: Adapted from Health Quality Ontario (2013).

- Balancing measures – intended to keep track of any unintended consequence of the improvement work, such as increased staff time required for completion of a discharge plan, or increasing the readmission rate because of premature discharge.

This can be accompanied by a measurement plan, which gives a definition of the measure, and describes how it will be calculated, analysed and displayed.

For example, staff in an outpatient clinic might start with the subsequent measures. They have had complaints about patient dissatisfaction with aspects of the clinic. When they asked patients about the problem, the single biggest issue noted was the length of time people had to spend in the clinic. The team designed an intervention to decrease waits at the clinic, with the aim of increasing patient satisfaction. Staff were worried that they miss breaks under the new arrangements, so a balancing measure of cancelled or shortened breaks was identified (Table 4.3).

4.5.3 What Changes Can We Make That Will Result in Improvement?

Generate ideas for methods of improving the problem. It is very useful to do this in a team – several heads are better than one – but it can be done by someone on their own. Do not jump straight to one solution – try to think

Table 4.3   Example of Measures in Work Intended to Improve Patient Satisfaction at an Out-Patient Clinic

Type	Measure	How to Calculate	How to Collect and Display
Outcome	Patient satisfaction with the outpatient clinic	Count the overall score using the five-point scale for each question. Work out the average score for each clinic by adding up the total and dividing by the number of patients who responded.	Approximately 20 people attend the clinic each week. Give every fourth patient leaving the clinic a Patient Experience Form and ask them to complete it and put it in the box on the desk. Plot the new score on the graph in the duty room.
Process	Length of time patients spend in the clinic – main complaint in the past	Subtract the arrival time from the departure time to work out complete time in the clinic. Add up the times from all the patients and take the average for the clinic. Note the longest and the shortest time spent in the clinic.	Receptionist notes the time of arrival, and the time the person came back to the desk to book new appointment at end of visit. Write shortest, longest and average times on the table in the Duty Room.
Balancing	Number of staff who missed break to keep up with the demand at the clinic	Count of number. No additional calculation.	Charge Nurse notes number of staff who miss break or have break curtailed. Write number for the week on the table on the wall of the Duty Room.

of as many as possible, and then decide which is the option you want to try first (NHS Improvement 2014).

In the mental health example explored in this chapter (Milligan 2015), the Occupational Therapist leading the work met with colleagues to talk over the problem, to create the Fishbone diagrams or Driver diagram, and to generate potential actions. Figure 4.3 shows the fourth version of a Driver diagram that seeks to identify the role of different issues in the quality of the handover provided for people transferring to care homes.

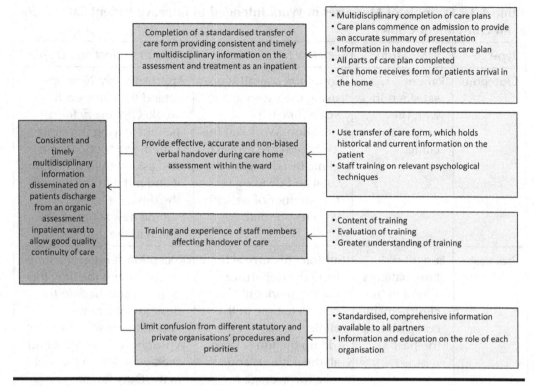

Figure 4.3 Driver diagram for a mental health services quality of handover project.

4.6 Conducting PDSA Cycles Using a Form

There are numerous forms available with which to record improvement cycles, including examples available from the Institute of Healthcare Improvement Open School. A form developed by Brian James of the University of Stirling, adapted from the Institute of Healthcare Improvement (IHI) version with permission, has the sections

Details of the Cycle

- Descriptive title
- Person completing the form
- Area
- Cycle number
- Start date and end date
- Objective of the cycle

Plan

- What change will be tested, and by whom?
- Prediction of the outcome of the test
- What data will be collected, how and by whom?

Do

- Observations and data
- What happened?
- Data table or graph

Study

- How does what happened match up to your predictions?
- Summary and conclusions

Act

- Based on learning from the cycle, what is your next action?

Taking these one at a time

4.6.1 Plan

The Planning stage is the most neglected phase of the process. Improvement cycles are much more straightforward if the preparation work had been thorough, as the aim of the work will be clear.

The Planning phase needs to include three things:

- A description of the nature of the change
- A prediction of the effect of the change
- A plan to measure the change

4.6.1.1 Description of the Nature of the Change

What, exactly, is going to be done? This needs to include a description of the change, who is going to do it and how and when it will happen.

For example, consider a community service that wants to combine two assessment forms into one, in an attempt to collect information in a more streamlined way. The description would include the details of which staff member is going to try the form out, at which location, and on how many patients the form will be used.

In the example of a hospital that wants to try a new discharge checklist, then 'Nurse Iain McDougall will use the checklist with the first patient to be discharged from Ward 11 on Wednesday morning' could be an appropriate description.

At this stage, ensure that there is no predictable hazard to a patient or staff member from the proposed change.

4.6.1.2 A Prediction of the Nature of the Change

This will follow from the aim of the work, and the development of ideas. In the example of a new form, the first prediction could be that the form can be used with a patient. If this is successful, then the next prediction could be that the form can be used in less time than the previous alternative.

In the discharge checklist example, the prediction could also be on usability, but in a later cycle it may relate to the number of items considered and recorded, compared to previous arrangements.

If possible, make a numeric prediction. So, for example, if previous work has found that only 80% of the required items are checked before discharge, the prediction might be that 100% of the items will now be considered.

4.6.1.3 A Plan to Measure the Change

In the previous examples, the time for completion has to be recorded in one instance, and the number of items completed recorded in the other. The plan has to include a clear statement of who will do this, and how it will be done. It is often useful to produce a simple form or tally chart that can be used to collect the information. In some cases, the person undertaking the work may not be the best person to collect the data – for example a receptionist, a ward or clinic supervisor, or student may be better placed to undertake monitoring.

4.6.2 Do

In the Doing phase, the plan is carried out. It is useful to record not only the main measurement, but any comments on the process. This can include clarifications and additional information, such as

'Two additional patients waiting at reception desk, so not able to get everything done'
'Question three seemed to cause confusion'
'Ran out of swabs after the third patient'
'Difficult to record everything and still see clients'
– and so on.

4.6.3 Study

Practicing the (improvement) cycle requires a certain discipline. If we do not practice this discipline but continue the practice of fire fighting – that is plan-do-plan-do – there will not be much progress. Plans will be tried out without coordination as if people were blindfolded.

Kiyoshi Suzaki (1993: pp 197–8)

The study phase requires reflection on the results found in the 'Do' phase:

■ Did the new process perform as predicted?
■ If not, is there anything to suggest why?
■ How large was the improvement?
■ Did the size of the improvement seem to be worth the effort required?
■ Were there any unintended results that need to be considered for the next stage of the work?

If the trial did not go as expected, do not despair. This is the reason that a small-scale trial was undertaken – so that learning could occur more quickly and changes be made.

Using charts is a good way of showing data over time. A run chart is a common way of presenting information.

4.6.4 Act

In the light of experience, does anything need to be changed, or can the process be scaled up and tried with a larger number of people?

If the process is to be changed: return to the 'Plan' phase for a second cycle. Identify the change to be made, document it, identify the measures, and agree when, where and by whom the change will be tried. Remember that the changes were tried because the team was not satisfied with the existing process: don't give up.

If the process change performed as expected, can it be scaled up or spread?

4.7 Scale and Scope: Learning from the IHI

The IHI distinguishes between scale and spread in PDSA cycles. Scale is used to refer to increasing the number of people involved, while spread refers to trying the process in different settings, or with different staff or patient groups.

For example, if after a satisfactory first cycle the number of patients on which a changed process is used is increased from one to five, then that is an example of scale. If the process is tried for the first time with a different staff member, then that is an example of spread.

The general advice is that it is best not to increase both spread and scale at the same time. For example, if a process has been tried by one staff member on one patient, and worked well, then trying it on five patients is reasonable. In trying it with a different staff member, however, it may be best to go back to trying it on one occasion first before seeking to increase scale.

4.8 Problems with PDSA Cycles

> Never stop thinking about the actual situation of actual service users at your actual workplace.
>
> **Adapted from Masanori Ino (Japan Human Relations Association 1992: pp 164–5)**

The purpose of improvement work, as the previous quote suggests, is to produce changes in practice, rather than in theory. Not all PDSA cycles result in change. Taylor et al. (2014) reviewed published PDSA cycles, and noted that

■ Less than 20% of papers reviewed described the use of repeated PDSA cycles
■ Not all work described as PDSA cycles focused on small-scale change
■ Only 15% described regular use of numerical information on progress

Speroff and O'Connor (2004) have also emphasised the importance of good measurement over time. The whole process can be improved by carrying through changes, measuring them and revising them as necessary to produce changes in the 'actual situation' rather than in theory or on a sheet of paper. Using the structure described in this chapter will help to avoid the problems experienced in the papers in this review.

4.9 Using PDSA in Practice

If newly established standards...and regulations are not revised in six months, it is proof that no one is seriously using them.

Kaoru Ishikawa (1985: p 65)

This chapter has set out common themes in running improvement cycles, focusing on the PDSA structure. Examples of real-life projects illustrate both the common issues that arise, and how the method can be adapted to a range of improvement work.

Using forms can help to provide a structure for the work, and to prompt consideration of issues such as the aim, time and place of an intervention, recording and analysis.

PDSA cycles, because they encourage recording of actions, contribute to standardisation (Ishikawa 1985). This, in turn, forms a basis on which to improve processes further. Like a process of pushing a wheel up a hill, standard processes act as a wedge to stop the wheel rolling back down the hill, but only until a new modification is developed to improve the process further.

Further Reading

Full references are included in the bibliography.

Langley et al. (2009) in *The Improvement Guide: A Practical Approach to Enhancing Organizational Performance* (2nd edition), San Francisco, John Wiley and Sons, provide useful information on the API Improvement Cycle, now also used by the IHI.

The IHI Open School has excellent materials on Improvement Cycles.

Chapter 5

Continuous Flow

One way in which Lean is different from traditional thinking is the focus on flow. Instead of asking people to work faster, Lean organizations focus on reducing delays and system barriers to flow.

Mark Graban (2012: p 152)

The basic concept in one-piece flow production is to send (work) along the processing sequence one at a time, adding value…at each process.

Shigeo Shingo (2009c: p 388)

5.1 Aims of the Chapter

The aims of the chapter are

1. To understand the concept of continuous flow
2. To be able to describe the problems associated with batching
3. To be able to distinguish between push systems and continuous flow
4. To know methods of seeking to improve flow

5.2 Introduction

5.2.1 Examples of Problems with Flow

■ Test samples arrive in a hospital laboratory in time with collection routes around the hospital, so there are lulls in the work over the course of the day, followed by prolonged bursts of activity. At the end of the day, large bags of samples begin to come in which have been collected from community clinics and general practices, and which could often not be processed until the following day. The team looked at timing of van pick up routes, and rearranged the routing to level flow (Chapter 6 – Levelling). The time at which staff were available was altered by negotiation, to match capacity to demand. These changes allowed samples to be analysed on the day of receipt in most cases.

■ A child needs an urgent mental health assessment. The assessment is undertaken that day, and care needs are identified. The service allocates cases in blocks, and it takes five weeks before the child receives an intervention. The service introduced daily huddles, visual controls and introduced a rolling case allocation process to reduce waits.

■ A General Practitioner refers a patient to a cardiology clinic. Various tests are booked at the same time. The tests are undertaken before the clinic appointment date. When the patient is seen at the outpatient clinic, the results of the tests have not been received, and the patient is asked to return once the test results are available, so that treatment can be recommended. The service shared information on the impact of delays; reduced batching of analyses to improve flow, and aligned the booking systems for clinics and tests to make it clear that a test result had to be available before an appointment. When it was clear at the time of referral that a test would be needed, General Practitioners were encouraged to initiate the tests, to reduce delays further.

■ A community care team receives several referrals each day. They prioritise referrals and try to see those they grade as 'urgent' as quickly as possible. People who are graded as less urgent fall further and further behind in the queue, and in some cases they are not seen for over three months. Some people in the 'non-urgent' group prove to have considerable needs, which have increased in the intervening period. The service worked on reducing overall waiting times, and to undertake rapid assessments on all people referred, allowing quick decisions on the degree of need and services required.

■ The clinical team decide at a Wednesday ward round that a patient can be discharged home on Thursday. An ambulance arrives to transport the patient, but the discharge medications have not yet been prescribed, and there is no discharge letter available. By the time the medications are prescribed and collected, the ambulance has been re-tasked to another duty, and the patient waits until a second ambulance arrives. The service introduced Estimated Dates of Discharge, using a visual control system (Chapter 8 – Visual Controls) which were reviewed as part of Daily Management (Chapter 11). This was linked to the production of Immediate Discharge Letters, timing and provision of pharmacy items, and booking of ambulances or patient transport.

■ An antenatal clinic sees a patient urgently after a telephone referral. The assessment is conducted quickly and a scan is needed. There is a delay of almost three hours before a scan can be undertaken because doctors were in clinics. The rota was amended to have doctors available at specific times to allow booking and levelled flow.

■ A specialist nurse sees a patient who needs an injection. The supplies they need to conduct the injection are not all present in the room, and they have to spend about 10 minutes assembling the required supplies and equipment before they can undertake the injection. The injection takes less than a minute. The service identified the equipment required, and arranged for procedure-specific packs made to their specification. Each pack cost less than £3.00. This halved the time for an injection, and doubled the clinic capacity.

These are examples of disruption to flow – flow of patients, flow of staff, flow of supplies and equipment, flow of medication and flow of information. These problems are common in health and social care services. Staff quickly learn to work around them, often making efforts above and beyond their required actions, to make things work for their patient, client or internal customer. Over time, staff may take the system for granted and forget that there is any other way of going about the service.

Chapter 1 described value. For an activity to be of value, it must meet a patient need, be done correctly the first time and change the product of the service in some way. The process by which patients pass through a service is known as a Value Stream, as it describes the series of connected activities which together deliver the service to the patient (Tapping et al. 2002; Nash and Poling 2008; Jackson 2013).

The way that patients, equipment or supplies pass along a value stream is known as 'flow.' The aim is to produce continuous flow, which Jackson (2013: 55) describes as 'the state of not waiting,' with patients moving seamlessly through the system, with staff, equipment and supplies available in the right place, at the right time, and in the right quantities. This is part of a 'Just in Time' approach (Hirano 1988; Shingo 2005; Hirano and Furuya 2006), where patients, service users and internal customers do not wait, and staff have what they need to manage the demand for their services. According to the Japanese Management Association (1989: p 66) the term 'Just-in-Time' was originally coined by Kiichiro Toyoda, the first president of Toyota.

5.3 Flows of Health Care

Some authors describe 'Flows of Health Care' (Black 2008; Provincial Health Authority 2011; Graban 2012). Commonly included categories include

- Patients/clients
- Families
- Health and social care staff
- Supplies
- Medicines
- Information
- Equipment

The precise flows will depend on the process being considered: for example, the Provincial Health Services Authority list (2011) also included flow of students, as the service being planned was a teaching hospital.

Figure 5.1 shows an example of a Process Worksheet being used to map out flows in an outpatient service. In this example, the movements of one service user, one staff member and of some key equipment and supplies have been mapped during a single outpatient visit. In this observation alone, the patient retraced their steps several times, and the main staff member involved moved repeatedly to look for supplies and equipment needed during the visit.

Keeping in mind the different people, supplies and equipment that need to come together to provide a good service is useful when reviewing flow through existing services. Mapping the flow of particular categories can help to identify problems and dislocations between processes.

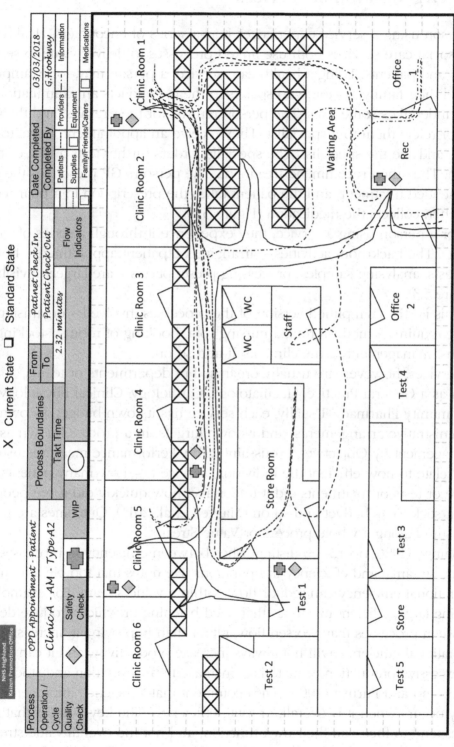

Figure 5.1 Flow in an outpatient clinic.

5.4 Organisation of Services

A person using a service experiences it as a series of encounters. Health and social care services both use linked processes to deliver value to service users and patients. Using a health care service, a person may, for example, attend their family doctor, who speaks to them, conducts an examination and undertakes some tests. The person returns for their results, and their doctor refers them to a specialist. They receive an appointment, travel to the clinic and see the specialist. The specialist orders further tests and sees them again. They then recommend treatment. The person's GP prescribes the recommended treatment, and the patient takes the prescription to a pharmacy and then collects the medication (Figure 5.2).

For a person using a service, they experience it through a series of touch points. The backroom activities – arranging outpatient appointments, booking tests, analysing samples, processing prescriptions – are largely invisible (Figure 5.3).

This is still a simplified version of the processes involved – organising a clinic requires a medical rota, a nursing rota, booking of rooms, stocking of rooms, management of the clinic itself and so on.

Services, however, are usually organised in departments or teams, such as a General Practice, Haematology, Cardiology, Clinical Physiology, Community Pharmacy. Usually, each service has its own budget, its own administrative arrangements, and its own targets, in a process known as 'Management by Objectives' (Toussaint 2015). Performance measures usually relate to how efficient the individual service is – how many patients did it see or tests or treatments did it undertake, how quickly did it see people, did it stick to its budget and so on (Maskell et al. 2011). Outcomes are rarely measured along a whole process or Value Stream.

Shingo (1986: pp 12–13) distinguishes between efficiency in processes (value streams) and efficiency in operations. He notes that too big a focus on operational efficiency can reduce flow within a value stream. For example, buying large, efficient machines that need batching or which produce delays between processes may worsen flow, rather than improving it: increasing operational efficiency will not always increase productivity, and it can result in excessive production of materials, increased transportation and stockpiling.

Hirano and Furuya (2006: p 46) comment that 'efficiency improvement only occurs when it is overall, or total, efficiency.' The key point is that services tend to focus on their own function, and not the overall value stream as experienced by the patient. This means that a focus on individual targets

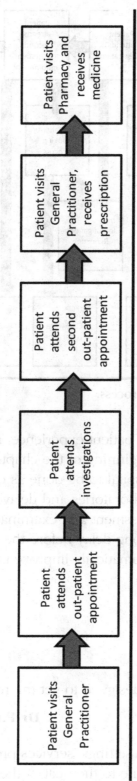

Figure 5.2 Visible steps in an outpatient process.

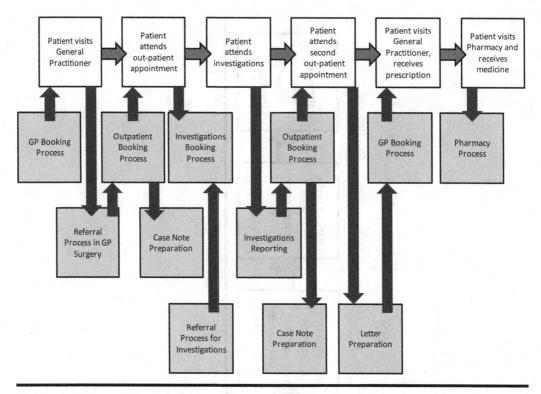

Figure 5.3   Expanded outpatient process.

without attention to the overall patient experience, may inadvertently worsen flow. In the examples at the beginning of the chapter, it was more efficient for blood collections in the hospital to be done as continuous routes, but this caused disruption in the laboratories and delayed samples. In the antenatal example, the clinical assessment and examination was conducted very quickly, but there was then a long delay before the scan: efficiency at one part of the process did not automatically improve the experience of the process for the patient.

5.5 Push Systems

> Every system is perfectly designed to get the results it gets.
>
> **Dr Paul Batalden (1996)**

In many health and social care settings, services providing component parts of the treatment pathway operate to the beat of their own drum. Staff often take pride in delivering their part of the process well and to a high quality. They may be less aware of how their process fits in to the overall value stream for the patient or service user. Often this is because the overall process is invisible to them.

5.5.1 *Example: Ophthalmology Clinic*

For example, consider an ophthalmology clinic. The key processes in the patient group at this particular clinic are

1. Arrive
2. Attend reception
3. A visual fields test by a nurse, who also dilated their eyes
4. A wait while dilation took effect, occasionally repeated if required
5. Assessment by an optometrist
6. Review by a consultant
7. Additional treatment undertaken by a nurse or doctor in a proportion of cases
8. Attend reception to book a further appointment, if required
9. Leave

Clinic appointment times ranged from 8.30 a.m. to 12 noon. At this clinic, the service started off calmly, but by 11 a.m. there were large numbers of people waiting. This happened on most occasions this clinic was run, and sometimes there were not enough seats for everyone between 10.45 a.m. and about 11.45 a.m. The staff caught up over lunch, and by the start of the afternoon clinic everyone has usually been seen, although occasionally the afternoon clinic was delayed because people were still being seen from the morning clinic. Staff often gave up some of their lunchtime to catch up, and some disliked this clinic because of its long-term problems.

During improvement work, staff on the unit identified the commonest time – the mode – that the different processes took to complete.

These times were then drawn together into the average timeline for patients – the first time this had been done. The average time at the clinic with no waits would be around 43 minutes. If an additional treatment was required and there were no waits, then the average time, including a further test that was often conducted, would be around 100 minutes. The average time at the clinic when recorded was over two hours. Observation indicated that the largest queues were when people waited to see a doctor. There were usually five doctors at the clinic to conduct the appointment stage.

The staff at the clinic then took the appointment times from a clinic and worked out how people would flow through the system if they were able to find the clinic at their appointment time, and if all procedures happened on time with no wait (Figure 5.4).

The staff found that, as the clinic was currently organised

- 70 patients were booked in to the clinic.
- No doctor was required until 8.55 a.m.
- By 11.20 a.m., seven doctors were required simultaneously, compared to the five usually available.
- By 11.30 a.m., 11 doctors were needed.

This explained the backlog that developed in late morning. In effect, each earlier process was pushing patients in to the next part of the system, which had no capacity to cope with it. The faster the earlier stages in the process worked, the bigger the queue later in the clinic process.

This is an example of a 'Push System,' where the previous process deals with its own process as efficiently as possible, and 'pushes' the patient,

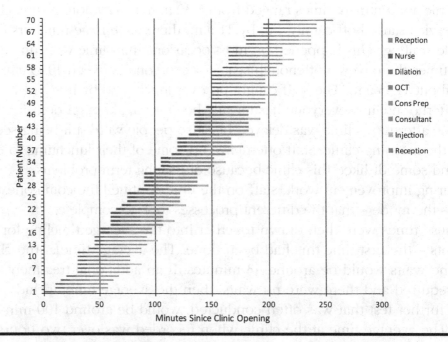

Figure 5.4   Ophthalmology clinic appointment times as currently booked.

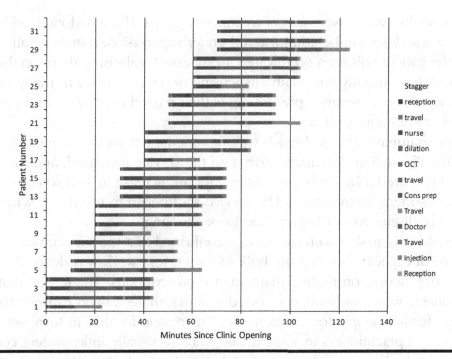

Figure 5.5   Impact of changing appointment booking times.

service user or item on to the next part of the process without explicit consideration of the system as a whole, or of the overall experience of the service user. The staff working on each process usually feel that they are doing their best to meet demand as quickly as possible. It demonstrates Batalden's adage that every system is designed to produce the results it gets – given the scheduling of the clinic, and the staff available, the build-up in waiting patients was inevitable. Reducing the number of patients attending the clinic would not improve the situation automatically: it was the timing of the appointments that provided the biggest influence on the clinic flow.

Rescheduling the start of the clinic and altering the time at which appointments were scheduled to level the flow (please see Chapter 6 for more information on Levelling) results in a more even flow of patients. As the people requiring injections are not always predictable, the flow would not be completely even, but it would be much improved compared to the existing appointment arrangements (Figure 5.5).

5.5.2 Example: Substitute Prescribing

Methadone is often used by substance misuse programmes for people who are addicted to opiates. The usual treatment flow is assessment of the patient by a specialist, with discussion of treatment options. If methadone is indicated, a test dose will be administered under supervision. Assuming all is well, the patient will then go through a process of stabilising them on the required dose, usually with daily dispensing of the treatment. In many programmes, the maintenance prescribing is then passed over to general practitioners or community clinics.

A programme began to breach waiting time targets for assessment consistently (Figure 5.6). Managerial focus on the service increased, and the service prepared a business case, asking for an increase in staff to conduct assessment for treatment. The service staff began to use the '5 Whys' approach, discussed in Chapter 7 on Error Proofing.

Detailed discussion with the service confirmed that the service was working at capacity, but that the bulk of the current work was devoted to monitoring people on routine maintenance prescriptions. The reason that assessments were not being conducted was that there was no capacity to take on further people for maintenance. The reason for this, in turn, was that general practitioners in some areas, who are usually independent contractors in the UK, were declining to take on the work. This then pushed the maintenance prescribing back on to the specialist service. The effect was that there was a visible queue of people waiting for assessment, because this was recorded in routine measures, but an unseen queue of people waiting for allocation to a community service (Figure 5.7).

Increasing the assessment capacity would have pushed more people into the system, and within a month or two the additional staff capacity would have been used up by the increased maintenance prescribing. The constraint in the

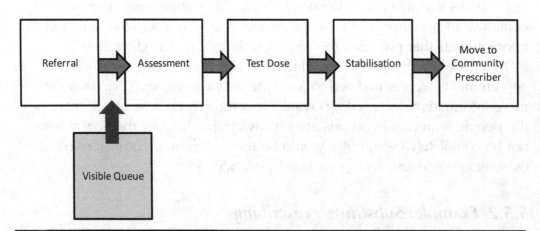

Figure 5.6 Substitute prescribing assessment and stabilisation process – location of perceived problem.

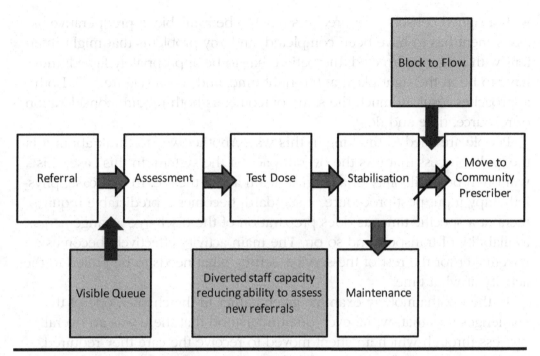

Figure 5.7   Substitute prescribing assessment and stabilisation process – actual problem.

service was in the community service capacity, and increasing specialist service capacity would have only provided a sticking plaster solution, which would have lasted a few months. The organisation redirected the planned investment to increase community service capacity, and it resolved the problem.

5.6 Pull Systems

Pull systems, by contrast, seek to pull the right staff, supplies and materials to the right place, at the right time and in the required quantities.

In industrial settings, this is envisaged as a process 'pulling' what it requires from the previous process. This can be a useful way of thinking about it in health and social care, particularly when reviewing a service (Jackson 2013b). For example, a theatre procedure will need to pull particular types of supplies and equipment for the day of the procedure. Experience suggests that giving staff the time to think through what needs to be pulled to the patient at each stage of the process also works well.

For a patient to be ready to go to theatre on a particular day, followed by an expected inpatient stay, there has to be an informed consent process, with a signed consent form; records have to be available; a preoperative assessment has to have been completed, and any problems that might interfere with surgery corrected; the patient has to be appropriately fasted; they have to be in the right place at the right time, and so on (Figure 5.8). Both approaches result in much the same outcome, as both require consideration of resource, time and flow.

People are used to thinking in this way. Another way to think about it is the 'pull' process that sets the overall pace of the system. In this case, this will often be availability of a surgical team and a theatre. In that case, physiotherapy input post-procedure, if standard, becomes a predictable requirement at a specific time, as does preparation of the discharge arrangements, availability of transport and so on. The main activity effectively becomes a pacemaker for the rest of the service, setting what needs to be pulled to the activity at what time.

In the ophthalmology example given earlier in the chapter, one of the challenges was that, while everyone understood that there was an overall process through which a patient moved to receive the care they required, the process operated as a series of largely independent actions. In most clinics, patients were given appointment times for the consultant, and a separate appointment time to see the optometrist. Some parts of the process went faster for some people, but they then waited until their consultant appointment time.

In this case, the medical appointment was the constraint (Goldratt 1980). Using this as the pacemaker for the service would mean that other appointments were then timed against this resource, as in the previously discussed surgical process.

5.7 Batching

> Batch production…is really an attempt to drive production at the convenience of the producer, rather than the customer.
>
> **Hiroyuki Hirano and Makato Furuya (2006: pp 118–119)**

5.7.1 Examples of Batching

- A Community Mental Health Team receives referrals over the course of a week. All referrals are kept for a Friday allocation meeting, attended by all staff. Referrals are passed to the relevant staff at the meeting, who

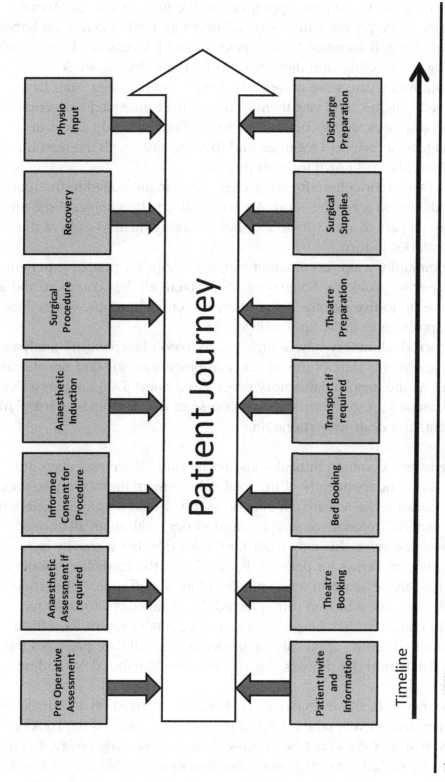

Figure 5.8   Pulling required inputs to the service user.

take them away and issue appointments the following week. About a quarter of the referrals are discussed in detail, while the rest are handed direct to a staff member. Some weeks, not all referrals can be dealt with during the meeting, and they are kept for the following week.

■ A community care team covers a wide geographical area. Staff have defined 'patches,' and visit them in turn. This is intended to decrease travel distances, and so be more efficient. Referrals and calls from specific areas are held together, and they are dealt with the next time a staff member is known to be in the area.

■ Blood taken for culture for suspected infection are added to the routine bloods due to leave the ward. A porter collects the samples three times a day, as part of a lengthy round, before taking them to each of the laboratories in turn.

■ A community team run different support groups for people experiencing specific problems. Some types of problem are less common, and it can be up to five months before there are enough people with a specific problem to make up a group.

■ A hospital laboratory buys a high-quality blood biochemistry analyser. The analyser is state of the art and can process up to 9000 samples an hour. As the hospital laboratory processes around 3000 samples a day, the samples are collected over the course of the day, unless particularly urgent, and dealt with at one time.

Batching is very common in health and social care. When processes are thought about independently of the total value stream for the service user, it seems to make sense to batch. It sounds as if it should be more efficient to save up material, referrals or samples, and to deal with them all at once.

In some instances, this may work for the service, but it usually introduces significant delays for patients. For example, the cardiology monitoring example made sense in terms of allocation of staff time, but introduced a delay in analysis, which in turn affected the availability of results for outpatient clinics, which then caused some patients to return for a further appointment. Batching approvals for higher cost social care packages introduced a delay in to the process, regardless of the likelihood of funding being agreed.

In the mental health example, if a patient was referred on a Thursday or Friday, they usually missed the referral meeting that week. If the backlog was such that they could not be discussed on the following Friday, it could be over a fortnight before they were allocated to a case holder. If there were issues in the referral that were not clear, and the allocated case holder called back to the GP or nurse who had referred the patient, they had often forgotten the details of the case and, in some cases, had to retrieve the case notes or recall the patient.

These examples have similar issues of delay for patients, because services are organised in a way that makes sense for the service, but they are not focused on value to the patient.

Protzman et al. (2011: 26–27) identify five types of approach, which lie on a spectrum:

1. Pure Batching – an entire batch of something – samples, application forms, patients and so on are moved through the process as one group.
2. Segmented Batching – producing a batch one piece at a time, such as processing all the ambulatory ECG results, then processing the ward ECGs and so on.
3. Period Batching – dealing with a batch of people or things in a specified period, such as dealing with all administration for the shift, at the end of the shift.
4. Group batching – in this model, people, tests or other items are divided into groups that have similar requirements, and they move down different lines. This is discussed further under 'Product Quantity Analysis' in the Levelling chapter. Protzman et al. (2011) regard this as midway between batching and true one-piece flow.
5. Mixed Model Sequencing – in this model, which is described in more detail in the 'Production Line Levelling' section in the Levelling chapter, each item or person is dealt with in turn, and the 'production line' is adapted quickly to be able to produce the different items – mixed models – without stopping production. In industry, the ability to make rapid changes to facilities is often called Single Minute Exchange of Dies (SMED). SMED is sometimes used as a generic term for rapid changeover.

5.8 One-Piece Flow

A system in which a person passes through the process with no delays, and no batching, is termed 'one-piece flow' (Shingo 2005). In one-piece flow at an outpatient clinic, for example, a patient may arrive and check in, and go straight to a clinic room. The clinician joins them there with no delay, and has the equipment and supplies to undertake the assessment straight away. This contrasts with the more common experience of delays at reception, waits in a waiting room, delays while the clinician finds the right notes, right equipment and right supplies and so on.

5.8.1 Examples: Problems Created by Lack of One-Piece Flow

■ An outpatient clinic was very busy, and often over-ran. It was common to run out of seats, and the service had thought about expanding into a neighbouring area to increase the size of its waiting room. There were four distinct areas of activity in the clinic, but as seating was so difficult to find, patients would sit anywhere that a seat was available. This meant that staff found it difficult to know who was waiting for which process. This, in turn, made it hard to know where the queues in the system were at any one time.

■ In an antenatal clinic for women whose pregnancies were judged to be 'higher risk,' the women went to a reception desk, and then waited in a waiting room. A midwife took them to a clinic room and assessed them. The women then waited in the room until an obstetrician saw them. The visible delay was in the waiting room, but during observations, it became clear that there could be three or four women waiting at any one time in the clinic rooms, after having been seen by a nurse. There was no obvious order in which the doctors saw the women. The design of the clinic produced a 'hidden' queue that could not be readily seen.

One of the major advantages of one-piece flow is that problems in the system are much easier to see. When a system is confusing, as in the subsequent clinic example, it is very difficult to see where the problems lie, and therefore to improve them. When flow begins to improve, it is easier to see blockages and disruption to flow.

Moving towards one-piece flow also has the significant advantage of decreasing or eliminating batching, and therefore decreasing built-in waits within the system (Suzaki 1987). One-piece flow is a general concept that can be applied to any system.

The advantages of one-piece flow (Hirano 1988; Shingo 2005; Hirano and Furuya 2006; Eaton 2013) are that it

■ Reduces waits
■ Decreases inventory

- Makes checking of errors and identification of cause easier
- Makes flow problems easier to identify
- Improves the speed at which changes can be made to the process

5.9 Creating One-Piece Flow

Placing workers here and there means they can hardly help each other. In allocating work and arranging workers, be sure to place them in such a way that they can help each other and combine their work.

Taiichi Ohno (Quoted in Japan Management Association 1989: p 116)

One-piece flow can be particularly relevant in production contexts, such as a laboratory or laundry, or even in the layout of a clinic. Shingo (2005: 101) notes that moving to one-piece flow requires consideration of levelling, reducing the number of people or items transported at once and improving layout to compensate for more frequent transportation.

To achieve this, the general principles of one-piece flow are (Hirano 1988; Hirano and Furuya 1996; Shingo 2005; Hirano 2009c)

- Lay out facilities in the order of the process.
- Create U-shaped lines (also known as 'cells').
- Avoid processing islands.
- Make machines small and mobile.
- Use multi-process operations and multi-skilled workers, who are trained to undertake the work.
- Separate human work from machine work, in relevant processes.
- Build error proofing and safety in to the process.
- Time activity against takt time (see Section 5.11 for an explanation of takt time).

Laying out facilities in the order of the process decreases transport of equipment and supplies, and the motion of staff and patients. It is common to see both patients and staff retrace their steps in a clinic (refer to Figure 5.1, for example). By organising the clinic, laboratory or office around the service flow, this can be markedly reduced (Tapping et al., 2002).

Processing islands are areas of activity that are largely unconnected to the main flow of the work, and are not synchronised with the other activities (Hirano 2009c). Examples given in this chapter include an outpatient service, in which the conduct and analysis of tests was not synchronised with the outpatient appointments, leading to delays when results were not available at the clinic appointments. Similarly, in a clinical assessment process, ECGs were conducted in a distant ECG department. This department was entirely separate, and was pulled in several different directions by competing demands. There was no alignment between its timings and that of the rest of the process, meaning that patients could experience significant waits at this part of their assessment.

In industry, it is common to arrange equipment in a U-shape, so that the completed product finishes its journey close to where it started (Hirano 1989). This again tends to reduce motion and transport. In some cases, one staff member undertakes all the processes in sequence. In health and social care, this sometimes occurs in laboratories, Accident and Emergency Departments, and in some types of assessments (Figure 5.9). In other instances, there can be several staff members who work at closely located stations (Figure 5.10).

One of the advantages of this type of arrangement is that it allows for one-by-one checking, so helping with error proofing (Hirano 1988). It is also easier to identify the cause of an error and to resolve it faster. In some situations, two parallel lines can be used (Hirano and Furuya 1996). This is

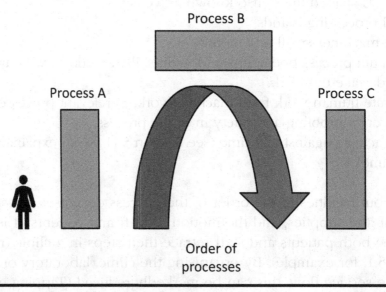

Figure 5.9   U-shaped cell, one staff member.

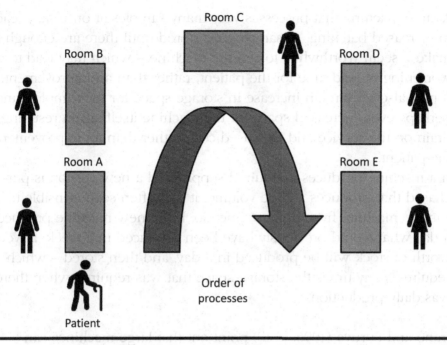

Figure 5.10   U-shaped cell, multiple staff members.

an option when one staff member is working on two distinct lines, such as might occur in a laboratory.

The equipment used in one-piece flow should be small and mobile, where possible. This allows for rapid rearrangement of equipment for different processes. It also helps to avoid batch processing or overproduction by better matching the machine to the demand. A large machine that can process many samples may seem better value, but it may worsen flow rather than improve it.

This apparent paradox arises because of the distinction between apparent efficiency and real efficiency (Suzaki 1987; Ohno 1988; Hirano and Furuya 1996). An improvement in efficiency is only an improvement if it adds value for the person using the service. There are many situations in which this may not be the case:

1. Purchasing a machine that works faster is only an advantage to the patient if the overall rate of flow is increased. So, for example, in a process in which there are long waits for an outpatient appointment, being able to run a test more quickly may make little or no difference to the lead time for the patient – there has been an apparent improvement in efficiency, but no improvement for the patient.

2. A large machine that processes very many samples at once may lead to increased batching, as samples are stored until there are enough to make it seem worthwhile to run the machine – which may lead to a worsening of lead time for the patient, rather than an improvement. It may also require an increase in storage space for the samples, and perhaps even increased space for the machine itself, again resulting in a drain on the service and increased cost, rather than an improvement for the patient.

3. If a machine produces a required supply, and a new version is purchased that produces a large volume, it will often seem sensible to only run the machine from time to time. So, if the new machine produces in a day what would previously have been produced in a week, a week's worth of stock will be produced in a day, and then stored – which requires many times the storage space that was required when there was daily production.

Hirano and Furuya (1996: p 48) point out that large machines can become a wider problem for several other reasons:

■ Their purchase can give the impression that the solution to most problems lie in investment in technology, rather than improving the process.
■ When large expensive machines have been purchased, it is very difficult to reverse the decision, making it difficult to change processes.
■ Making maximum use of the equipment can become the purpose of the exercise, rather than the equipment being used only to support the process.

5.10 Drum–Buffer–Rope Systems

In Lean, the general aim is to produce one-piece flow to reduce delays for the service user, and to help to level work for the staff members.

There are some circumstances in which some batching may help flow, at least until the problems in the system can be improved (Inozu et al. 2012). Goldratt (1990) built on earlier work to coin the idea of the Theory of Constraints.

The argument Goldratt advances is

1. Any system has a step which is the single most constraining step.

2. If this step does not operate to its full capacity, then the whole system slows because it cannot produce faster than this most constrained step.
3. For the system to operate as efficiently as possible, the use of this step must be maximised.

The intention will be to increase the capacity or efficiency of this step. Until that can be done, this step acts as the overall drum beat of the service, as the system can go no faster than this step. This 'Drum' therefore drives the whole service.

To maximise the use of this step, it makes sense to keep it operating at its maximum capacity. Any system will have delays from time to time related to machine breakdown, lost or delayed materials and so on. Goldratt argues that, to maximise the use of the constrained step, the time that can be lost from the system because of delays should be calculated. A Buffer, equivalent to this time, is then created in front of the constrained function, or Drum.

For example, consider a process in an outpatient clinic that it limited, for example because only one test machine is available, and which takes six minutes on average. If delays in the rest of the system of up to ten minutes occur, then it could be appropriate to keep two pieces of work – probably two patients, in effect – ready for the constrained step. In that way, if the system slows, the whole clinic can still recover because the rate of the most constrained step never slows.

In Lean terms, this builds in an automatic wait for patients. It may make sense to do this, at least in the short-term, if by doing it the overall flow in the clinic, and the average wait for patients, is reduced. The longer-term aim would be to resolve the constraint.

There is no advantage to exceeding the planned capacity of the Buffer. Thinking of an industrial example, if the work earlier in the process produces more items than are needed for the buffer, the stock accumulates in front of the Drum. As the Drum is the most constrained part of the process, it can never catch up, unless the whole process is stopped. In Goldratt's analogy, a 'Rope' is used to control the gateway into the process. When the Buffer is full, the Rope pulls the gateway into the process closed, opening it again when the Buffer is no longer full.

This produces the whole term of Drum–Buffer–Rope. In a clinic example, there is no merit in bringing people in early for their appointment, once the equivalent of the Buffer is full – it will only result in an increased lead time for the patient.

5.11 Takt Time

Takt time is the rate of output required…to satisfy demand.

Hirano and Furuya (1996: 35)

The pace at which a service needs to work to meet demand is known as takt time (Ohno 1988). 'Takt' is a German word that can be translated as 'beat' or 'rhythm.'

The takt time is calculated from the time in which a service is open, divided by the demand for a service. For example, if a service operates Monday to Friday, 9 a.m. to 5 p.m., there is a total time of 40 hours. It may be completely closed at lunchtimes for 30 minutes a day, however, reducing the available time by two and a half hours per week, making the time available 37.5 hours (2250 minutes). If the demand for this service is 4000 samples a week, then the takt time is 2250 divided by 4000, which is just under 34 seconds per sample (Figure 5.11).

As another example, if an outpatient clinic is open for four hours (240 minutes), and must see 30 patients in that time, then the takt time is 240 minutes divided by 30, giving a takt time of 8 minutes.

Key points about takt time

Open hours per ~~day /~~ week / ~~month~~	=	40:00
The time that an area is open to provide a service		
Minutes per ~~day /~~ week / ~~month~~	=	2400
Minutes per day	=	480
Breaks per day	=	30
Department is closed for all staff attending breaks at same time		
Set-up Time / Huddle / Other per day	=	0
Other time where department is closed due to initial Set-Up or all staff attending an activity such as Team Huddle		
Minutes available per day	=	450
Demand per day	=	800
Takt Time (Minutes/Unit)	=	0.56
Takt Time (Seconds/Unit)	=	33.75

Figure 5.11   Example of takt time calculation.

1. Takt time does not take in to account rework. For example, if a laboratory must repeat 5% of tests because of quality control problems, the takt time is calculated from the original demand, not for the demand plus the rework.
2. The opening hours of the service are used, minus any breaks or other planned stoppages. For example, if a service closes completely, then the time of the closure would not be included in the available time. If, however, a service has rolling breaks, where one or two staff go on a break at a time but the service remains open, then these would not be taken in to account in identifying the time available (Hirano and Furuya 1996).
3. Takt time is a measure of demand and time available, not a measure of the actual performance of the current service. So, for example, if the outpatient clinic described previously only sees 25 patients at the clinic, then that does not change the takt time.

Takt time does not mean that there is only that amount of time to be spent on each person/sample/process. In the previous example, if the process took 24 minutes, then three staff would be required, and so on (Eaton 2013).

If a service could operate with no waste at all, then the number of staff required equals the sum of the cycle times/takt time. So, for example, if the outpatient appointments take an average of 16 minutes, then two staff would be needed to deliver the required service to takt time. Eaton (2013) introduces the useful idea of 'minimum headcount' – making the point that an allowance has to be made for holidays, breaks and so on.

5.12 Multi-Process Handling and Multi-Skilled Workers

> Multi-process operations are the key that opens the door to one-piece flow production.
>
> **Shigeo Shingo (2009: p 389)**

Multi-Skilled Workers and Multi-Process Handling are related ideas that complement one another (Suzaki 1987; Hirano 2009c). In multi-process handling, one staff member undertakes more than one process. In a laboratory, this could involve one worker running two or three different machines. In a clinic or other assessment setting, this could be undertaking two or three distinct processes such as an interview, blood pressure check and taking blood.

To do this, the staff member needs to be multi-skilled. Multi-skilled workers are essential. The core reason multi-skilled workers are so important is that it allows the number of staff working in an area to be moved up or down in response to patient demand.

Consider, for example, a clinic that is usually staffed by five staff members. If the staff members have very specific roles, then if the number of patients is expected to be lower on a specified day, it is not possible to reallocate staff to other duties as at least some of each process will be required. If the staff are multi-skilled, however, then a lower volume of work can be covered by a lower number of staff, allowing rotas to be organised around this, or staff to be reallocated to work in another area.

There are other advantages of multi-skilled workers, however. If staff can perform a variety of duties, then it is easier for them to support a colleague if there are problems in flow. For example, in an Assessment service, there were some duties that were conducted by a Health Care Assistant, and some that required a trained nurse. The staff identified which of the actions could only be undertaken by a trained nurse, and then taught the Health Care Assistants to undertake the other actions. This meant that, if a nurse was under pressure, the Health Care Assistants could undertake a greater number of the required tasks, letting the nurse concentrate on the aspects of care that required their specialist skills.

Training people to be multi-skilled requires clarity on the nature of the task, and therefore the development of Standard Work, discussed further in Chapter 9. Having standard work requires the identification of standards, and usually incorporates self-inspection (please see Chapter 7 on Error Proofing for further discussion of types of inspection). This means that errors are much less likely to be passed on to the next stage of the process, and therefore less likely to result in defects that affect patient care.

It is important that the required processes are as clear as possible. Hirano (2009c: p 405) comments, 'nothing should be left to…(the)' oral tradition 'of know-how that gets passed from person to person. Everything must be explicit.' If it is not possible to explain the process clearly, then it is very difficult to learn it. As Hirano notes, this has to include the 'givens' that people are 'just expected to know.'

In health and social care, the situation will often be that the person being taught already has relevant professional skills, and it is then the sequence of activities and how they are to be recorded that is being taught rather than,

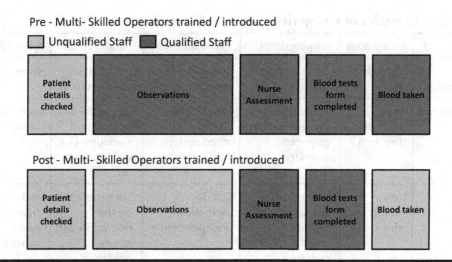

Figure 5.12   Impact of multi-skilled operators.

for example, having to train a nurse to take a blood pressure or to teach a social worker to have interviewing and interpersonal skills. In other cases, particularly with new staff with no previous professional training, a whole skill may need to be taught (Figure 5.12).

5.13 Multiple-Skills Training Schedules

A Multiple-Skills Training Schedule (Hirano 2009c) is often used to show which staff are able to undertake a procedure, and the target date for training others. Various formats are used, such as circles divided into quarters, sides of a box or a cross within a box. The types of categories used vary by organisation and process. Table 5.1 gives examples of categories from published examples. A version used by NHS Highland is shown in Figure 5.13, adapted from Hirano (2009c: 409–410).

5.14 Training Staff in Multiple Skills

There are four stages of training people in new tasks (Suzaki 1993):

- Preparation
- Explanation and demonstration of the job
- Execution of the job by the trainee
- Follow-up

Table 5.1 Examples of Categories Used in Skill Matrices

Speed 2013	Instep 2009	Instep 2009	Jackson 2012	Hirano 2009c	Speed 2013
Not competent	No skills	Can complete the task	Unable to do operation	Unable to do the operation	None
Competent	Partly trained in this area	Can complete the task to the required standard	Can do with assistance/ need review	Able to do the operation if someone else does the set up	Low/very basic
	Fully trained in this area	Can complete the task to the required standard, in the required amount of time	Can do operation independently	Can generally do the operation, but needs guidance	Under training, or need refresher
		Could do all of the previously mentioned and train others	Can do operation well/ instruct	Can do the operation well, except under unusual conditions	Reasonably competent
				Can do the entire operation well	Highly competent
					Expert

5.14.1 Preparation

This stage requires a clear statement of the standard work required for the process. The person who will be teaching the method must run back through the task using only the guidance, to make sure that it does include all the relevant actions, including any unspoken 'givens.'

The staff member must be prepared, so needs to understand the advantages to patients of the increased flexibility.

5.14.2 Explanation and Demonstration of the Job

The trainer explains the task to the trainee and describes its purpose. They demonstrate the job, then go over the standard work with the trainee, step by step. They then run through the whole process again to let the trainee see the work against the standard work. This will include

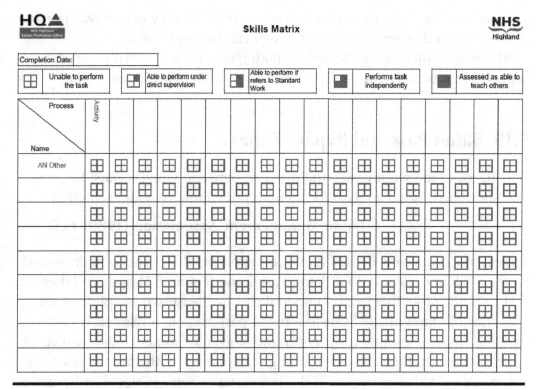

Figure 5.13 Example of a skills matrix.

explaining and demonstrating any inspection or other error proofing work that must be done, including describing the reason for the error proofing actions.

5.14.3 Execution of the Job by the Trainee

The trainee carries out the procedure. The trainer corrects any errors and allows the trainee to repeat the task. The trainee explains the whole task to the trainer and then repeats as often as required. Suzaki (1993) points out that the trainee, in seeing the job for the first time, may identify ways of improving the process which can be taken in to account, and incorporated into revised standard work if useful.

5.14.4 Follow-up

The trainee needs to know who to ask for help or advice and to understand their responsibilities. Questions that are asked as the person becomes familiar with the technique are often very useful, as they may show up parts of the process that are not clear or which can be improved.

This stage will involve the trainee taking on the task, initially under supervision, but reducing as the trainee gains confidence (Figure 5.14).

5.15 Baton Pass and Bypass Zones

> To make the work easier, the distance between workers must be shortened. Make it easier for them to communicate with each other.
>
> **Japan Management Association (1989: 115)**

Baton Pass Zones and Bypass Zones are concepts that relate to multi-skilled workers (Hirano 2009d). In a Baton Pass Zone (Figure 5.14 and 5.15) there will be some tasks that can be undertaken by at least two people in a process. Taiichi Ohno likened this to a baton pass zone in a relay race, commenting, 'in a swimming relay, faster and slower swimmers must each cover a set distance. In the case of a running relay, however, the faster person can cover for a slower person in the baton (pass) zone' (Quoted in Japanese Management Association 1989: 115). Baton Pass Zones are also known as Baton Touch Zones (Hirano 2009d) and Relay Zones (Suzaki 1987).

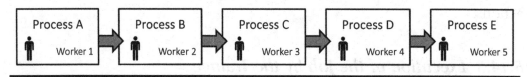

Figure 5.14 Existing process.

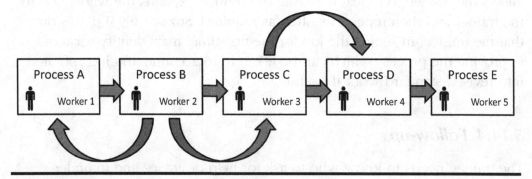

Figure 5.15 Process with options for support – Baton Pass.

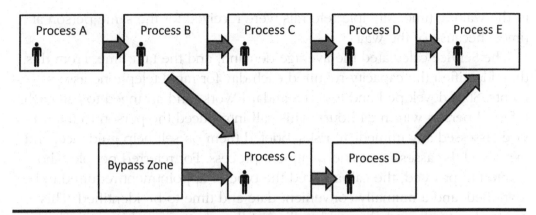

Figure 5.16 Process with options for support – bypass zone.

In this example, Worker 2 can perform Processes A, B and C. Worker 3 can perform both Process C and Process D. This means that Worker 2 can help out Worker 1 and Worker 3 when needed, and Worker 3 can support Worker 4 if required.

If workload means that one person gets behind, the fact that they have shared skills means that the second person can pick up some of the work usually undertaken by the first staff member – to pick up the baton. This will usually be temporary. It is easier when the service is organised using cells with closely located processes, as it makes it easier to both identify the problem and to take on the work.

Bypass Zones are lines of parallel processes that are opened when there is a major constraint in the system. Many services have one or two procedures in a process that work close to capacity. This can be reviewed (see the discussion on Line Balancing) but it may be necessary to temporarily open a second, parallel process undertaking the same procedures (Figure 5.16). In the example in Figure 5.16, there is a known constraint in Processes C and D, so in a time of increased demand, two additional workers can be allocated to undertake duplicate processes to keep up with demand and so meet takt time. This is much easier if there are already multi-skilled workers. Having a skills matrix also makes it easier for staff to see at a glance who already has this skill, and who could be allocated to the task.

5.16 Practice Example

A drug and alcohol treatment service had long waiting times for first treatment, and a high rate of non-attendance, which staff believed was linked to the waiting time. Multiple referrals were received for the same person at times, because of the wait.

The Service calculated the average demand, and the takt time. From this, they identified the capacity required each day for rapid telephone assessments. Staff developed and tested Standard Work, and arranged to call each referred person within 24 hours. This call introduced the person to the service, assessed any immediate risks, briefed them on self-help guidance, and explained the assessment and treatment process. For referred people who wanted to proceed, the call allowed the type of appointment required to be identified, and a mutually convenient date and time to be identified. This reduced re-work, and allowed levelling of flow, better matching capacity to demand. Treatments were now commenced at the first face to face appointment. The average wait to commence treatment reduced by 65% (Beattie et al. 2018.)

5.17 Conclusions

Continuous flow is one of the key components of the Lean approach to work. Improving flow reduces delays for patients, decreases frustration for staff and makes problems in the system much more apparent. It also improves the ease with which errors can be identified, corrected and the root cause resolved.

If continuous flow cannot be achieved, then creating a pull system is preferable to allowing a push system to continue. In some cases, buffers and other methods of coping with constraints may be required. Where demand is uneven, having multi-skilled workers allows more flexibility in staffing, and in supporting parts of the system which are under pressure.

Further Reading

Full references are included in the bibliography.

Mark Graban's book, *Lean Hospitals* (2016) has a good section on flow, with numerous examples.
Hirano and Furuya's book *JIT Is Flow* (1996) has a wealth of practical knowledge and can often be found second hand. Hirano discusses flow in several volumes of the *JIT Implementation Manual* (2009).

Chapter 6

Levelling

6.1 Aims of the Chapter

The aims of the chapter are

1. To understand the distinction between process and demand variation
2. To know how to apply product quantity analysis in health and social care
3. To be familiar with approaches to load levelling

6.2 Introduction

> The fundamental principle driving levelled production is that the rate of flow and the mix of products being produced must mirror the rate of customer demand as closely as possible.
>
> **Hiroyuki Hirano and Makato Furuya (2006: p 123)**

Health and social care services exist to meet patient and service user need. Services do not, however, always align with individual need. Where there are mismatches, either service users wait for services, or staff wait for service users or both. The improvement aim is to 'create stability in the workload,' (Eaton 2013: p 29) a process often referred to as *heijunka* (Japan Management Association 1989; Tapping et al. 2002; Nash and Polling 2008; Jackson 2013).

There are two main causes of variation in workload (Bicheno 2008):

■ Process variation
■ Demand variation

Process variation is variation introduced by the way the service is run, while demand variation is caused by true variation in demand for the service itself. The service may have limited control over the overall demand, so it needs to consider how to adjust to smooth the way activity flows into the system, or how the service responds to the demand.

6.3 Process Variation

6.3.1 Examples: Process Variation

■ Patients saw a haematologist who assessed whether further chemotherapy was needed. If it was, the patient went to the chemotherapy unit. They would wait until a chair was available, the treatment preparation had arrived and a nurse was free to commence the infusion. As this process took at least 90 minutes and often longer, over half the treatment chairs were usually empty until after 10.30 a.m. By noon, there was often a queue of people waiting for a chair.
■ A preoperative assessment service was busy when patients began to flow through from outpatient clinic appointments, but it was quiet at other times.
■ A hospital had discontinued the practice of admitting people routinely the evening before surgery. Most people were now admitted on the morning of their surgery. As the surgeons and anaesthetists liked to see the patient prior to their surgery, and were in theatre most of the day, all the patients were asked to come in at 7.30 a.m., no matter what time their surgery was scheduled. This produced congestion in the waiting area and a significant increase in activity for nurses. It meant that patients who were not due for surgery until early afternoon could have to wait over five hours for surgery, and they had often fasted for far longer than was recommended.
■ An outpatient clinic was very quiet and flowed well at 9.30 a.m. By 11 a.m., the same clinic had long queues, disgruntled patients and harassed staff.

▪ A large general practice kept a small number of appointments for people who wanted to be seen urgently. Patients had learned that they needed to call at precisely 8.30 a.m. to have a chance of getting an appointment. Extra administrative staff had to be put on at 8.30 a.m., who were not needed in the remainder of the morning, to answer the large number of simultaneous calls received.

The way these services, or an adjacent service operated, caused these variations. In effect, the service design forced the unevenness to occur.

Unevenness caused by service design can also be undone by altering the system. Figure 6.1 shows chairs in use in the haematology chemotherapy service by day and hour over a one-week period. Figure 6.2 shows the average number of chairs in use by hour over the week. The week was typical of other, recorded, weeks.

The graphs show that there is variation by day and by hour. Mondays and Fridays are the quietest days, with Fridays being particularly quiet. Figures 6.1 and 6.2 also demonstrate substantial variation by hour, with substantial unused capacity after 2 p.m. and before 11 a.m.

The service identified the balance of planned versus unplanned work, quantified average attendances and ranges, and rearranged the

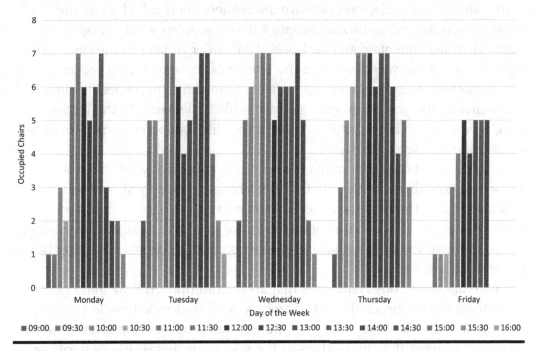

Figure 6.1   Patients being treated in a haematological chemotherapy service, by day and hour over a one-week period.

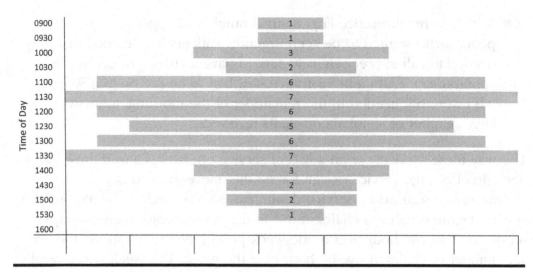

Figure 6.2 Patients being treated in chemotherapy service, average number by hour.

appointments. Some people know in advance that they will have a specific number of treatments. These people can be booked into slots at times when other patients will not yet have emerged from clinics. Clinic appointments themselves can be more widely spread over the day, and the medicines preparation flow was also improved.

In a similar issue, the preoperative assessment service had some pre-booked attendances, and some people who came from wards to be assessed. Ward patients could be booked in earlier or later in the day, help-ing to even out the workload over the course of the day. It also proved pos-sible to identify the usual range of patients who came from specific clinics, and so match the staff numbers against the likely demand. In the longer term, it would also be possible to look at the distribution of outpatient clin-ics over the course of the week.

In the surgical example, a first round of improvement work did not remove all batching, as the clinicians felt strongly that they should see patients prior to the list. It was possible, however, to change afternoon patients to arrive closer to lunchtime, to make clear the guidance on fasting, and to improve the flow within the theatre process to decrease waiting both for patients and for staff.

There are numerous challenges that arise from uneven flow introduced by systems (Protzman et al. 2011). Services need to decide how to organise staffing. If demand arrives unevenly, then to keep up, staffing levels may be organised to meet this demand, as in the telephone answering example or the pre-theatre example. If this is done, to cope with peak demand, then the same level of staffing may not be required for the rest of the shift, leaving people with time on their hands. If the staffing resource is not increased, then delays are likely, and staff will often be harassed and pressured, trying to keep up with demand. Either approach has the risk of disrespecting staff, by not making best use of their time and skills, or by expecting too much from them.

This kind of uneven demand, resulting in batching, also requires greater space. When the theatre suite reduced batching, they were also able to free up the space to create same sex waiting areas, which had been thought to be impossible without capital expenditure.

Finally, it also produces problems elsewhere in the system. In the theatre example, people were being processed as they arrived, which was not necessarily the order in which they were to go to theatre. This meant that some people were ready many hours in advance, while others were not ready when the theatre suite called for them. This disruption to flow, and lack of visibility, can cause significant problems for services, which staff often work hard to work around.

6.4 Demand Variation

6.4.1 Examples: Demand Variation

- A service providing radiotherapy for people with breast cancer referred people after they had gone through the diagnosis and multidisciplinary team assessment process. Over a four-year period, the number of new people presenting each week varied from zero to 10. Some of the changes in demand related to an annual breast cancer awareness week, which often brought a surge of new referrals.
- A Child and Adolescent Mental Health Service consistently received fewer referrals during the school summer holidays, because many referrals came from school staff and associated workers.
- An accident and emergency department had marked variation in average attendances, by time of the day, day of the week and month of the year.

In these cases, the service has little or no control over the rate at which people come into the service. They can, however, affect to at least some extent how they respond to the demand (Eaton 2013).

In looking at the radiotherapy example, the service was contending with long waits for some patients, partly related to uneven workload and the consequences of it. When the service looked in detail at new diagnoses by week (Figure 6.3), they found that the average number of patients, the mode and the median, were all three.

The service then used this information to identify the cumulative number of weeks in which each number of treatments was required (Figure 6.4).

So, for example, 46% of weeks have two new treatment requirements or less (line 'A' – Figure 6.4); 71% of weeks have three new treatment requirements or less (line 'B'), and 84% of weeks have four new treatment requirements or less (line 'C').

The service then tried to decide what would be an appropriate number of treatment slots to be able to provide per week. After some experimentation, they concluded that four treatment slots would be reasonable (Figure 6.5).

Using real weekly data from the previous 17 quarters, they found that, in 22 weeks, this could be expected to be the precise number required (0 difference); in 40 weeks, this would be one slot more than required (i.e. there would be a free slot), and in 11 weeks one additional treatment would be required and so on.

The team then took the data, and went through their information working out how quickly people would have started treatment, compared to the

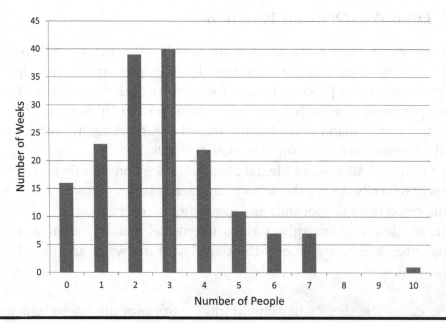

Figure 6.3 Number of new people requiring breast cancer radiotherapy, by week, over 17 consecutive quarters.

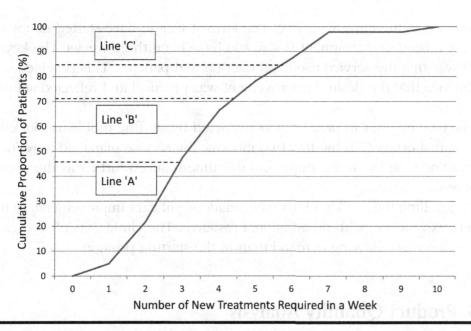

Figure 6.4   Radiotherapy numbers by cumulative proportion of weeks.

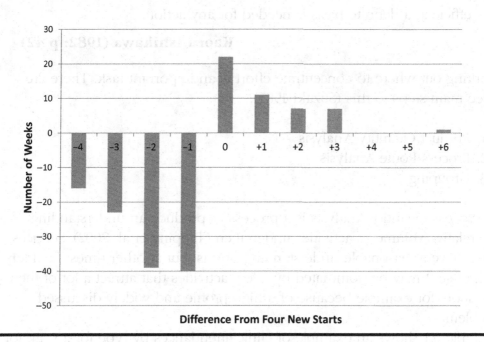

Figure 6.5   Difference from four new start treatment slots.

experience in the current service. The longest wait to have started radio-therapy related to a treatment slot would have been three weeks. The key point was that the service used real data on real patients. This provided confidence that the desired improvement was practical and reflected actual experience.

The true number in practice was restricted by staffing problems, but even with staff shortages, in the first two months, the service managed to reduce the waiting time by over a third, and this time reduced further as the system improved.

By levelling the workload, the staff made significant improvements to the patient experience, with no additional resource. The clinic slots offered came much closer to following demand than in the starting position.

6.5 Product Quantity Analysis

> Each problem consists of so many smaller problems that it is dif-
> ficult to know just where to begin solving them. In order to be
> efficient, a definite basis is needed for any action.
>
> **Kaoru Ishikawa (1982: p 42)**

Working out where to concentrate effort is an important task. There are three main steps to this (Suzaki 1987):

1. Product Quantity Analysis
2. Process Route Analysis
3. Grouping

Process Quantity Analysis is a process to produce an understanding of the relative volume of activities undertaken (Tapping et al. 2002). Services often have a reasonable understanding of this, but at other times the attention of staff may be dominated by a few activities that attract a lot of their attention, for example because of a high profile and widely discussed problem.

Table 6.1 shows an example of clinic attendances by type for a year, for a hypothetical service.

Stage One: Product Quantity Analysis: a common way to do this is by producing a Pareto chart (Juran 1995: pp 47–58). A Pareto chart is a bar

Table 6.1 Example of Annual Attendances by Appointment Type

Appointment Type	Number
A	544
B	204
C	678
D	85
E	321
F	26
G	177
H	379
I	32
J	102
K	823
L	164
M	367
Total	3902

graph, which has a second line showing the cumulative percentage. This allows staff working in a service to see both the actual number of events or attendances, and the percentage of all events/attendances that they comprise. This allows a discussion of relative priority.

The steps to construct a Pareto chart are (adapted from Ishikawa 1982: pp 42–43)

1. Decide the classifications you want to use in the chart.
2. Decide on the time period to be covered by the graph.
3. Add up the frequency of occurrence of each category for the period.
4. Draw horizontal and vertical axes on graph paper, and decide on the scale to be used, and the divisions in the scale, based on the totals from Step 3. Write in the titles of the axes.
5. Draw in the bars, beginning at the far left with the most frequent items. If there are several categories with limited numbers, you may decide to group them together as 'other.'
6. Under the horizontal axis, label each of the bars.

7. Plot a line showing the cumulative total reached from the addition of each category.
8. Title the graph and state the source of the data on which the graph is based.

It is not necessary to use a computer spreadsheet or other software programme, unless it makes the task easier – a hand-drawn chart is perfectly acceptable, if it helps in decision-making.

Ishikawa (1982: p 44) comments that,

> A Pareto diagram is very useful in drawing the cooperation of all concerned. As the type of diagram clearly and distinctly exposes the relative magnitude…it provides the workers with a base of common knowledge from which to operate.

There are various uses for this type of graph, including plotting errors by type and demand by volume. In the previous ophthalmology example considered in Chapter 5, the number of people attending each clinic was known. There were many small clinics or types of attendance that, while important to the people concerned, were not the main work of the service. As with other work in Lean, focusing on getting the large volume work to flow well can free up time to spend on complex, low volume work that can otherwise be squeezed out by high volume work.

Juran (1992: pp 57–61) notes the 'vital few – for whom planning is to be done on an individual basis' and the 'useful many – those for whom planning is to be done on a group basis.' Juran (1995) also makes the point that the information needed to identify a problem will rarely be sufficient to also identify likely solutions. For this, further work on the shop floor – the *gemba* – is required.

Using the example in Table 6.1, putting the appointment types in order of frequency produces Table 6.2. The third column shows the percentage of the total for each category, and the fourth column shows the cumulative percentage.

If this is then put into a graph as described previously, Figure 6.6 can be produced.

From Table 6.2 and Figure 6.6, it can be seen that three clinic types – K, C and A – make up 52% of the total number of appointments. If three more clinic types are included – H, M and E – then the six categories together make up 79.7% of total appointments. In this example, just under half of the

Table 6.2   Appointment Types Ordered by Numerical Size

Appointment Type	Number	Per cent	Cumulative Percentage
K	823	21.1	13.9
C	678	17.4	38.5
A	544	13.9	52.4
H	379	9.7	62.1
M	367	9.4	71.5
E	321	8.2	79.8
B	204	5.2	85.0
G	177	4.5	89.5
L	164	4.2	93.7
J	102	2.6	96.3
D	85	2.2	98.5
I	32	0.8	99.3
F	26	0.7	100.0

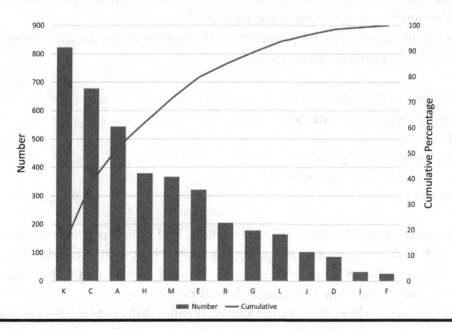

Figure 6.6   Pareto chart of clinic appointments from Table 6.2.

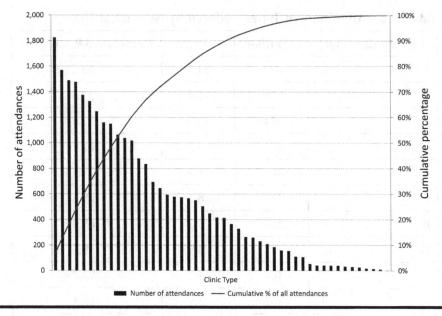

Figure 6.7   Pareto chart of appointment types and numbers, for an ophthalmology service.

appointment types make up almost 80% of all appointments. In some real-life cases, this can be even more striking. Figure 6.7 shows appointment types and numbers for an ophthalmology service for a year.

Stage Two is Process Route Analysis. At this stage, processes through which different categories pass are identified.

For example, the type of processes within ophthalmology, discussed in Chapter 5 – Continuous Flow, include

- Visual field examination
- Eye pressure measurement
- Dilation
- Fluroscein angiography
- Review by ophthalmologist
- Treatment

The order in which these are undertaken, and which procedures occur on which visit, vary. People attending the same clinic may have different experiences of the process, related to the type of appointment, the stage of their condition and their individual clinical needs

Stage Three – Grouping. As people with quite different conditions may have very similar processes as part of their visit to a clinic or service, it may be possible to group several apparently different conditions, because they make use of the same processes. For example, in a macular degeneration clinic, some people may be coming back only for injections, while others may be having a series of procedures to make a diagnosis or to help decide on continuation of treatment. Categories can be plotted on a Process Grouping Diagram (Figure 6.8).

In this case, conditions 4 and 5 follow the same process. Ishikawa (1982) points out that, once routes are identified, it may be possible to produce services where people needing the same processes flow through a dedicated line. This tends to reduce constraints that arise from multiple value streams flowing through the same processes at the same time. This is not always possible, but being aware of competing demands on key points of the system is important. Sometimes these processes are not those that are anticipated before observations are conducted.

In working out demand, it is useful to distinguish between Value Demand and Failure Demand, discussed previously (Bicheno 2008). Value Demand is demand direct from patients, service users or from processes that serve them. Failure Demand is demand that results from a problem in the process.

For example, an antenatal service organised detailed scans which followed on from dating scans. It would have been possible to agree on an appointment at the time of the dating scan, as the detail scan date depended

	Process 1	Process 2	Process 3	Process 4	Process 5	Process 6	Process 7
Condition1	X	X	X			X	
Condition 2	X	X	X				
			X			X	
Condition 3	X	X	X	X	X	X	
Condition 4	X	X	X			X	X
Condition 5	X	X	X			X	X
Condition 6	X	X	X		X	X	
				X		X	X

Figure 6.8 Example of process routing diagram.

on the stage of pregnancy identified at the dating scan. The staff rotas were not known far enough in advance to allocate clinic dates sufficiently far in advance, however. This meant that patients were told that they would be sent a date. Many people called in the following weeks to ask if their appointment date was now known. It took time to respond to each call, and patients were usually dissatisfied with the answer, as dates could not yet be allocated. When the staff rotas were released, the administrative staff booked all the appointments that they had stored over the previous month, in two days of very hard work, and then posted all the appointments out at the same time.

Over the next few days, as appointments were received, they had a large volume of calls from women asking to change the time or date of their scan, because it conflicted with school, nursery or work times, or because their partner could not be present at that time. Almost all of this work – the calls to ask about allocation of appointments, the two days of intense work to collate and issue appointments, and the constant interruptions over the following few days as people called to change their appointment – would have been avoided if the appointments could have been agreed on directly with the woman at the time they left their booking scan. The root cause of this additional demand – failure demand – was the timing of agreement of staff rotas, and therefore the inability to offer clinic appointments.

In some cases, unevenness in demand and unevenness in response interact. For example, patients present to outpatient clinics at different rates, although it is often possible to predict the overall rate (please see the Product Quantity Analysis section for an example). Services often then compound unevenness in demand by using very set return intervals – for example, three months or six months – rather than an interval tailored to the patient's needs, assuming they need to return to the outpatient clinic at all.

6.6 Production Line Levelling

Production Line Levelling is a technique that is widely used in industry (Ohno 1988; Japan Management Association 1989), and that can be applicable in some health care situations.

The challenge for a production line is to turn uneven customer demand into relatively level scheduling of work. Eaton (2013: p 293) comments 'hei-junka (levelling) aims to provide a balance between responding only to customer requests in the sequence they arise, and the need to obtain efficiency from your people and processes.'

Services sometimes respond to uneven demand by large changes to contracts, or even redundancy. Lean organisations aim to respect staff, which includes treating staff in a responsible manner. This means that some levelling of activity is inevitable, to keep staff working. Not all unevenness can be eliminated, and it is in these circumstances that using staff in brief improvement projects in their clinical area, or in work such as 5S, can be very valuable.

There are numerous guides to the principles of levelling (Japanese Management Association 1989; Hirano and Black 1988; Hirano and Furuya 2006; Hirano 2009d) and the subsequent example is based on these descriptions. The idea is to bring activity into line with customer demand, while decreasing batching, decreasing waiting, increasing flow and increasing flexibility.

Consider, for example, an industrial production line that has an expected overall demand of 10,000 items a month. The average demand is 5000 of Item A, 3000 of Item B and 2000 of Item C.

If the production line used a monthly production schedule then, assuming that it could produce the items at the same rate over a four-week month, then it could make Item A for the first fortnight, Item B for the next six days, and then Item C for the last four days.

There are several drawbacks to this:

- If an order for item C is placed towards the end of the month, then it will probably be at least three weeks before it can be filled.
- Storage space is needed for all of the product produced.
- Materials are often received in large batches to cope with the expected demand for materials to build one type of product in volume.
- The stockpile of materials and completed goods can act to conceal problems in the system: because there is a buffer, it is easier for the system to cope with problems. This is not good, because it makes it more difficult to identify problems in the system and to resolve them.
- A large number of faulty goods may be produced before a problem is identified.
- It is very difficult to change the design of an item at short notice, or to adjust the production schedule.

In effect, the system is organised for the benefit of the organisation, rather than focusing on lead time for the customer.

The Batching section in the Continuous Flow chapter described types of batching (Protzman et al. 2011). Rather than production planned around a once-a-month cycle, the cycle can be two weekly, one weekly or daily (Hirano 2009d), in a 'segmented' production (Shingo 2005). Suzaki (1987: pp 126–7) describes these periods as 'time buckets' – periods of time that 'hold' a certain amount of production. Examples of different schedules are shown in Table 6.3.

In two weekly productions, using the previous example, the production line would plan to produce 5000 items a fortnight. Looking at these schedules

- A fortnightly schedule would produce 5000 items in two weeks, split 2500 of Item A, 1500 of Item B, and 1000 of Item C.
- A one weekly schedule would produce 2500 items, split 1250 of Item A, 750 of Item B, and 500 of Item C
- A daily production schedule would produce 250 of Item A, 150 of Item B and 100 of Item C.

All when scaled up would produce the same monthly quantity as the once-a-month production schedule but would reduce at least some of the problems of the monthly schedule, as less inventory would need to be held, less storage space for completed product would be needed, and average lead time would reduce.

So, taking the daily production requirement of 250 of Item A, 150 of Item B and 100 of Item C, and assuming a ten-hour production day, the line could produce Item A from 8 a.m. to 1 p.m., Item B from 1 p.m. to 4 p.m., and Item C from 4 p.m. to 6 p.m.

The final option, described as Mixed Model Sequencing or Mixed Production (Suzaki 1987, Schonberger 1987; Protzman et al. 2011) is to spread the production over the course of the day. The production line needs to produce items in a ratio of 5:3:2. So, it would be possible to space these out so that, in each group of 10 items, 5 of Item A are produced, 3 of Item B and 2 of Item C. This could be arranged as a production sequence of AABCABCABA, for example. This is as close to level production as can reasonably be produced, and spreads the work across the day as evenly as possible. It does depend on a very rapid set up, and this is discussed further subsequently.

Table 6.3 Examples of Production Schedules

Schedule	Week One					Week Two					Week Three					Week Four				
	M	T	W	Th	F	M	T	W	Th	F	M	T	W	Th	F	M	T	W	Th	Fri
Monthly	A	A	A	A	A	A	A	A	A	A	B	B	B	B	B	B	C	C	C	C
Fortnightly	A	A	A	A	A	B	B	B	C	A	A	A	A	A	B	A	B	B	C	C
Weekly	A	A	AB	B	C	A	A	AB	B	C	A	A	AB	B	C	A	A	AB	B	A

Thinking of takt time, if 500 items have to be produced every day, and the production line is open for 10 hours, then the takt time for an individual item, overall, is 1 minute 12 seconds (72 seconds). To produce a block of 10 items should take 12 minutes (720 seconds). This 12-minute time period to produce 10 items can be considered as a 'pitch' – a work increment that can be monitored. This allows an overall view of whether the system is keeping up with demand.

In health and social care, the concepts are also relevant. The proportion of groupings identified in Product Quality Analysis (previous section) can be combined with takt time to identify pitch. It may not be practical to move to true Mixed Model Sequencing, but it can be very useful to know how many appointments of each type need to be available a day, how many procedures of each type in a week, and so on, to meet demand. When combined with the idea of pitch – of a meaningful time period in which a certain number of activities should, on average, be completed – it becomes much easier to know if your service is keeping up with demand or is falling behind.

6.7 Jargon Buster

(Services should) remove excess work, eliminate waste, unevenness and unreasonableness (muda, mura, muri) and raise their productivity

Japanese Management Association (1989: p 65)

Muda, *Mura* and *Muri* are very similar words, and often cause confusion. They were described briefly in Chapter 2, and this section develops the concepts further.

Muda means 'waste,' and is often used in books and articles on Lean as an alternative to the use of the word 'waste' (Eaton 2013).

Mura means unevenness (Japan Management Association 1989), irregularity (Imai 1997) or inconsistency (Ohno 1988). Graban (2012) gives examples of this in matters such as planned hospital discharges, which tend to happen in a lumpy, uneven manner.

Muri refers to unreasonableness or strain (Imai 1997). 'The (employer) may be forcing their workers to do what they need not do, or what is very difficult to do' (Japan Management Association 1989: p 149).

The three problems are interconnected (Ohno 1988: p 41). Bicheno (2008: p 13) notes, 'unevenness causes overburden, which in turn causes many other forms of waste.' When people are overburdened, they are more likely to pay less attention to quality, to reduce preventative work, which in turn increases errors, which results in further burden to the service and so on.

6.8 Set-Up Reduction

Set up time – the time to prepare for a process and to clean up after it – is important in thinking about Just in Time. Reducing set-up time can help improve flow, can reduce Lead time, and is essential in running Mixed Model Sequencing, where different activities occur on the same 'production line.'
    Examples of set-up time include

- The time to clean a room from the last patient, and the time to prepare it for the next patient.
- Time to read case notes in advance of the next patient or service user.
- Time to collect together equipment and supplies needed to work with someone.
- Time to turn on computers and have them boot up before a clinic.

There are two main ways of addressing set-up time in a health and social care context – by reducing set-up time in sequential processes, and by moving set up to a parallel process.
    In the pre-theatre example discussed earlier in the chapter, patients were called to theatre when the previous operation was completed. There would be set-up time in the theatre, in cleaning and in preparing equipment and supplies, but there is also time taken for the anaesthetic process. In this case, the staff moved some of the anaesthetic process to a parallel process, by calling the patient earlier, a pull process, and by starting the anaesthetic induction in a separate room. Moving the set up parallel in this way means that the activity is still conducted, but the Lead time is reduced.
    Another example of this is in using two clinic rooms. In one instance, one doctor worked across two clinic rooms. A nurse assessed the person and prepared them in one room, while the doctor was seeing a person in a second room. The doctor then saw the patient in the first room, while the

second room was being prepared, and then the patient assessed, and so on. In this manner they leapfrogged the clinic rooms.

This approach does not automatically reduce the lead time for patients, but it may do so if the doctor's time is better managed, so that they are not waiting on a patient to become available.

In each of these examples, one process – the theatre time and the doctor's time – is being used as the pacemaker for the overall service. In each case, this is because it is the most constrained. As discussed in Chapter 5, Eliyahu Goldratt (1990) noted that all systems have constraints – bottlenecks – that limit their performance. He suggested that, by identifying the bottleneck and focusing on it, improvements in flow can be made. In the Theory of Constraints, 'buffers' are used, which are put in place to make sure that the constrained process is used to maximum effect. The example of having a patient ready for the doctor and waiting in a separate room is an example of a buffer, in this sense. This may not improve the overall Lead time for the person using the process, but it can improve flow.

In Lean terms, this does tend to focus on processes, rather than people's experience of the complete service. It can be useful to think about constraints, but keeping patient experience and the total value stream at the forefront of one's mind, rather than thinking only about how to maximise capacity, is important. It is possible to optimise one part of a value stream without optimising overall flow.

As well as moving set-up time externally, it is possible to decrease set-up time that is internal to the process. This is done by removing waste from the system, and a focus on 5S and careful consideration of value is important.

Hirano and Furuya (2006: p 210) note, 'having the set up and the...area properly planned is essential.' They identify principles of set up and change over which, adapted to health and social care can be taken as

■ Ensure that little or no motion is required during set ups.
■ If preparation can be done in advance, then do it.
■ Make set up parallel if at all possible.
■ No adjustments – get the set up right the first time.

As an example, we can develop the example of injections at an ophthalmology service, discussed earlier, in more detail. The service undertook ten or more ocular injections at each clinic. By 80 minutes into the clinic, a queue had developed, and by two hours after the clinic had commenced, this had lengthened further.

The service undertook process mapping and observations, and realised that several different problems occurred:

■ The staff member who undertook the injections was available from the start of the clinic.
■ Some patients only knew an injection was required after they had seen a doctor, and the process leading up to this meant that it was over an hour from the start of the clinic before they began to present for an injection.
■ Patients for whom it was known in advance that an injection was required, tended to be given appointments later in the morning – which was exactly when patients began to arrive from their medical appointment to receive an injection.
■ The preparation for the injection took an average of 17 minutes. Most of this time involved staff collecting together the supplies to administer the injection.

The service took several actions, which together improved flow and decreased patient waits:

■ Patients for whom it was already known that an injection was required were booked towards the start of the clinic if possible, before patients began to arrive from their doctor's appointment (Load Levelling).
■ Packs containing the necessary equipment and supplies were prepared in advance, reducing the set-up time from 17 minutes to less than five (the time to clean the room, and to complete the case notes, bring in the new patient, settle them and explain the procedure). This was further reduced, as a nurse began to show the patient into the room while the doctor or specialist nurse completed the case notes from the last patient at a separate station.

6.9 Responding to Variation in Demand

Despite the best laid plans, variation in demand or mismatch between capacity and demand will still happen from time to time. There are two main approaches to increased demand (Shingo 2005):

■ Planned changes to capacity, based on predictions
■ Rapid unplanned changes related to unexpected increases

In the first instance, there are many changes to demand that can be anticipated. For example, the Child and Adolescent Mental Health Service mentioned earlier had a significant decrease in demand in the summer, and an increase in demand after school returned and around school examination times, although this was less predictable. Reducing capacity in the summer by scheduling holidays is relatively straightforward, as many staff members will want to take leave during school holidays.

Admissions to acute hospitals tend to be higher in the winter, and again this can be anticipated and staffing adjusted in advance.

Some fluctuations are much less predictable and require rapid action. In Lean systems, designing the capacity in advance is a worthwhile consideration. For example, Shingo (2005: p 115) gives the example of increasing overtime between shifts at Toyota to cope with a short-term increase in demand without scheduling entire additional shifts.

Coping with decreased demand is more of a challenge, in some ways, as it is less visible. Overproduction is often regarded as one of the most problematic wastes, and so continuing to produce is not a viable option. Services do not want to lay staff off, however, and respecting staff is a key aspect of the Lean approach. It is disrespectful, however, to create a situation in which staff feel that they need to try to keep busy to avoid criticism. As noted previously, there are various activities that can be undertaken, including

- 5S audits, sweeps and improvements
- Small improvement projects
- Maintenance of equipment, preparation of materials

Making respectful use of spare staff capacity to drive improvements can have benefits for the whole system, and as it attracts recognition can result in staff feeling less need to simply 'look busy' to avoid criticism.

6.10 Practice Example

6.10.1 Surgery

An operating department opened for elective surgery 8.30am – 9pm five days a week, 8.30 – 5pm on Saturday, and 8.30am – 1pm on Sundays. Overall weekday utilisation was an average of 70%. Weekend utilisation was

22%. The cost of theatre utilisation was around £25 a minute. The optimum utilisation for elective theatres was calculated as 92%.

The staff reviewed the use of individual theatre lists, and booking patterns particularly for weekend surgery. Making use of the underutilised weekday capacity allowed all of the weekend activity to be accommodated on weekdays without exceeding the recommended utilisation rate. Activity was also levelled within sessions, allowing smoother workflow and reduced variation.

6.10.2 Community Assessment Service

A service offering community assessment used a suite of offices. It was often difficult for staff to book a room, and the service believed that additional accommodation was required, which would have had to be purchased at commercial rates, or would have required building work. When they measured their overall room utilisation, they were surprised to discover that it was only 49%. There were peak times when all rooms were used, and other times when very few rooms were in use.

Mapping the room use in detail, and comparing it to demand, allowed them to identify sufficient room capacity The service worked out the volume of activity required to deliver specific activities, and level their delivery across the week. This allowed all required room capacity to be delivered and also reduced waits for clients because it levelled the delivery of services. Rates of non-attendance also reduced, because it was possible to offer definite appointment slots rather than staff having to check room availability and to notify clients later.

6.11 Conclusions

Levelling is an important concept in Lean, and contributes to Just in Time. Variable demand leads to overworked staff, frustrated patients and patchily used capacity.

There are two main types of unevenness – that related to the process itself, and unevenness caused by external factors such as true varying demand. Variation arising from the process is mainly tackled by improving the process itself, to reduce batching and unevenness, and to promote one-piece flow.

Unevenness that results from true variation in demand can be smoothed to some extent, such as by identifying capacity that balances under and overcapacity, and by adjusting staff availability to reflect likely expected need.

Further Reading

Full references are included in the bibliography.

There are numerous books that give an account of Levelling in industrial settings, such as the *JIT Implementation Manual: Volume 4 Leveling Changeover and Quality Assurance* (Hirano 2009d) and *A Study of the Toyota Production System* by Shigeo Shingo (2005).

Chapter 7

Error Proofing

> As long as there are errors in the organization of processes…flaws
> will result no matter how perfectly operations are performed.
>
> **Shigeo Shingo (1986: p 12)**

7.1 Aims of the Chapter

The aims of the chapter are

1. To understand the importance of error proofing
2. To know the main approaches to error proofing
3. To be familiar with the links to improvement cycles and identification of
   cause

7.2 Introduction

No one wants errors in any sphere of activity, but in health and social care,
where the consequences of errors can be catastrophic, there is an even
greater focus on identification and prevention of errors.

The key insight on errors is that it is work itself – the process – that
causes the errors (Shingo 1986). Errors do not exist independently of the
work. Examples include

- A treatment planning system included three successive checks. When
  patients went to commence their treatment, there were errors in 14%
  that prevented their treatment being commenced on the planned date.

■ A patient was being discharged from hospital for palliative care at home. A hospital staff member identified a number to call and left a message on an answering machine. There was no system for monitoring the answering machine, and the patient returned home with no support in place, to be readmitted urgently less than 48 hours later.

■ A woman attends for a surgical procedure that requires the use of X-ray equipment. Her assessment says that a pregnancy test has been conducted, but on checking, this is incorrect. The surgery has to be delayed.

■ Community alarms automatically notified a central service when their batteries ran down. The central service sent a list to a maintenance service. In some cases, the call had been logged several times because there was confusion about the interpretation of the information being transferred

All of these errors arose from the course of the work. This realisation – that preventing errors means making changes to processes – is important.

Error proofing is part of a group of activities that are often described using the Japanese word *Jidoka* (Japanese Management Association 1989). *Jidoka* is usually regarded as one of the two major pillars of the Toyota Production System, the other being 'Just in Time' (Sugimori et al. 1977).

Jidoka, as it is used in most Lean literature, refers to building quality into the system, and it includes ideas of prevention, identification and response to problems. Kitazuka and Moretti (2012) note that, as used in industry, it can also refer to development of a system that flows with minimal external supervision, because the quality parameters are well established and understood by the people working in the system.

7.3 History Note

In its original meaning, *Jidoka* was used to describe 'autonomation,' a word coined to describe 'automation with a human touch' (Japan Management Association 1989), also known as 'autonomous automation' (Kitazuka and Morreti 2012). This is used to refer to a system that allows machines to identify errors and respond to them by stopping the process to allow a human to correct it. The original term was probably coined by Sakichi Toyada, the founder of the Toyota group, in relation to a self-monitoring loom.

Sakichi Toyoda developed a loom company and pioneered technical innovations (Rose 1991). Japanese loom sales were dominated by UK and US companies, who sold iron looms. These were expensive for the small weaving companies that predominated in Japan, and there were technical issues around the usual width of Asian fabrics compared to other countries, and the relatively lower strength of the cotton available in Japan that affected some of the overseas made looms. Toyoda's technological developments targeted these unidentified weaknesses in the business models of the UK and US companies (Rose 1991) a process similar to the 'loose brick' strategy the eventual Toyota Motor Corporation that was descended from Toyoda's company later used to target UK car sales (Hutchins 2008).

Toyoda's work also resolved a major problem in mechanical weaving. If a thread breaks, the loom will continue to operate, and it can produce many metres of fabric with an error running through it. In order to reduce error, it was common to have a worker standing beside the machine, waiting to identify the error, stop the machine and reset it.

Looms use a system of threads running the length of the fabric (the warp) and threads that are woven at right angles to this (the weft). Problems arose when the tension in the warp thread dropped, increasing the risk of breaking and also reducing cloth quality. The Toyoda loom included a warp halting device that stopped the loom automatically if the warp thread broke, and a weft halting device performed the same function for the weft thread (Toyota Motor Corporation 2012).

The 1905 loom handbook, edited by Sakichi Toyoda, pointed out that this meant that the loom did not need to be watched constantly (Toyota Motor Corporation 2012). The handbook also commented,

'(There is) no need for reworking of defects, therefore there is no waste of weft thread.'

And noted that the loom –

'Prevents breakage of the warp thread.

Reduction in warp thread breakage means less stopping time and improved machine output.

…Eliminates unevenness, creates excellent texture…'

This includes, therefore, concepts of error proofing by poka-yoke devices (see later in the chapter); prevention of error, defect identification, stop the line, one by one confirmation of defects, increased efficiency by decreased rework, and a focus on quality. Taiichi Ohno, in a 1969 internal Toyota article, identified this as the origins of the *jidoka* concept (Toyota Motor Corporation 2012).

7.4 Zero Defects

Errors will continue to be made. Accidents, on the other hand, can largely be prevented by intelligent and imaginative use of additional cues that announce that an error has occurred and that make it possible for the error to be corrected before damage has been done. Where possible, physical design should be used to prevent error from being translated into injury.

Senders and Senders (quoted in Grout 2006)

Defects are results, and errors are the causes of these results.

(Hirano 2009d: p 545)

In health and social care, the only acceptable number of defects is no defects at all. This idea – Zero Defects – sounds impossible and can be met by disbelief that defects can be prevented.

Errors, however, do not automatically result in defects in processes. Sometimes errors pass through the system without causing any harm. In other cases, they are spotted by another staff member, by the system or by the patient, and harm is avoided.

The aim of error proofing, therefore is to

1. Reduce errors as far as possible.
2. Identify any errors that do occur.
3. Take remediable action to prevent identified errors causing defects in care.

As errors result from work processes that can be altered to reduce or eliminate the likelihood of errors arising, and errors that do occur can be identified and prevented from turning into defects, this means that defects can be eliminated over time.

Hirano and Furuya (2006: p 185) comment,

> When one (defect) occurs there are likely to be more and it is
> essential that production stop immediately until the underlying
> problem is identified and resolved. If the (service) still flows by
> simply removing the defective part or product, an effective solu-
> tion is not possible.' Kitazuka and Moretti (2012: p 44) concur: 'the
> best way to achieve the "perfect process" is to stop the process
> and fix every small error after it occurs and before it reaches a
> critical level.

This leads to the concept of 'stop the line' discussed later in the section.
Health care staff feel caught in two pressures – not to have harm occur to
patients, and pressure to keep the service flowing. Safety has to come first.
As discussed in the 'Value and Waste' section, part of value is doing things
right first time – a service delivered quickly has little or no value if there is
an error that results in harm to the patient.

7.5 Types of Inspection

Inspection is defined as comparison with a standard. Comparison
of actual conditions with standards tells whether or not outcomes
are acceptable and reveals any abnormalities.

Shigeo Shingo (2005: p 147)

The aims of inspection vary (Shingo 1986, 2005). They can be intended to

- Detect defects (judgement inspections, also sometimes called 'contain-
  ment inspections').
- Reduce defects (informative inspections).
- Prevent defects (source inspections).

For a health care example, consider a sterile set of instruments for an
operating theatre:

- Checked in theatre when opened and rejected if incomplete – judgement inspection.

■ Checked in an inspection in the sterile processing unit, a problem identified and the missing item added – informative inspection.
■ Checked in sterile processing, an item found to be missing, and the process reviewed to reduce the chance of a future error – source inspection.

In practice, an inspection process may include one or more of these intentions. It is useful to consider what type of inspection is being conducted. All have their place, but preventing an error becoming a defect, or preventing the error occurring in the first place, is obviously preferable to simply identifying a problem.

Statistical methods are often used to monitor error rates over time, and this can be useful in prompting improvement. This might include information, such as hand washing rates or infection rates on a ward. This information is collected and displayed on charts in the area so that it can inform the work of the clinical team. Figure 7.1 shows an example of a run chart produced as an output of a Rapid Process Improvement Workshop (RPIW).

Run charts and other methods of displaying performance over time can be quite distant in time from the original error, so they have a more important role in overall monitoring, in sharing information with the team and in demonstrating continued attention to a problem than they do in immediate error correction and defect prevention.

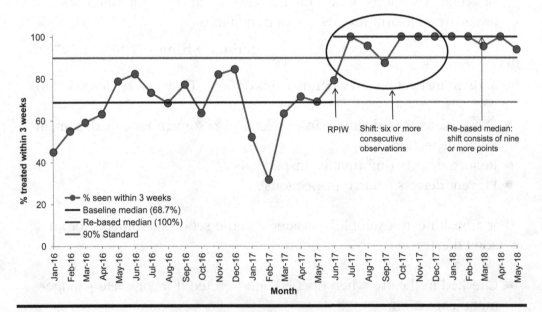

Figure 7.1 Percentage of clients seen within three weeks of referral - Run chart.

7.6 Identifying Errors

Error proofing needs to be specific to have its maximum impact. Many organisations exhort staff to greater safety efforts – 'try harder,' 'increase safety,' 'make fewer errors.' These demands can increase in tempo and volume after a prominent defect in care. General 'advice' like this is rarely useful, however – error proofing requires attention to detail.

Identifying errors before they can become defects in care depends on an understanding of what care should be like. If there is no clear view on what constitutes best practice, then identifying an error becomes very difficult.

Developing standard work helps with this, and this is discussed in Chapter 9. Standard work provides a current view on best practice. An example of a 'best practice' care bundle in patient safety is shown subsequently. This includes details of steps and actions that should have occurred, giving all staff the knowledge to identify an inadvertent omission and to act to stop the error becoming a defect.

Components of Central Line Care Bundle (Institute for Healthcare Improvement 2009)

- Hand hygiene
- Maximal barrier precautions upon insertion
- Chlorhexidine skin antisepsis
- Optimal catheter site selection, with avoidance of using the femoral vein for central venous access in adult patients
- Daily review of line necessity, with prompt removal of unnecessary lines

So, for example, if having conducted and recorded the results of a pregnancy test is a key step in the work on an Early Pregnancy Assessment Unit, and this is not recorded as having taken place, then the person seeing the woman next should take immediate action.

The point of bringing feedback closer to the time and place of the original error is not to identify staff to blame: it is to increase the likelihood of prevention, and to increase the chance of understanding the underlying problem that caused the error.

There are several times at which inspection can make a difference and prevent an error becoming a defect (Figures 7.2–7.4 through 7.5) (Hirano 2009d).

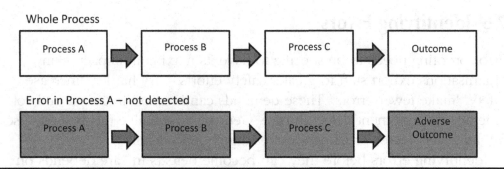

Figure 7.2   Opportunities to Identify an error and prevent a defect [1].

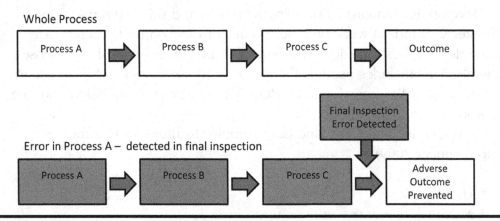

Figure 7.3   Opportunities to Identify an error and prevent a defect [2].

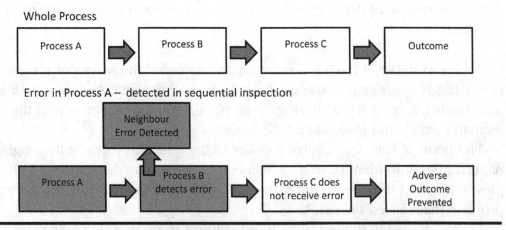

Figure 7.4   Opportunities to Identify an error and prevent a defect [3].

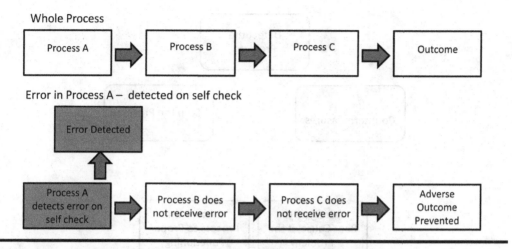

Figure 7.5 Opportunities to Identify an error and prevent a defect [4].

7.6.1 *Final Inspection*

The role that an inspector must set...is not to throw away defective (items), but to eliminate totally their production. This must be established as the criterion for judging (their) performance.

Japan Management Association (1989: p 147)

A final inspection, such as the operating instrument error identified in theatre in the previously mentioned example, happens at some distance in time and space from the original error. This can be recorded and illustrated on a run chart, and this is likely to have some effect on the efforts of the team as a whole. It can, however, still be quite distant from the original error which can make both feedback, and identification of the cause, more difficult (Figure 7.6).

7.6.2 *Inspection by the Next Person*

In sequential or neighbour assessment, the next person in the process inspects the work. This tends to happen closer in time to the original error, and so the opportunity for feedback and learning is increased. It again depends on their being a clear view of what constitutes appropriate practice.

Immediate feedback to the previous person in the process allows the error to be corrected quickly before it can cause a defect, and it also allows rapid learning. The priority is not to pass an identified error on to another part of the process.

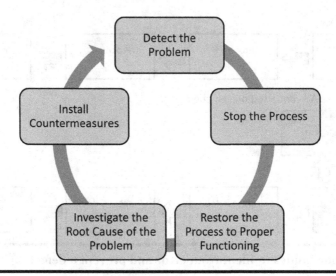

Figure 7.6   Stop the line.

In practice, it may not always be possible to undertake the check at the next process, but it should be done as quickly as possible, and the result of any error shown to the person who undertook the process at which the error occurred, so that they can identify the problem and correct it.

Some errors may be so important to avoid that more than one person in the process may check it. This happens, for example, in blood transfusion where some checks are conducted by more than one individual in sequence.

7.6.3 Self-Inspection

> Inspection done by inspectors…does not produce added value. Therefore those who are actually engaged in (providing the service) must be the ones responsible for full quality assurance.
>
> **Japan Management Association (1989: p 144)**

Self-inspection requires the person undertaking the process to check the output themselves. This will often involve a procedure to allow them to compare to a standard, such as a checklist. The previously mentioned SPSP bundle is a good example of such a checklist. Some errors may only be identifiable by the person undertaking the action: for example, 'Skin is cleansed with a single-use antiseptic containing 70% isopropyl alcohol and left to dry before insertion' can only be identified by the person undertaking the process, the patient or by someone directly observing practice, which will not often happen. This means that, even in systems using some type of later inspection, self-inspection is essential.

7.7 Care Bundle Example

A bundle is a structured way of improving processes of care and patient outcomes. It is a small straightforward set of practices – generally three to five – that, when performed collectively, reliably and continuously, have been proven to improve patient outcomes.

Institute for Healthcare Improvement

In patient safety, there are groups of activities – bundles – that, if undertaken together, will reduce the risk of an adverse event happening to a patient. An example are the bundles of activities used when inserting and maintaining a 'drip' – a Peripheral Vascular Catheter (PVC).

The bundle used when putting in the catheter is

1. Ensure that a PVC is clinically indicated for this patient.
2. Hand hygiene has been performed immediately before PVC insertion procedure.
3. Skin is cleansed with a single-use antiseptic containing 70% isopropyl alcohol and left to dry before insertion.
4. Aseptic technique is maintained throughout the insertion procedure; that is, critical parts are not touched.
5. The catheter site is covered with a sterile transparent semi-permeable dressing.

Once the catheter is in place, there are a further set of activities to undertake (Scottish Patient Safety Programme 2014):

1. The clinical need for the PVC has been reviewed and recorded today.
2. Medical staff have reviewed the need for intravenous therapy including antibiotics and switched to oral, if possible today.
3. The PVC site has been assessed; PVC has been removed if there are signs of inflammation or phlebitis at the site and has been considered if in longer than 72 hours.

4. The PVC dressing is intact.
5. The access hub has been cleaned with a single-use antiseptic containing 70% isopropyl alcohol before accessing ('scrub the hub').

7.8 Source Inspection and Stop the Line

Failing to shut down the line and take corrective action is just the same as subduing the symptoms of appendicitis with ice. The ice will work, but the pain will recur and eventually considerable time will be lost...it is extremely important to take basic, thorough corrective action when abnormalities appear.

Shigeo Shingo (1985: p 72)

Primum non nocere: First, do no harm. When in doubt, is the best action no action at all? Though one of the best-known dictums in healthcare, this maxim is not a statement about what to do at all; rather, it is a statement about what not to do. Sometimes it makes sense to cause healthcare processes to stop rather than to let them cause harm.

John Grout and John Toussaint (2010: p 150)

In some industrial production lines, when a staff member encounters a problem they cannot resolve, they can slow down their section of the production line by pulling a cord, to give them time to try to resolve it. If they cannot resolve it, they can pull the cord again and this stops their section of the line or the whole production line. Senior staff, such as supervisors, go to their assistance and work to resolve the problem. Part of this work is trying to understand why the problem arose in the first place and to identify how to prevent it arising in the future (Ohno 1988,2013).

The line that is not stopped is either a tremendously good line, or an absolutely terrible line.

Taiichi Ohno (Japan Management Association 1989: p 73)

The Virginia Mason Medical Center, having seen this process in use in industry, introduced it into health care (Institute for Healthcare Improvement 2005; Kenney 2010). They asked all staff who encountered a patient safety problem to immediately 'stop the line' and to call a central point. Senior staff then joined them to review the problem, and to take any required actions. Their experience was that the number of calls was large at first but decreased over time as systems improved. Staff confidence in the response they would receive was very important: a dismissive or blaming attitude would have squashed the likelihood of further alerts being received. Staff need to be sure that the process is the focus, not individual staff members. Ohno (1989: p 73) commented, 'what is needed is to make sure that the line can be stopped. And then continue to improve the line in such a way that it becomes a line that need not be stopped.'

7.9 Identifying Causes

Nothing is more dangerous than an idea when it is the only one we have.

Émile-Auguste Chartier

Do not confine your thoughts…but think freely: the actual cause or the hint for a cure will come out of this kind of free thought. Enumerating a large number of likely causes reduces the probability of overlooking a major problem area.

Kaoru Ishikawa (1982: p 25)

When problems arise or errors occur, people usually have views about why they have happened. These ideas will be drawn from previous experience of the problem, by drawing analogies from similar situations that have happened in the past, from things people have read in professional journals, from anecdotes related by others, or just by applying common sense.

Asking 'why?' five times – the 'five whys' – is a commonly used tool to try to get to the root cause of a problem (Ohno 1988). Graban and Swartz (2012: p 321) describe the process as follows:

1. Ask why the problem occurred at the time and place it happened.
2. Ask why the event described in the first step happened.
3. Keep on until you have reached the root cause.

As Graban and Swartz note, there is no 'rule' that this has to happen five times: in some cases, the root cause is reached more quickly, while in others it takes longer.

7.9.1 Example of a Root Cause Analysis

A patient waits in a department for over three hours, and when this is identified, it is too late to see them.

Why did this happen?

Because the patient did not tell the receptionist they had arrived.

Why did this happen?

Because they reported to a central reception and assumed that this meant they had reported into the clinic. They could not see the separate clinic reception desk.

Why did this happen?

Because they sat at the first chairs in the clinic that they came to, which are on the other side of a doorway from the reception desk and not in direct sight of the desk.

Why did this happen?

Because there is nothing to indicate to patients that there is a reception desk beyond the doorway, and no reason for them to think that they might have to report to two desks.

Sometimes the initial assessment of the problem will be correct: in others, it will be incorrect or incomplete. In the previous example, it would be possible to go further – why, for example, does the patient need to use two separate reception desks? Is this needless duplication that could be avoided?

Applying improvement cycles protects against problems arising from this process, at least to an extent. The process, described in Chapter Four, requires a statement of the problem and an explanation of how the planned intervention is intended to resolve it, or at least contribute to resolve it. The person or team takes baseline measurements, makes a prediction of impact, undertakes the intervention on, initially, a small number of people or events and then measures to see if the system has improved.

This system is self-correcting. If the initial assessment has been incorrect, then at some point, it becomes obvious that no improvement has happened. If problems are tackled without using a PDSA cycle or similar process, then it can take far longer for it to become clear that the selected intervention has not had an impact. Sometimes purported solutions which had no beneficial effect are left in place for weeks, months or even years on the assumption that they must have helped – sometimes despite evidence to the contrary.

Even when the solution is an important part of the problem, it may not be the only approach, or necessarily the most beneficial one. Improvement cycles accompanied by measurement can help to identify this, but thoughtful consideration of possible causes at the beginning of the process is also valuable.

Cause and Effect diagrams are a useful visual way of representing influences on a problem and can be used in groups when discussing possible causes, and with teams to share ideas visually.

Cause and Effect diagrams were developed by Kaoru Ishikawa in the 1940s (Ishikawa 1982, 1985), and look a little like the bones of a fish, giving the alternative names of 'Ishikawa Diagrams' and 'Fishbone Diagrams.' 'Cause and Effect diagrams' best captures the intent of these diagrams, and so that term is used in this book. Ishikawa (1982) describes three types of Cause and Effect diagrams – Dispersion Analysis, Production Process Classification and Cause Enumeration. It is this last type, designed to identify and record possible causes of an outcome, that tend to be used in health and social care.

Ishikawa (1982: p 25) comments that 'all possible causes are...listed. When doing this, everyone's ideas are necessary.'

When constructing a diagram with a group, the easiest way is often to list all the possible causes on Post-it notes, and then to group them in to main categories. As the previously mentioned Ishikawa quote indicates, the identification of possible causes should be as wide as possible, to reduce the chance of missing an important cause. Group discussion can help to agree which are the same issue by a different name, and how they can best be grouped. This type of discussion with a team can be invaluable. It encourages discussion and lets people hear different perspectives on the problem. Knowing what other people think, and hearing other possible causes of a problem that may not have been considered previously, is often very helpful. Ishikawa commented (1982: p 20), 'group members must speak, openly with one another' and the sharing and discussion can be as valuable as the final diagram.

These ideas can then be used to draw a Cause and Effect diagram. The process (Ishikawa 1982) is the following:

1. Write the quality issue on the right side of the paper and draw a broad arrow to it across the page (Figure 7.7).
2. Using the groupings you have identified, draw the required number of branch arrows diagonally against the main arrow.
3. Use the information on your individual Post-it notes to form the twigs coming off these main branches.

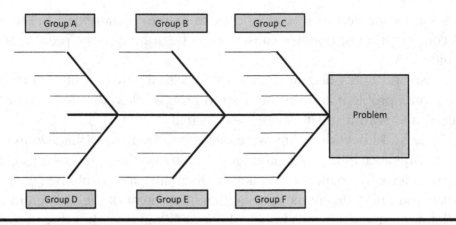

Figure 7.7 Structure of an Ishikawa diagram.

The group can then agree which of the issues seems most important to tackle first. Generally, this will be decided by consensus, based on a combination of the probability of the factor being strongly implicated in the problem, the likely size of its impact and a view on how easy it will be to influence it.

7.10 Error Proofing Devices

The remedy is in changing systems of work. The remedy is in design.

Don Berwick (2001: p 247)

If healthcare is to improve patient safety, systems and processes must be designed to be more resistant to error occurrence and more accommodating of error consequence.

Patricia Spath (2002)

Error Proofing devices, known as 'poka-yoke' (POH-kah YOH-kay) have an important role in error prevention. These can range from automated alerts, to checklists, to physical devices. If you cannot take a picture of it, it's probably not poka-yoke (adapted from Grout 2006).

Examples include

■ An automated prescribing alert which appears when two drugs with an adverse interaction are prescribed, and which has to be overridden before the prescription can happen.

- A checklist used before discharge, to ensure that relevant actions have been taken.
- A connection on intra-spinal catheters which is not compatible with syringes for intravenous injections.
- A brightly coloured bib with 'do not disturb' worn by a nurse when dispensing medications, to reduce interruptions which could result in error.
- A needle which cannot be re-sheathed into its original cover, decreasing the risk of a needle stick injury.

In some cases, devices are designed to promote 'benign failure' (Grout 2003, Grout and Toussaint 2010). This is very common in everyday life, where, for example, lawn mowers are often designed to start only if two levers or buttons are pressed simultaneously, washing machines will not open while they contain water, and food blenders stop immediately if the lid is removed.

Health care examples include mobile X-ray machines that stop moving as soon as a lever is released, and fittings that do not allow an oxygen outlet to be connected to a nitrous oxide supply. The Pin Index Safety System consists of holes on the cylinder valve positioned in a semicircle below the outlet port. Pins on the pressure regulator are positioned to fit these holes. Unless the pins and the holes are aligned, the port will not fit (Figure 7.8).

7.11 Autonomation

The objective of Autonomation is to facilitate one-piece, flexible, high quality flow with as little operator involvement as possible.

Hiroyuki Hirano and Makato Furuya (2006: p 187)

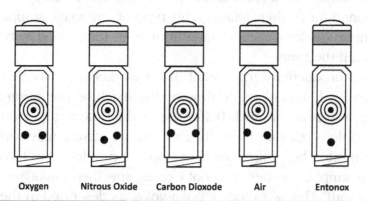

| Oxygen | Nitrous Oxide | Carbon Dioxode | Air | Entonox |

Figure 7.8   Example of error proofing devices.

Autonomation is an important consideration in the use of machines. Autonomation is described as 'automation with a human touch' and is a translation of a term attributed to Sakichi Toyoda (Japan Management Association 1989).

The problem with automation is that, without human judgement, machines carry on with their function, regardless of problems. Simple pumps continue to pump, whether there is a leak in the system or not, basic sterilisers continue to operate whether or not there is a problem with their settings, and so on. A result of this is that people are tied up watching machines and waiting for something to go wrong. This is an enormous waste of human talent – people should be used for tasks that require judgement and intelligence.

Hirano and Furuya identify four stages to the move from manual work to full 'autonomation':

1. All the work is done by hand.
2. Some of the work is done by a machine, but typically a person has to operate the machine.
3. The machine performs more of the work, allowing the operator to move away from the machine, but the machine will not identify problems.
4. Once the machine is set up, the person can move away knowing that the machine will stop if a problem occurs and will alert them to the problem, for example by a warning light or a sound.

Toyota originally manufactured textiles. Looms kept functioning even when a problem developed, meaning that, if there was not a human to spot it, many metres of cloth could be produced with a defect. Toyota developed a loom that stopped when a thread was broken or was no longer in the loom (Japan Management Association 1989 – see the 'History Note' previously mentioned for further details). This type of automatic stopping – an error prevention device – meant that a human no longer had to be beside the machine all the time.

In terms of productivity, this meant that a worker could look after several machines, and only had to spend time on the machine preparing it for work or resolving problems – a much better use of the time of a person.

This principle is relevant in health care, where increasingly sophisticated machines can often be programmed to stop if a problem develops. Syringe drivers, for example, can be set to not exceed specified limits, reducing checking for staff. This is a type of poka-yoke, as described in the previous section.

The main idea, however, of not letting errors become defects and of 'stopping the line,' have become important principles in Lean, and are discussed in more detail in the 'Continuous Flow' chapter.

7.12 Practice Examples—Early Identification and Prevention

A service managed complex assessments on children with significant needs. Assessments from several professions were required to help develop the best possible care plan in partnership with families. Delays in one assessment caused delays in other parts of the assessment, and in developing a plan. In some cases, meetings with families were scheduled, but had to be rearranged or repeated because assessments were not complete.

When the extended team reviewed their processes, they found that assessments from individual professions were not visible to the process as a whole. The team developed a visual control board (Figure 8 Chapter 8 – Visual Controls) that showed progress of the assessment of each patient. Alerts were established to identify assessments at risk of being delayed, and the team developed Standard Work to escalate actions when required. Patterns of delay were collected, and this information used to identify problems that were then targeted for action.

7.13 Conclusions

> Don't sit in your office looking at your Excel spreadsheet and imagine that you are improving productivity – that is management by looking in the rear view mirror. Instead, "get your butt to the Gemba" and learn to anticipate problems.
>
> **John Bicheno (2008: p 57)**

The aim in health and social care has to be to reduce defect to zero. This requires a focus on reducing errors, detecting errors, preventing the error leading to a defect and then learning from the error to reduce the likelihood of future errors.

Stopping errors from passing on down the process is very important. Judgement inspections at the end of a process can in some cases prevent an error becoming a defect, but they will not usually improve the process, or retrieve the work that has gone in to the process since the original error.

Building inspection in the process is important and requires agreement on what standards and actions are expected. Some risks are so important that sequential checking by more than one person – for example, blood transfusion – may be appropriate.

Not all errors can be identified by a later check, however, so a self-checking process is important.

This combination – of reducing the likelihood of error, increasing the identification of error, decreasing the impact of an error (e.g. by benign failure) and actively learning from errors and changing the process in the future – can markedly reduce defects.

Further Reading

Full references are included in the bibliography.

Shigeo Shingo's book *Zero Quality Control: Source Inspection and the Poka-Yoke System* (Shingo 1986) is an excellent technical resource, although it uses industrial examples.

Healthcare Kaizen by Mark Graban and Joseph Swartz (Graban and Swartz 2012) has good examples of error proofing in health care settings.

Mark Graban's book, *Lean Hospitals* (Graban 2012) included the comment that 'Errors occur, often as the result of a system, in which a mistake is defined as "a wrong action attributable to bad judgment or ignorance or inattention." Not all errors are necessarily caused by bad judgment, ignorance or inattention.' It was as a result of this comment, suggesting that mistakes are a sub-group of errors, which resulted in the term 'error proofing' being used in this volume.

Kaoru Ishikawa's *Guide to Quality Control* (Ishikawa 1982) is out of print, but it contains much useful advice on the use of Cause and Effect diagrams in different contexts.

John Grout's 2007 ARHQ publication, *Mistake-Proofing the Design of Healthcare Processes* has excellent examples of mistake proofing devices in use in health care settings.

Chapter 8

Visual Controls

8.1 Aims of the Chapter

The aims of the chapter are

1. To understand the role of visual signals in Lean
2. To be able to describe the main types of visual signals that can be used
3. To be familiar with kanban and their use in supply chains

8.2 Introduction

> Make your workplace into a showcase that can be understood by everyone at a glance.
>
> In terms of quality, it means to make the defects immediately apparent. In terms of quantity, it means that progress or delay, measured against the plan, is made immediately apparent.
>
> When this is done, problems can be discovered immediately, and everyone can initiate improvement plans.
>
> **Taiichi Ohno (as cited in Japan Management Association 1989: p 76)**

Visual controls are methods of making a situation visible. One of the great challenges in health and social care is that problems are often difficult to see. In other cases it is obvious that there is a problem – for example an overflowing waiting room and dissatisfied people – but it is far from apparent where in the system the problem exists.

The purpose of visual controls is to make problems obvious. Suzaki (1987: p 107) comments,

> Whenever an abnormal condition exists, the system will give a signal requiring that timely corrective action be taken...In order to develop such a system, andon, kanban, production control boards and the like are used to facilitate the transfer of important information as quickly as possible.

This is not what happens in most existing health and social care systems. Problems in flow may show up as the number of people on waiting lists, people waiting on trolleys in an Accident and Emergency Department, or complaints from service users. These tend to happen after the problem has developed, and in some cases very long after. As the 'Error Proofing' chapter discusses, identifying problems in the system as quickly as possible and working to resolve them is a critical part of the Lean process.

Hirano (2009c: p 454) summarises the use of visual control methods as follows:

■ Learning to distinguish promptly between what is normal and what is not.
■ Making abnormalities and waste obvious so that everyone can recognise them.
■ Constantly uncovering the need for improvement.

8.3 Process Boards

Process Boards are often used to display the overall status of a process. This can be very useful when it is difficult to see an entire process at once, and when it is useful to convey the current status to people as quickly as possible. (Hirano and Furuya (2006) use the term 'Production Control Boards.' Hirano also uses the term 'Production Management Boards' (2009c).)

Figure 8.1 shows a Process Board for a theatre loan kit, developed by a local team after improvement work. In some cases, services do not hold all the equipment necessary for every procedure, and this is hired from the

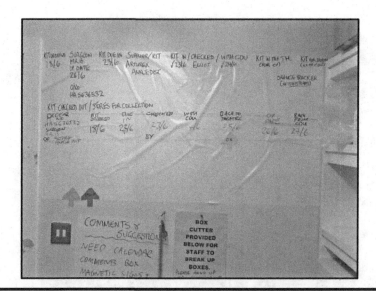

Figure 8.1 Production board for theatre loan kit, in development.

relevant surgical equipment provider. For example, in orthopaedics, this may be the company that makes a particular type of hip prosthesis.

The steps would be that the person is identified as requiring a particular surgical procedure. If the equipment is not available locally, this has to be identified and the equipment requested from the company concerned. It then has to be logged in, checked, sterilised, received back in the theatre suite, used for the procedure, cleaned and returned to the company. The lead time for this process can be long, as there may be a considerable delay between the identification of the need and the operation date. In other instances, it can be brief because of urgent clinical need. Different staff – administrative, procurement, theatre, portering, sterile services – will be involved, so it can be very difficult to know what stage in the process each request has reached. This all needs to be balanced against the date on which the equipment is required (the pacemaker for the whole process).

Figure 8.1 gives a view of all the current loan equipment requests and the stage of the process, together with the planned procedure date. In the past, information had been communicated in a book which required staff to remember to read it, and which contained information relating to numerous different sets of equipment. The new Process Board made it more straightforward to see the status of loans at a glance and to identify delays.

Figure 8.2 shows a straightforward Process Board for a respiratory ward. This Board shows the actions that are required for the care of each person, including planning to support discharge. The Board lets the staff see at a

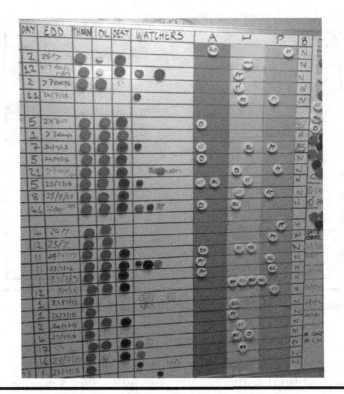

Figure 8.2   Process board in use in a respiratory ward.

glance what has been done for each patient, and therefore to understand the overall state of the process. This does not mean that care is identical for every patient – the details of discharge planning will vary markedly, for example – but there are some common processes that have to happen on every occasion. The Board includes an Expected Date of Discharge (EDD). The EDD lets the team reflect on the reason for variation from the expected EDD. There could be an apparently unavoidable reason, such as an unexpected worsening of the person's clinical condition. Other reasons, however, might include

- Delays in obtaining tests
- Delays in test results being reported
- 'Batching' of decisions on discharge to ward rounds, leading to delays in the date of discharge
- Delays in medication availability
- Delays in arrangements for the return home, such as re-commencing or arranging domestic support services or community nursing
- Delays in transport

Each of these types of delays can be considered, and improvement work undertaken to seek to prevent its occurrence on the next occasion. Some causes of delay will be out of the control of the specific service, but if the delay is apparent, it can be logged with the service managers who can identify a need for work across a value stream, for example by means of a Rapid Process Improvement Workshop.

Figures 8.2 and 8.3 show Process Boards used in a Respiratory Ward, designed by the staff. This Board was still being refined. As seen in Figure 8.1, it is useful to develop a Board, use it over time and amend it as required before investing in expensive printed Boards.

Figure 8.4 shows a huddle in front of a Process Board used to track overall caseload.

Figure 8.5 shows the template of a Process Board used as a 'Patient Tracker' (Graban 2012). This was developed for use in a Neurodevelopmental Service and allowed the administrative coordinator to see at a glance the stage of each process and to identify delays.

Variations of this idea that may be useful in particular contexts include Scheduling Control Charts that show when particular activities are planned to happen, and Operation Control Charts that show the overall activity required (Hirano 1988).

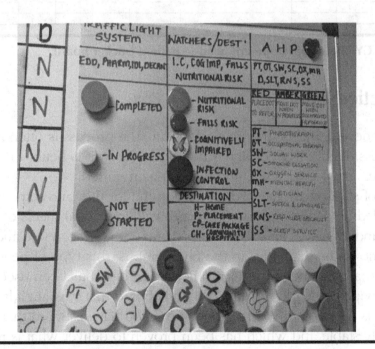

Figure 8.3   Detailed view of part of a respiratory ward process board.

Figure 8.4   Process board used in an orthopaedic ward team huddle.

Overall Status	Days to Outcome	Days to First Appointment	Name	CHI Number	Referral Received (Date)	Vetting Complete (Date)	Consent Obtained (Date)	MDT Planned (Date)
O	141	87	A.N. Other	123456789	03/01/2017	03/01/2017	03/01/2017	24/02/2017
	0	0						
	0	0						

Figure 8.5   CYP neurodevelopment needs – patient tracker board.

8.4 Practice Tip

1. When developing Boards that add value, the process is often a work in progress. Rather than design a Board on paper, it is better to develop the idea, try it in practice and refine it as required.
2. Roles of stick-on whiteboard are very useful for this, and some makes can be rolled onto, and peeled off, a ward wall. Individual sheets costs very little, and this gives an excellent opportunity to refine, revise and improve.
3. In some of the examples in the photographs, this type of peel-off whiteboard has been used. In other cases, tape has been used to mark out a wipe-on, wipe-off standard whiteboard that was already present. There is no need to spend money until you have a Board that it is reasonably stable and which has been proven to deliver what is required to improve efficiency, effectiveness, safety and flow.

8.5 Andon

An Andon is a visual signal that 'alerts supervisors to (a) problem immediately' (Hirano 1988, Hirano 2009c: pp 456–457). The term was initially used for signal lamps that turned on when a worker 'stopped the line' in an industrial setting (Japan Management Association 1989), but has become used more widely. Hirano (2009c: 464–465) lists four types of Andons. These include paging andons, which light up when supplies are needed; emergency andons which signify abnormalities; operation andons that show the current status of the process; and progress andons that show the progress of the overall process.

An example of an Andon is shown in Figure 8.6. This alert, in a theatre, shows the operating suite in which an emergency has occurred. The light flashes, accompanied by an audible alarm, which means that the additional staff arriving to help know which theatre to go to straight away.

Figure 8.7 shows the use of a visual signal in a hospital clinic.

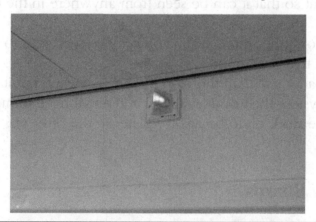

Figure 8.6   Andon (signal lamp) outside an outpatient clinic room.

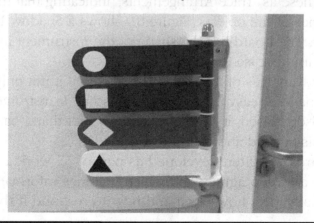

Figure 8.7   Use of a visual signal in a hospital clinic.

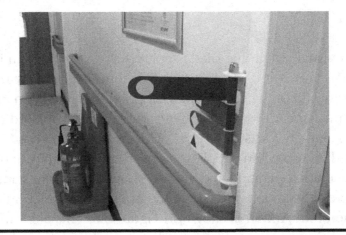

Figure 8.8   The signal in use.

When a problem is encountered that needs additional input, the relevant tab is flipped out so that it can be seen from anywhere in the corridor (Figure 8.8).

This then allows the shift coordinator to move resources to deal with the additional need that has arisen.

This is a broader use than the 'stop the line' concept, but it has a similarity in that the system then deals with the additional need immediately, rather than passing the work on to be resolved later in the process.

8.6 Shadow Boards

Shadow Boards show the planned location of an object. Hirano and Furuya (2006) refer to these as 'Trace Arrangements,' indicating that the markings 'trace' the outlines of the objects. Figure 8.9 shows a Shadow Board in use in a fracture clinic. The board has the shape of the instrument indicated, and it is also labelled in this case.

One of the advantages of a Shadow Board is that it not only shows what is there, but it makes it easy to see what is missing. If instruments or other equipment is disorganised, it can be difficult to spot that a particular item is missing until it is needed and cannot be located.

Shadow Boards are often developed as part of 5S work and can be combined with a Sweep agreement, which includes information on who checks in advance, how often and how to respond if there is an abnormality.

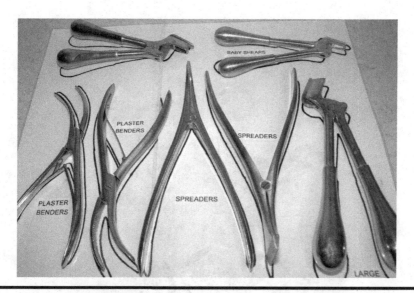

Figure 8.9   Shadow board.

8.7 Demarcation Lines and Other Markings

White Demarcation Lines (Hirano and Furuya 2006, Hirano 2009c) are floor markings designed to show the location of equipment and/or supplies (Figure 8.10). Other demarcation lines are used to show pathways, to show areas on which no supplies or equipment should be placed, usually to increase safety. A variation of this is Traffic Lines, which show the direction of travel in confined areas, again to increase safety, particularly where staff may be carrying items that can obstruct their view.

Red Demarcation Lines (Hirano 2009c) are used to show the maximum level of stock for a particular item. This can give a good visual indication of excess stock.

Tiger Marks (Hirano and Furuya 2006) are striped lines, often red or orange, which show potentially dangerous areas (Figure 8.11). This may include areas which cannot be accessed because of moving equipment, for example within the swing area of the arm of scanning equipment.

Door Swing Lines, as the name suggests, are used to show areas within the sweep of a door which has no hatch, allowing staff pushing a trolley to see if someone is on the other side (Hirano and Furuya 2006).

Footmarks around machines are used to show the location of a piece of equipment without heavy lines (Hirano and Furuya 2006). This may simply be four coloured dots on the floor, which correspond with the location of the feet of the machine or equipment trolley.

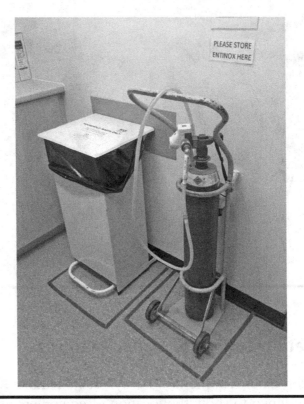

Figure 8.10   Demarcation line showing position of cylinder and waste bin.

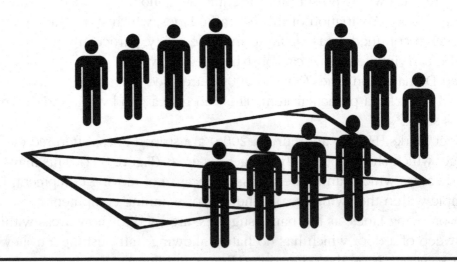

Figure 8.11   Tiger markings showing exclusion zone.

Figure 8.12   Diagonal strip used to show position of folder.

Diagonal lines can be used across folders when it is important to be able to identify that a folder has been removed (Figure 8.12). This also makes it straightforward to restore a folder to a required position, if this is important.

8.8 Practice Point

Visual Indicators have to have a purpose. It is easy to become carried away, and to begin to see indicators as an end in themselves. There are several examples of services apparently confusing neatness with purpose. Areas that use 5S are tidy – but they are tidy for a reason. The purpose of 5S and of Visual Signals is to make it easier, safer and more efficient to undertake a procedure, not neatness for its own sake.

There are reported examples of desks being '5S'd' with marking showing where monitors should be placed, where the computer mouse should be located, the telephone placed and so on. The main question is how this improves function.

There can be good reasons for clearing desks, such as when several people use the same desk. In treatment rooms, it usually makes sense to keep clutter to a minimum and to have different treatment rooms arranged in the same way, so that people can find things easily and quickly, but the reason why it is being done is to make the service easier and quicker to deliver – not to keep marking tape manufacturers in business.

The key is identifying what is needed to improve service delivery. The quote from Shingo (1988: p 94) in the introduction indicates that the purpose of Lean is to make things, 'easier, better, faster, and cheaper.' In this context, 'better' can be taken to include 'safer.' If the change does not get you closer to one of these aims, then don't do it.

8.9 Location Boards

Location Boards give an overall 'map' of an area, so that items can be located as quickly and easily as possible. In a storage area, for example, they can be used to show which supplies are located in which section. On a larger scale, they can be used to show the location or equipment and supplies on a ward or a warehouse. Figure 8.13 shows a Location Board.

8.10 Kanban

The commonest use of Kanban in health and social care is to ensure that supplies are available in the right place at the right time to allow staff to deliver a good service.

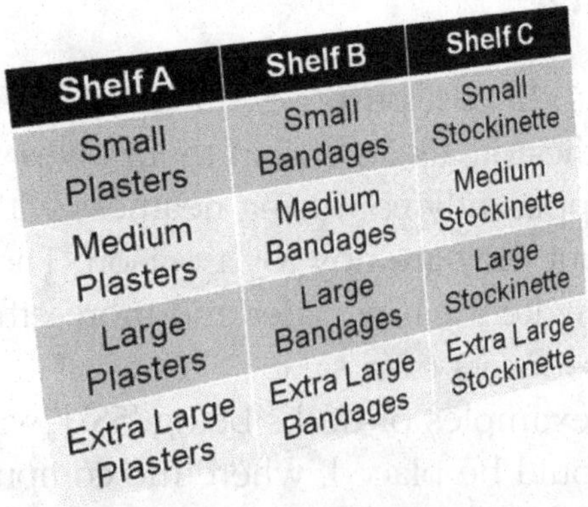

Shelf A	Shelf B	Shelf C
Small Plasters	Small Bandages	Small Stockinette
Medium Plasters	Medium Bandages	Medium Stockinette
Large Plasters	Large Bandages	Large Stockinette
Extra Large Plasters	Extra Large Bandages	Extra Large Stockinette

Figure 8.13   Location board.

Kanbans originally referred to a slip of paper on which supervisors wrote the work they were producing, which were then shared with other supervisors to get a complete idea of what was being produced (Japan Management Association 1988: pp 86–87). Kanban in health and social care are used as visual indicators of what supplies are needed. An example of a kanban is shown in Figure 8.14.

Reordering is a common problem in health and social care, and supplies run out from time to time in many services. On the other end of the supply spectrum, some services stockpile large amounts of supplies, some of which go out of date and have to be destroyed. This then ties up resources in unused stock and in replacing expired materials. This is expensive and produces waste. For patients, there can be long delays if staff try to access required equipment or supplies and find that it is not there, causing waits and frustration while staff – often equally frustrated – try to find the materials that they need. This becomes even more of a delay in a community service, where a second home visit or second clinic attendance may be required.

Surprisingly, apparently well-stocked wards and units can still run out of items. This is often because there is no overall plan to the stocking: there

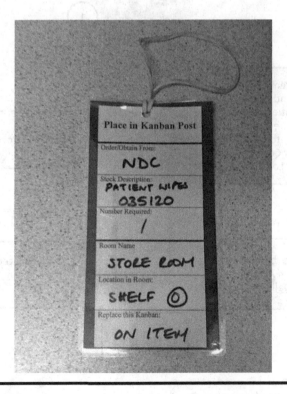

Figure 8.14   Kanban.

is often limited information on what material is required when, resulting in overstocking of items – some of which are never used-- while at the same time, other items run out.

Kanban are often used to create a reordering system based on use. Figure 8.15 shows a kanban reordering cycle.

A common model is the twin bin system, where two identical containers have the same contents'

In this arrangement, the stages to using a kanban are

1. Work out how many of an item are used within the restocking period. For example, if it is possible to obtain a restock within one day of a request, then two days stock is needed in total (one day to use, and one day to last until the new stock is received). In this example, each day's stock would be in one of the containers.
2. Identify the type of supply, including the stock order number of the item.

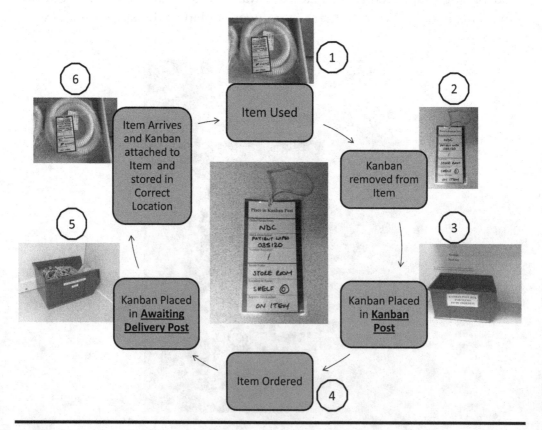

Figure 8.15　Use of Kanban.

3. Attach a ticket or label – a kanban – showing the item, the part number, the volume of items needed, the ward or area from which the item(s) are needed and the place in the ward it is to be stored (Figure 8.14).
4. When the first batch of items are used, the staff member takes the empty container and drops it (or in some cases the kanban alone) into a 'kanban post' (Figure 8.16). The second, full, container is pulled forwards so that there is a supply to use, readily visible.

The ward has an arrangement where either the supply staff or a ward staff member, checks the kanban post daily and refills the supply in the first, empty bin. In some cases, this will be from a local supply, which then needs its own reorder system. In other cases, it will be from a central supply area.

If objects are too large to be stored in bins, then a card system is used, in which the card attached to the object is dropped into the kanban post. When the supply returns, the kanban will be attached to it.

Kanban achieve several different aims (Hirano 2009c):

■ They create a 'pull' system, where the downstream process pulls only what it needs to perform its function.

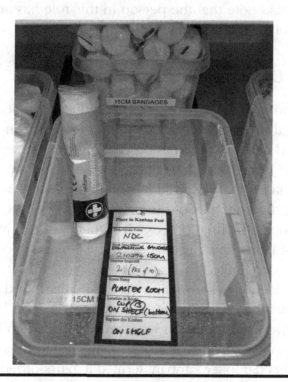

Figure 8.16 Twin bin system in use, with second bin located behind first.

■ The upstream process – the supplier of the material – can reduce the stock held as, generally, the demand for supplies becomes more level, as there are fewer peaks and troughs of demand.

■ The kanban that travels from the ward or area to the supply store has precise details of what is required – the type and amount, and which area the request came from. This reduces the likelihood of incorrect orders, as can occur when staff manually transcribe order details.

■ The kanban includes details of where on the department it is to be stored, and so reduces the likelihood that the material is stored in a different area, with the likelihood for confusion.

■ The kanban decouples the flow of supplies from direct supervision – the system established allows supplies to flow without separate supervision of the process. (Kitazuka and Moretti 2012).

The system may be used within a ward, clinic, office or care home. In that case, there will often be a designated person who checks the kanban post and restocks. The Japan Management Association (1989) refer to a similar role in an industrial setting as 'a whirligig beetle' that moves on water and changes direction rapidly – which gives a good impression of rapid movement. They also note that the person in this role has an important function in also conveying information.

8.10.1 Further Details: Production Kanban

In industry, kanban are used to control the production schedule. Kanbans indicate to the final process what needs to be produced, and other kanban then 'pull' required items to the final process – for example, the suspension required for a car (Japan Management Association 1988: pp 79–99). This ensures that only items that required for the final process are produced. It also means that the only part of the process that needs to know exactly what is being made is the final process. It is therefore relatively quick to change the mix of items being produced. In health and social care, Kanbans generally have a more limited role.

Hirano (2009c) identifies two main types of kanban used in production: kanbans that show when parts are to be moved (Transport kanban) and kanban used to give instructions on what procedures are to be performed (Production kanban). He divides Transport kanban into those used as orders for outside suppliers (Supplier kanban, termed a 'parts-ordering kanban' by the Japan Management Association [1989: pp 84–85]) and those used between internal processes (In-factory kanban). Production kanban are subdivided into Signal kanban, used in batch production, and Production kanban, showing what is needed from the previous process.

8.11 Kanban Examples

Example One: As mentioned previously, an outpatient clinic kept a large stock of supplies. When asked about this, the team explained that it was very important that they did not run out of items that were needed for the clinic. The team explained that their supplies came weekly. When asked whether this was one week's supplies, they felt that the stock was considerably more than one week's supply, but it became clear that there was not a clear idea of what stock was used in an average week. Rather, nurses tended to order 'just in case' as supplies began to look lower.

The service called the portering and supplies service, and asked whether their weekly delivery had to remain at that frequency. The supplies service explained that they passed the door of the department several times a day: they came weekly because that was how often the department submitted an order. It became clear that the clinic staff had thought that only weekly delivery was available, but it had not explored this with the supplies service. The supplies service, for their part, had assumed that the clinic staff knew that delivery several times a day was possible, but preferred not to use it.

There was variation in what was used in a day, because the nature of the outpatient clinics and the number of patients and staff present changed. The clinic staff realised, however, that use was relatively predictable on a specific day. With the assurance that delivery was possible at short notice, the clinic staff reduced the stock held by over 60%, moving to a kanban system.

Example Two: A clinical physiology department found that investigation rooms often lacked the supplies needed for the day's clinics, and staff would have to take time to look for the appropriate supplies. In some cases, it was not obvious at the start of the clinic, and supplies would run out mid-clinic, leading to significant delays for patients, and annoyance and stress for staff.

The staff used 5S to separate the necessary from the unnecessary and to work out the best location and quantity of supplies. They then introduced a kanban system to maintain required supply levels. After some additional concern about a possible increase in workload, staff reported satisfaction with the system and noted much reduced disruption to their clinics.

8.12 Process Tracking Charts

> Visual controls and the process surrounding them represent the nervous system in Lean Management.
>
> **(Mann 2015: p 75)**

Process Tracking Charts can be used to show the performance of the overall system. In some cases, Process Boards, discussed previously, will fulfil this function. In other cases, a different process may be required. Mann (2015) points out those visual controls are particularly important in types of work where the process cannot be easily seen.

A common way to monitor performance is to compare actual to expected and to record comments. This is often done in relation to a 'pitch,' which in this context refers to a division of time (see Chapter 6 for more information on the idea of a 'pitch'). For example, Table 8.1 shows a Process Tracking chart for an outpatient clinic.

It is essential that this information is then used to guide root cause analysis and action to prevent recurrence.

A common way to use the information is to use it to construct a Pareto chart showing the most frequent causes of interruptions, and then prioritising them for action (Mann 2015). The way the information is used is important. The information is feedback on the state of a system, not a criticism of individuals.

Table 8.1   Outpatient Clinic Process Tracking Chart

Pitch	Expected Number of Patients	Actual Number Completed	Comments
9 a.m.–10 a.m.	10	6	Late start. Material missing, had to be located, and doctor delayed.
10 a.m.–11 a.m.	10	12	Began to catch up. Delay before some patients saw the doctor.
11 a.m.–12.00	10	9	Clinic flowing well.
12.00–12.25 p.m.	0	3	Lunch delayed because three patients still in the clinic process. Set up for the next clinic delayed.

8.13 Conclusions

Visibility is important. Knowing the status of a process and being able to make decisions about immediate improvement actions, and longer-term improvement work, are part of the quality improvement process. Identifying abnormalities, responding to them and learning from them help to drive improvements.

Kanban are a straightforward way of supporting processes by helping to ensure availability of supplies and equipment.

Further Reading

Full references are included in the bibliography.

Healthcare Kaizen (2012) by Mark Graban includes good examples of visual controls in use in health care.
5 Pillars of the Visual Workplace by Hiroyuki Hirano (1995) and *5S for Operators* by the Productivity Press Development Team (1996), based on Hirano's book, include examples of visual controls in place in industry. Also by Hirano, *JIT Is Flow* (2006) includes other good industrial examples.

Chapter 9

Standard Work

The first step toward improvement is standardisation. Where there
is no standard, there can be no improvement.

Japanese Management Association (1989: p 56)

9.1 Aims of the Chapter

1. To understand the purpose of Standard Work
2. To know the components of Standard Work
3. To be familiar with the forms used to measure and document Standard
   Work

9.2 Introduction

Mindless conformity and the thoughtful setting of standards should
never be confused. What solid SOPs do is nip common problems
in the bud so that staff can focus instead on solving uncommon
problems.

John Marriott (Quoted in Graban 2012: p 70)

There is a useful distinction between Operation Standards and Process
Standards (Hirano and Furuya 2006). Process standards refer to the entire
value stream. They identify the volume of work required, the time in which
they can be conducted and the resources that can be used to deliver them.

Process standards will change in a dynamic process, in response to demand, and as a result of scheduling changes.

Operation Standards, by contrast, will include the details of the individual operations that make up the overall value stream. Process Standards are necessarily set at a relatively high level, as they cut across departments and functions. Operation Standards, by contrast, describe the expert functions needed at local level within a department or a function to deliver the overall process.

As is often the case, the terms are used in different ways by different authors, but regardless of the terms used, the distinction between the standards for the overall process and the standards for an individual procedure or operation is helpful.

9.3 Process Standards

Process standards describe

- The processes on either side of the current process in the value stream – for example, a Stroke Unit may receive patients from an Accident and Emergency Unit, and move patients to a community rehabilitation ward, while a community team may take self-referrals, and pass the person on to relevant support services
- The expected volume of use – whether this be service users, blood samples or some other relevant measure.
- The expected sequence of operations within the process (e.g. assessment – investigation – treatment plan – intervention – discharge planning or receipt of sample – centrifuge – analysis – results reporting).
- The expected time and resource needed for each part of the process.
- The takt time for the process (see Chapter 5 'Continuous Flow' section for further details).
- For relevant processes, the Standard Work in Process (see Chapter 5 'Continuous Flow' section for further details).
- Standards required of the process – such as required measures of quality.

Some industrial literature uses the terms uses the term 'Production Standards' rather than process standards (Hirano 2009e: p 624) and this can be useful to know to avoid confusion when reading other literature.

9.4 Standard Work

To avoid potential confusion with surgical operations, the term 'Standard Work' is used in this volume as the term for Standard Operations.

Examples of problems arising because of a lack of Standard Work include

■ During preparation for improvement work, observations revealed that both nurses and doctors in a clinic performed the same test on patients. A quick calculation suggested that, in the four years the clinic had been running, there had been over 5000 duplicate measurements. Each of the measurements took around two minutes, so this was 10,000 minutes work, or almost 170 hours of staff time – equivalent to over four weeks of full-time work.
■ An integrated rural community team had a shared office. If staff were out of the building, colleagues sometimes answered telephone calls on their behalf. If no one answered, calls diverted to an answering machine. In some cases, if the person answering the phone had the same training, immediate actions were taken. In other cases, they left notes for their absent colleague in a notebook. Staff sometimes found that key information had not been recorded, because the person taking the call was not familiar with the issue and did not know what questions to ask.
■ In a hospital assessment clinic, nurses had different ways of working with Health Care Assistants. Some liked to do specific measurements themselves; others preferred the Health Care Assistant to undertake the measurements. As the Assistants could not be sure which nurse would see the patient they assessed, they conducted all observations on all patients to avoid criticism from the nurses. In at least a third of the patients, observations were repeated unnecessarily.
■ Nurses on a hospital ward took calls for an urgent outpatient Service. There were one or two calls a shift on an average night, and whichever nurse was closest to the telephone answered it. Different nurses asked different questions, recorded it in different ways, and left the information in different formats.

Standard Work describes the detail of an operation within a process.

Further Detail: There are a series of useful descriptions and measurements that can be used in manufacturing processes, and which are well described in standard textbooks, for example Hirano 2009e. Some of these measures are relevant in specific situations in health and social care. The suggested steps (Hirano 2009e: p 629) are to create a capacity work table, showing the current capacity of each production 'cell;' create a standard operations combination chart; produce a standard process sheet, and finally produce a standard operations chart. Hirano uses slightly different terms than those used in this volume, but the original source material is very valuable and well worth reviewing if the situation arises.

Figure 9.1 shows a Standard Work Description document.

HQ▲
NHS Highland
Kaizen Promotion Office

Standard Work Description

NHS Highland

Process Name:	
Location / Dept:	
Completed by:	
Date:	Review Date:

Task #	Description of activity	Equipment / Tools	Role	Time (Mins)

Figure 9.1 Standard work description.

9.5 Components of Standard Work

There are three components of Standard Work (Ohno 1988; Japan Management Association 1989; Shingo 2005):

- The sequence of operations to be conducted
- The time the operations will take
- The required supplies needed for the operation

This section considers these in turn.

9.5.1 *Sequence of Operations*

This is a statement of the activities to be conducted, and the agreed order. This is often important, as if there is lack of clarity on the order of activities, they may be done twice. In the previously mentioned examples, not knowing who was going to do which procedure resulted in confusion, duplication and delay.

The idea of 'Standard Work' often causes concern for staff. People worry, understandably, about 'cookie-cutter medicine,' with the same processes being applied to everyone, regardless of need.

This comes partly from memories of Standard Operating Procedures, confined to dusty shelves and rarely reviewed, if ever, and recollections of 'guidance' on how to conduct clinical activities, helpfully provided by 'higher authorities.'

Mark Graban (2012: p 67) suggests a definition of what he terms 'standardized work':

'The current one best way to safely complete an activity with the proper outcome and the highest quality, using the fewest possible resources.'

There are several important aspects of Graban's definition that are worth considering. Standard work is not low-quality work – rather, it tries to capture the best way of doing the work within the resources available. Lean assumes that delivering a high-quality service not only benefits patients by doing things right first time, but also reduces costs by decreasing rework, complications and waste.

The second matter to note is that standard work is not set in stone. It should be a live document that is updated when new ways are identified of improving the process, rather than a fossilised set of Standard Operating Procedures, confined to a never-to-be-consulted folder.

It follows that, while the overall process is not within the control of individual work areas, wards or teams, the work within their area, and the Standard Work, should be designed by them, as they know their operations best. It is important, however, that staff are aware of the work feeding into them and the next stage of the process, as well as evidence on effectiveness, when relevant. There is little value in optimising the work in one section of a process, if it causes greater delays in another process than it resolves, or of optimising work that will not deliver the expected outcomes.

Important considerations in developing Standard Work are

1. Knowledge of the whole process. What might have already been done by someone else? The previously mentioned test example is an illustration of this. Staff working in the same clinic for over four years did not know what each other did. In our experience, it is common to find that staff know very little about parts of the process elsewhere, even in the same building. In one piece of work, it emerged that a staff member who worked in a specialist hospital ward had never visited the Accident and Emergency Department from which most of their patients emerged. Similarly, in another specialist unit, few staff had visited the community units to which many of their patients moved, and so had limited knowledge of the services on offer in these units.
2. What is done at present? As the examples illustrate, staff are often not completely clear on what everyone does. Even people doing apparently the same task are sometimes surprised to find that other people do it differently from them, or have a different understanding of what is required. Describing the current process, and the variation in it, is usually a good way to start.
3. The relative workload and timings of different staff members and operations. If there is a highly constrained service (see the Drum–Buffer–Rope discussion in Chapter 5 'Continuous Flow') then it may make sense to move part of the work to a part of the service, and therefore a staff member, with more time. In services with constraints, it is common to see other staff standing waiting for work. If any of this work can be rebalanced from the capacity limited part of the process to another part, then this may improve the overall flow of the service.
4. Avoiding Over-Specification. As discussed in Chapter 3, it is possible to go too far in specifying activities. There are some critical operations that have to be done in a very particular way to ensure safety, and these do

need careful specification – see the example of a Safety Bundle in the Error Proofing section, for example.

In many other cases, professional staff know perfectly well how to conduct an activity. If someone is known to be competent to take a blood pressure, for example, then it is not necessary to explain to them how to do it – they need to know that they undertake the blood pressure measurement, and perhaps that they record it on a specific form, but they do not need instruction in the basic method: if they do, they should not be conducting the activity unsupervised in the first place.

In industry settings, it can be essential to give very clear guidance, for example on which hand to reach across to undertake a particular process. This type of detail is seldom necessary in health and social care settings, and when it is necessary, it will usually be obvious to everyone concerned.

5. Make Safety Checks Clear. When a process needs to include a particular safety check, it should be very clear in the process what is to be done, and that this is the responsibility of the staff member undertaking that specific task.

6. Build Error Proofing in to the Process. The Error Proofing section discussed this in more detail. Error Proofing is very difficult until there is some idea of Standard Work. Once it is clear what is to be done at what stage of the sequence, Error Proofing becomes easier.

As discussed in detail in Chapter 7, 'Error Proofing,' it is appropriate to consider

   a. What check should the person conducting the operation perform on their own work? Are there key aspects that they need to check before they pass the work on to the next person in the process?

   b. What check should they conduct on the work they receive? Anyone can make an error, and it is essential that systems can cope with this without patients coming to harm.

7. Be prepared to revise the work. Standard Work that is not revised is probably Standard Work that is not being used. Staff regularly think of new ways of doing things, and if these are found to be improvements, usually using a Plan – Do – Study – Act (PDSA) cycle, then the work should be changed to accommodate it. This is not a criticism of the original work, but a natural part of the process of continuous improvement.

9.5.2 *Timing of Operations*

Staff who are used to a system that does not specify time can find the idea of identifying an average time for a process oppressive. This is not a timing of an individual, however, but a collective view on how long an operation is likely to take. If there is no notion of approximate timing, then scheduling of an outpatient clinic for example becomes impossible. Similarly, in a complex clinic with several different components, there needs to be an idea of how long individual operations take, so that the parts of the clinic can be scheduled to flow as well as possible.

Everyone understands that people are not cars, and that requirements vary by person, but observations usually reveal a 'commonest time' for each part of the process. Averages can be deceptive, and looking at modes is often helpful if there are sufficient observations to make this appropriate. Damiani (2012) describes a variant of this used by Toyota in Brazil, where five timings of each activity are made. The longest and shortest are discarded, and the average of the other three measurements is taken.

Averages, or arithmetic means, are calculated by adding up all the values and dividing by the number of observations. Averages can be skewed by a few outlying observations, and so they are not always the best choice for describing a process. Medians are the numbers that occur in the middle of a series (for example, in a series of eleven observations, put in order of time, the median would be the sixth observation. In a series of twelve observations, the median would be the average of the sixth and seventh observations, after they have been placed in order of time). The mode is the most commonly occurring number. Which best represents the observations is usually clear when the observations are reviewed.

Attaching a time to the activity also helps to give people a feel for what is expected in the activity, and how it fits with the other parts of the process.

9.5.3 *Supplies*

The description of Standard Work includes the equipment and supplies that are needed for the work, and which therefore defines standard stock (Japan Management Association 1989: p 104). This will include consideration of the number of items that are needed for a procedure.

9.6 Recording Timings

Timing operations is not something that people are used to in health and social care. While waiting times and other high-level measures are familiar, it is much less common to measure the time taken for particular tasks.

It is important that staff understand that it is the time for the operation that is being measured: this is not an attempt to measure their individual efficiency, but rather to understand the times needed for parts of a process.

Process Mapping and Value Stream Mapping are discussed further in the Value Stream Mapping section. For timings of operations, Time Observation Records are used. These forms (Figure 9.2) are used to record the steps in a process, the times for each operation within a process (called 'Cycle Times') and the total time for the process (termed the 'Lead Time').

Paradoxically, when using a Time Observation Record, it is important to start by not using the form at first. It is easy to assume that you understand current work. As the previously described examples indicate, it is very common not to know exactly what other parts of a process, or even co-workers, do, or how precisely they tackle a problem. Watching a process through, from start to finish, is important. Ideally, this should be done several times before beginning to time operations.

Scope of Operations	From:												Date/Time:		
	To:												Completed By:		
#	Activity	1	2	3	4	5	6	7	8	9	10	11	12	Most Frequent / Mode Time	Notes
	Total for One Cycle:														
	Less Wait and Walk:														
	Processing (Value) Time:														

HQ▲
NHS Highland
Kaizen Promotion Office

Figure 9.2   Time observation record.

After several rounds of observation, a description of the process can be drawn up. The steps in the process, the individual operations, are then written down the left-hand side of the Time Observation Record (Figure 9.3).

In timing a process, the commonest way to record times is to record the time each process, including waits between operations, begins. The time of an individual operation can then be calculated by subtracting the starting time of the following process from the starting time of the previous process (Figure 9.3). This is the Cycle Time, the time taken for one operation, often by one person.

The total time for the process is then calculated by subtracting the end time from the start time of the process, to give the Lead Time. Reading from left to right across the page allows an average or mode to be identified for each Cycle Time, and an average or mode Lead Time to be identified. This begins to give a good idea of the time taken on average for the complete process, and for individual operations within the process.

In some cases, several different routes may be followed (see Chapter 6, 'Levelling,' for a discussion of different 'families,' and of Product Quantity Analysis). This can usually be accommodated on a Time Observation Record. Figure 9.4 shows a form that records how people pass through a process in several different ways.

9.7 Forms Used in Standard Work

There are a series of forms that are useful in developing and describing Standard Work (Suzaki 1987; Hirano 2009e; Hirano and Furuya 2006; Jackson 2012; Hadfield et al. 2012). Time Observation Forms are described in the previous section.

Process Work Sheets (or Standard Operation Sheets/Charts, or Standard Operating Sheets/Charts) are used to describe an operation pictorially. Figure 9.5 gives an example. The sheet shows the operation, displays the sequence of actions, identifies the activities that occur before and after it, and gives information on safety requirements and quality checks. Some versions also show the details of the process at the side of the diagram (Hadfield et al. 2012).

Standard Work Descriptions give a step-by-step account of a process, including expected times, and can include photographs of the process (Figure 9.6). As with Process Work Sheets, important information on checks and safety requirements can be emphasised.

Time Observation Record

Process	CPN 2 & 3 - Administration			Observation Time					Observer			Derek Leslie / Gavin Hookway			
Step #	Description of Operation	1	2	3	4	5	6	7	8	9	10	11	12	Most Frequent task time (mode)	Notes
1	CPN 2 Admin Start	00:00	00:00	00:00	00:00	00:00	00:00	00:00	00:00	00:00	00:00	00:00	00:00	86:00	Average
		111:00	61:00	00:00	00:00	00:00	00:00	00:00	00:00	00:00	00:00	00:00	00:00		
2	CPN 2 Admin Finish	111:00	61:00												
				00:00	00:00	00:00	00:00	00:00	00:00	00:00	00:00	00:00	00:00		
		00:00	00:00	00:00	00:00	00:00	00:00	00:00	00:00	00:00	00:00	00:00	00:00		
1	CPN 3 Admin Start			00:00	00:00	00:00	00:00	00:00	00:00	00:00	00:00	00:00	00:00	45:00	Admin
				45:00	00:00	00:00	00:00	00:00	00:00	00:00	00:00	00:00	00:00		
2	CPN 3 Admin Finish			45:00										00:00	
					00:00	00:00	00:00	00:00	00:00	00:00	00:00	00:00	00:00	00:00	
					00:00	00:00	00:00	00:00	00:00	00:00	00:00	00:00	00:00		
1	Leave Caladh Centre				00:00	00:00	00:00	00:00	00:00	00:00	00:00	00:00	00:00	08:00	Travel
					08:00	00:00	00:00	00:00	00:00	00:00	00:00	00:00	00:00		
2	Arrive MA Hospital				08:00	00:00	00:00	00:00	00:00	00:00	00:00	00:00	00:00	01:00	Travel
					01:00	00:00	00:00	00:00	00:00	00:00	00:00	00:00	00:00		
3	CPN 3 Clinical Supervision Start				09:00	00:00	00:00	00:00	00:00	00:00	00:00	00:00	00:00	79:00	Admin
					79:00	00:00	00:00	00:00	00:00	00:00	00:00	00:00	00:00		
4	CPN 3 Clinical Supervision FinishStart				88:00	00:00	00:00	00:00	00:00	00:00	00:00	00:00	00:00	01:00	Travel
					01:00	00:00	00:00	00:00	00:00	00:00	00:00	00:00	00:00		
5	Leave MA Hospital				89:00	00:00	00:00	00:00	00:00	00:00	00:00	00:00	00:00	08:00	Travel
					08:00	00:00	00:00	00:00	00:00	00:00	00:00	00:00	00:00		
6	Arrive Caladh Centre	111:00	61:00	45:00	97:00	00:00	00:00	00:00	00:00	00:00	00:00	00:00	00:00	00:00	
	Time for one observation	111:00	61:00	45:00	97:00	00:00	00:00	00:00	00:00	00:00	00:00	00:00	00:00	78:00	Average
	Minus walk/wait time	00:00	00:00	00:00	08:00	00:00	00:00	00:00	00:00	00:00	00:00	00:00	00:00	08:00	
	=processing time	111:00	61:00	45:00	89:00	00:00	00:00	00:00	00:00	00:00	00:00	00:00	00:00	76:00	

Figure 9.3 Completed time observation record.

Time Observation Record

Observer: Gavin Hookway

Process	Social Work Receipt of Referral	Observation Time												Most Frequent task time (mode)	Notes
Step #	Description of Operation	1	2	3	4	5	6	7	8	9	10	11	12		
1	Review Telephone Message	00:00	00:00	00:00	00:00	00:00	00:00	00:00	00:00	00:00	00:00	00:00	00:00	00:30	Value
2	Check Care First	00:30	00:30	00:35	00:16	03:50	00:35	00:00	00:00	00:00	00:00	00:00	00:00	01:26	Value
3	Telephone Call to Client / Relative	00:42	01:23	00:07	02:21	01:45	02:18	00:00	00:00	00:00	00:00	00:00	00:00	04:16	Value
4	Telephone Call Ends	01:12	04:15	12:19	03:28	00:00	02:53	00:00	00:00	00:00	00:00	00:00	00:00	02:35	Wait
5	Log information on Care First	07:20	17:32	20:35	06:35	05:35	07:54	00:00	00:00	00:00	00:00	00:00	00:00	07:50	Value
		09:30	09:32	10:03	15:38	15:25	07:31								
6	Submit Initial Contact	16:50	20:07	16:07	00:21	01:24	00:03	00:00	00:00	00:00	00:00	00:00	00:00	01:58	Value
		00:05	07:59												
7	Create Activity on Care First	16:55	28:06	16:28	17:02	15:28	02:00	00:00	00:00	00:00	00:00	00:00	00:00	01:20	Value
		01:05	01:00	02:00	00:33										
8	Print Activity	18:00	00:00	00:00	00:00	17:35	17:28	00:00	00:00	00:00	00:00	00:00	00:00	00:28	Value
9	Save File	18:50	00:50	00:00	00:00	00:53	00:38	00:00	00:00	00:00	00:00	00:00	00:00	00:33	Value
						18:28	18:06								
10	Print Initial Contact	19:40	00:50	00:00	00:00	00:34	01:22	00:00	00:00	00:00	00:00	00:00	00:00	00:53	Value
		00:10	00:00	00:00	00:00	19:02	19:28								
11	Collect prints – leave office	19:50	00:00	00:00	00:00	04:07	00:06	00:00	00:00	00:00	00:00	00:00	00:00	01:17	Travel/Walk
		02:10	00:00	00:00	00:00	23:09	19:34								
12	Return Office with Prints	22:00	00:00	00:00	00:00	01:55	02:22	00:00	00:00	00:00	00:00	00:00	00:00	24:07	Travel/Walk
		00:03				25:04	21:56								
13	Process End		22:03	29:06	18:28	00:14	00:19	00:00	00:00	00:00	00:00	00:00	00:00		
		22:03	29:06	18:28		25:18	22:15	00:00							
	Time for one observation	02:52	22:03	29:06	18:28	25:18	22:15							20:00	Average
	Minus walk/wait time	00:00	03:25	04:31	00:30	07:44	03:49							03:20	
	=processing time	02:52	18:38	24:35	17:58	17:34	18:26	00:00	00:00	00:00	00:00	00:00	00:00	16:40	

Figure 9.4 Time observation record with different routes through a process.

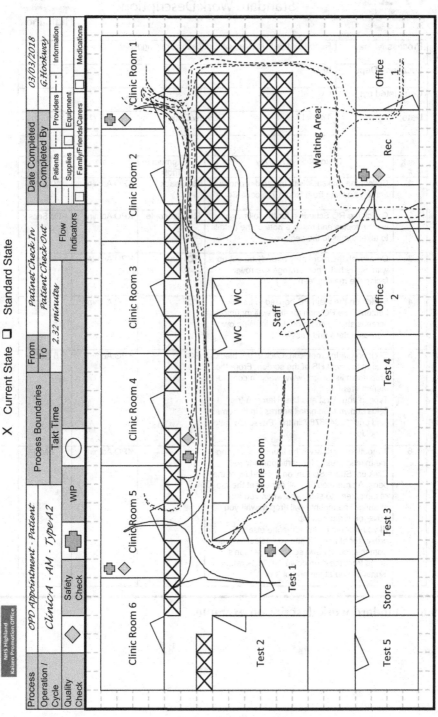

HQ△
NHS Highland
Kaizen Promotion Office

Process Work Sheet

X Current State ☐ Standard State

Process	OPD Appointment - Patient		Process Boundaries	From	Patinet Check-In	Date Completed	03/03/2018		
Operation / Cycle	Clinic A - AM - Type A2			To	Patient Check-Out	Completed By	G.Hookway		
			Takt Time		2.32 minutes				
Quality Check		Safety Check	WIP		Flow Indicators	Patients	Providers	Information	
			○			Supplies	Equipment		
						Family/Friends/Carers		Medications	

Figure 9.5   Example of process work sheet.

NHS Highland
Kaizen Promotion Office

Standard Work Description

NHS
Highland

Process Name:	Report Out Set Up (Medical Education Training Room)		
Location / Dept:	KPO		
Completed by:	GC		
Date:	12/05/17	Review Date:	19/02/18

Task #	Description of Activity	Equipment / Tools	Role	Time (Mins)
1	Collect the rucksack with the spider phone and a visualiser from Room 7, Scotia Court	Rucksack	KPO Admin	10 Secs
2	Check the RO Schedule for the following week's topics and make a note of the details to take across to the session	RO Schedule	KPO Admin	30 Secs
3	On arrival, the room may already be set up with chairs but if not, arrange five rows facing the main screen	PC	KPO Admin	5 Mins
4	Switch on the main PC housed in the Lectern. The PC monitor and wall mounted screens should come on. Log in using own sign-on details and password	PC	KPO Admin	5 Secs
5	Click on the Internet icon. Click in the blank field at the top LHS of the screen. From the drop down list select 'www.webjoin.com' to launch WebEx Type in your First and Last Name in the fields shown then email address in the email field and '123456789' in the 'Passcode' field, click 'Join'	PC	KPO Admin	5 Secs
6	A meeting window will be launched starting the meeting ready for participants to join. Click on 'Share Screen' on the middle of the page. A green toolbar will appear at the top of the screen to show you when you are sharing. The tool bar will drop downif you hover on the green tab (If you want to make someone else the presenter at another site you select 'Assign' from this toolbar and select the person's name from the drop down list. They return 'rights' to you at the end of their	PC	KPO Admin	1 Min

Figure 9.6 Standard work description example.

The times for the individual operations can then be combined to show the total process, using a Work Combination Sheet (or Operations Combination Sheet). An example is shown in Figure 9.7. It is usual to show waiting times, and walking/movement times for patients, separately from the times of individual operations. This gives a visual display of the proportion of the time spent in operations, and the proportion of time spent waiting or moving from place to place or room to room.

In some health care examples, machines work unattended, allowing a staff member to undertake a second part of the process. This is common in laboratories, for example. In that case, the usual method is to show a dotted line for the work of the machine carrying on while other activities occur.

9.8 Service Examples

Returning to the examples given previously in 9.4, the response to each of these issues was:

- Duplicate tests: The introduction of Standard Work across the clinic setting was agreed with the full team of clinicians, nursing staff and the administration team. In the development of this standard work, the team identified multiple wastes within their processes. When the team reviewed the whole value stream for their service and the associated wastes, they were able to develop a suite of standard work which eliminated over-processing of tests on patients which freed up valuable clinical time. The standard work was scheduled for review three months later.
- Community team: The team reviewed the content of calls, and found that a small number of topics and requests accounted for a large number of calls. They created and tested Standard Work for these situations, and agreed recording mechanisms. Where calls could be dealt with immediately, this was done. For other queries, Standard Work was agreed on how to escalate the problem to the relevant professional if required, or to notify the relevant staff member on their return, if non-urgent. The process reduced markedly the number of required follow ups when the staff member returned to base, and also provided faster responses for clients.
- Health Care Assistant Roles: The nurses and Health Care Assistants reviewed their roles and responsibilities. Once the roles had been

Work Combination Sheet

X Current State ☐ Standard State

NHS Highland

| Scope of | From: Patient Arrival in Department | Date: 5th October 2017 |
| Operations: | To: Patient Departs for Theatres | Completed by: Gavin Hookway |

| 1 Sq = | 2 | M | Time (draw vertical red line at Takt Time) | Takt = | 18.36 | Mins |

| # | Activity | Task Time | | | | Time (draw vertical red line at Takt Time) |
		Value	Non V	Walk	Wait	
1	Patient Checks into Department	3		1	21	
2	Patient Admitted to Hospital	11		3	21	
3	Discussion with Surgical HO	4		2	16	
4	Anaesthetic Assessment	11		1	20	
5	Surgical Team & Consent Process	7		1	14	
6	ECG Test	2		1	6	
7	Theatre Check & Depart for Theatres	4		5	9	
	Totals:	42	0	13	107	162
	%:	26%	0%	8%	66%	100%

Key: Value — GREEN   Non Value — AMBER   Walk — BLUE   Wait — RED

Figure 9.7 Standard work combination sheet example.

reviewed and agreed, Standard Work was produced, tested and shared to clearly define the activities to be undertaken by nurses and the Health Care Assistants. This reduced duplication, improved consistency and flow, and increased the time available for added value work with patients during their visit.

■ Ward Messages: The specialist service reviewed the calls that arrived, and produced draft Standard Work. They discussed this with the ward staff, and tested the Standard Work over three PDSA cycles. The final product was an information collection form which included the questions to be asked, information to be offered, and the criteria and process for emergency response if required. Standard Work was also developed for the restocking of forms and the daily collection and use of the forms by the specialist service. In the longer term, it was possible to develop an electronic system which avoided double entry of the information, but the paper system worked well, and safely, for over a year.

9.9 Using Standard Work in Practice

Standard Work is an essential component of the quality improvement process. Developing Standard Work with a team helps to ensure a common understanding of processes. It also makes it easier to identify variation and to spot problems, as there is an agreed way of doing things. It also forms the basis of future improvements, where quality improvement ideas can be tested against existing Standard Work using PDSA cycles, to establish whether it is an improvement.

Standard Work also gives a basis for problem-solving, as it contributes to clarity on what is happening, and therefore the steps to be improved.

In order for Standard Work to have an impact, it has to be incorporated into Leader Standard Work and Daily Management, discussed in Chapter 11. Visual Controls (Chapter 8) allow use of work to be monitored and problems to be identified. This supports root cause analysis and problem-solving (Chapter 4) and keeps Standard Work current by identifying required improvements.

Managers need to pay careful attention to the use of Standard Work, and to ensure that they show interest in its use, including direct observation and feedback where possible.

Further Reading

Full references are included in the bibliography.

Standard Work for Lean Healthcare (Jackson 2012) provides a useful discussion of these tools. Hirano's *JIT Implementation Manual. Volume 5: Standardized Operations* (Hirano 2009e) and *JIT Implementation Manual. Volume 6: JIT Implementation Forms and Charts* (Hirano 2009f) include greater technical detail if required.

Chapter 10

Value Stream Maps

> Taking a Value Stream perspective means working on the big picture, not just individual processes, and improving the whole, not just optimizing the process.
>
> **Rother and Shook (1999: p 10)**

10.1 Aims of the Chapter

1. To understand the role of Value Stream Maps
2. To know how to obtain data for a Value Stream Map, including the role of direct observation
3. To be familiar with the symbols used in a Value Stream Map
4. To know the stages of construction of a Value Stream Map

10.2 Background

The advantages of value stream mapping are

- Seeing an overall process, rather than isolated functions.
- Being able to identify the role of activities in relation to the total value stream.
- Providing a visual representation that can be shared and discussed.
- The method can also be used to develop and present a future state for the value stream.

The key principle is that value streams are centred on delivery of what patients or service users require, and which is identified by asking the people using the service. Value streams do not focus on functional operations (e.g. booking a laboratory), but rather on the process as required by the patient or service user. This helps to avoid any assumption that an operation, as currently delivered, is necessarily the best way of meeting the person's need.

Dean (2013) uses the phrase 'Healing Pathways' in preference to Value Streams to make the point that there is a positive health purpose to the value streams. This is an important observation, but 'Value Stream' is used widely in health care, so the term has been used in this volume to avoid possible confusion with Clinical Pathways, Managed Clinical Networks and similar terms.

Nash and Poling (2008: p 1) comment, 'A value stream is the process flow from the "point of requested need" to "closure of all activity" after the product or service has been provided.'

10.3 History Note

Toyota used maps of 'material and information flows' (Liker and Hoseus 2008: p 183; Martin and Osterling 2014: p 4), but Value Stream Mapping was not a key Toyota concept. A book describing internal Toyota tutorials in the 1970s makes no mention of them (Japan Management Association 1989), and Shingo's 1981 account of the Toyota Production System also has no reference to them (Shingo 2005). Rother and Shook (1999) note that Toyota use 'Materials and Information Flow Maps' which include flows of material, information and people/processes, which provides some of the same functions.

The use of Value Stream Maps (VSM) in improvement was described by Rother and Shook (1999) and extended to service industries by Tapping et al. (2002) and Kyte and Locher (2004). The remarkable success of the VSM in the time since, and its ubiquity in much improvement work, is testament to the versatility of the method.

10.4 Differences from Process Maps

Process maps are useful tools that show the steps in a particular process. The added components of VSM are that they show information flow; include times for activities ('cycles') and for waits; show the people or items currently in the system ('Work in Process') and focus on the service as experienced by the patient or service user.

A current state map is a snapshot of a system as it currently exists. A key feature is that it is often impossible for an observer to see an entire value stream at one time: information has to be collected and shared to allow the whole value stream to be understood, particularly when it may happen over a long period of time and in different locations, as could be the case in an outpatient system, for example. This means that, for many people involved in a system, the preparation of a current state VSM will be the first time they will have 'seen' the entire process to which they contribute.

10.5 Complaints Handling Process Map Example

The service wanted to look at the way that complaints were handled. This involved several teams and happened over a large geographical area.

The process steps were identified by meeting with staff, and reviewing documents and examples (Figure 10.1). The Process Map later helped the team to produce a Value Stream Map.

In practice, there were differences in how complaints were handled, with multiple rework occurring at the 'Enquiry/Concern' stage, and also at the logging of the complaint centrally (indicated by red 'swirls'). This caused delay in complaint investigation commencing, and a subsequent delay in the patient/client receiving a response.

The handling of the complaint across three separate area teams had some commonality, but it was evident that there was variation in processes with no standard work across the whole process.

10.6 Developing a VSM

> The point of value stream mapping is not the map, but understanding the flow of information and material.
>
> **Rother and Shook (1999: p 11)**

Constructing a VSM of the current state of a process requires close observation of the process. When working with a team, it is common to have people describe to you how they feel things should work, rather than what happens in practice. In some cases, staff are surprised when they lay out

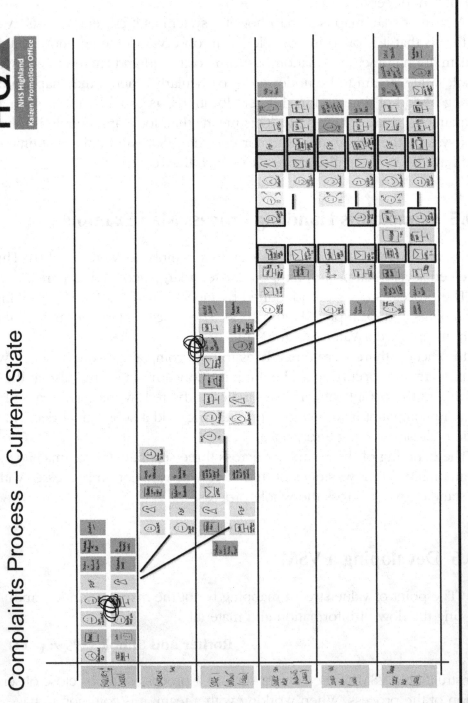

Figure 10.1   Current state process map.

the current state, as it may differ markedly from their previous understanding of it. In some instances, this is because they are unaware of the whole process or precisely what happens at different stages. In other instances, it is because they are used to describing the expected practices, without reflecting on how seldom they are actually applied.

10.6.1 Scope

Decide the scope of the value stream to be mapped. Some value streams of interest will be part of larger processes. For example, an outpatient referral pathway may include several stages, one of which is the process of booking an appointment. This stage may represent a whole process in its own right, and it may be appropriate to develop a VSM specifically for this stage. In other cases, it may be the entire value stream that is of interest, in which case the booking process may be represented by one cycle. The degree of resolution to be applied depends on the scope and nature of the process of interest.

The first stage is to identify the main cycles of activity that occur. For example, for an outpatient process, the steps may be

- A person goes to their GP.
- The GP assesses them and refers them to a Consultant Outpatient Clinic.
- The referral is received, logged and an appointment sent.
- The patient attends the appointment.
- The Consultant refers them for tests.
- Referral for tests received, logged and appointment sent.
- The person attends for diagnostic tests.
- Test results are received, logged and a further appointment set.
- The patient attends appointment.
- Consultant asks GP to prescribe a medicine.
- The patient attends their GP and receives a prescription.
- The patient takes the prescription to a pharmacy, where the prescription is dispensed.

Some of these stages could be described as value streams in themselves. For example, the process in the GP surgery, or the arrangements to receive, log and arrange diagnostic tests will both have multiple steps within them.

The scope of the work, and the extent of the value stream being reviewed, will depend on the focus of the particular improvement work being undertaken. This will relate to the problem assessment, and decision on prioritisation, discussed in the 'Improvement Cycles' chapter.

For the purposes of this example, we will assume that we are mapping the entire previously mentioned value stream, in order to decide where to prioritise improvement efforts.

10.6.2 Observations

To map a value stream, direct observations are essential (Rother and Shook 1999: p 10). Observations are conducted using standard forms, described in Chapter 9, 'Standard Work.'

Once you have an understanding of scope, walk the whole process, as far as possible. Going to the *gemba* – the place the work is done – is essential. Use big eyes, big ears and a small mouth – you are there to observe and to learn, not to criticise or comment. The only exception to this is if you observe something that appears to be an immediate threat to patient or staff safety, in which case the observer needs to bring it to the direct attention of the relevant supervisor.

Observation etiquette is important (Stark 2016).

10.6.3 Observation Etiquette

In an ideal state, everyone in a work area knows that improvement work is happening, has been asked their opinion, and has an opportunity to discuss and contribute in advance. This is the ideal, but it doesn't always happen. It is common for there to be 60 or more staff associated with a single ward area in one way or another, for example, with multiple shifts and staff who work across several areas.

With holidays, illness and general communication delays, it is common to find that not everyone has heard about the work. In other cases, people have heard, but haven't entirely understood what is happening. Lean has a fundamental value of respect for staff, and going the extra mile to demonstrate this is always worthwhile. People are very quick to identify a dissonance between what you say and what you do.

The effect is that, if you turn up in a service area to help with observations, all may not be as you expect. It is useful to have Standard Work fir observations.

10.6.3.1 *Advance Planning*

Work out when you are likely to be in the area. Tell the relevant manager and shift lead that you intend to be there, and discuss any issues they want to raise. If at all possible, meet with them and show them the forms you expect to use, explain their purpose and show examples of previous use so they can see how the information comes together to support their change work.

Offer the opportunity to help with the observations – more on this later. The more people understand about the process, the more transferable skills they acquire. Lean is not something you 'do to' people – the intent is to support people to understand the principles and methods so that they can apply them to their own service.

If work is underway on an event, such as a Rapid Process Improvement Workshop (RPIW), it can be easy for people to feel they are being 'done to' rather than being supported to develop new skills. When you have learnt about Lean, there is a temptation to run the whole thing yourself – resist this temptation at all costs. If you are helping with an RPIW, perhaps as Team Leader or Workshop Leader, the skills the team acquire are at least as important as the outcome of the event itself.

10.6.3.2 *Identification and Introductions*

Wear a name badge, showing your name, job title and organisational affiliation: you can't expect everyone to know you. Strive for humility.

As soon as you arrive in an area, ask for the person in charge, introduce yourself and explain the purpose of your attendance. If the person already knew you were coming, that is an added bonus. Don't assume that the discussion with the manager or team lead will have been passed on. Things happen: people are ill, are hurried, forget things – make no assumptions about what staff have already heard.

Use the opportunity. Every person you speak to is another person you can talk to about the process, about the principles and about their role in the work. Explain the structure of the work, timescales, the aim, and ask their thoughts. If they have time, show them the forms and explain how they are used. You can ask if they would be interested in collecting any information themselves, if time permits.

It can seem tedious, but this has to be repeated every single time you go into an area, at least as much as making yourself known to the person in charge and the relevant people on the shift. It is common to discover that people have forgotten some of what you told them, in any case, or have misunderstood it. Engagement does not happen by accident: demonstrate interest, listen and value the information and advice you are given.

10.6.3.3 Observations in Clinical Areas

If you want to follow a patient or other service user, always ask permission. There are a very few occasions on which this may not be possible – with an unconscious or anaesthetised patient, for example – but even there, it is often possible to explain what you are doing to a relative of the person, and to seek their agreement.

A standard script can be useful – your name, your role, the purpose of the current work, a guarantee of anonymity and a clear explanation that the focus is on the process. It is uncommon for people to decline, but if they do so, respond courteously, thank them for their time and move on. Respect their decision.

When people do agree, it is often unnecessary to enter a consulting room. The focus is frequently on delays between processes. Even when a process is being timed, it may be unnecessary to enter the clinic room itself. If it would be useful to observe a clinical process involving a patient, then explain this – and explain why – and check that the permission you have been given also covers this interaction. Some people will be willing to have you take timings of waits, walks and so on, but unwilling to have someone else present at an examination, interview or test. Again, respect this decision.

People using services have often used the service before, and may want to tell you of their experiences. This is useful: take careful notes of any information the person volunteers to share. Generally, it is possible to separate observations from patient feedback, but sometimes people are so keen to tell you about their experience that it would be discourteous to decline. Make sure notes are anonymised, unless the person specifically wants you to bring something to the attention of the service. It is useful to know the specifics of the complaints procedure for the organisation, so that you can explain it if asked.

In other cases, you may want to look at the flow in an entire area, rather than following individual patients. In this case, where you are recording timings for several cycles at once, it may be possible to put a notice in the room explaining that observations are being conducted, and how to ask for more information. Members of the public are used to the idea of quality control, and they often find it reassuring to know that someone is observing processes, even if the detail is not completely clear to them.

In this situation, you may find service users looking across at what you are doing, and even squinting to see the observations you are making. This can again be a useful opportunity for interaction. If it is not disruptive to care, you can make eye contact, introduce yourself, and ask if the person would like to see what you are recording. This gives instant assurance that no individually identifiable information is being collected, and it often evolves into a discussion of the person's experience of the service.

10.6.3.4 Sharing Observations with Staff

As with service users, if a staff member looks curious, it is useful to show them what you are doing and to talk it over with them. Even if you have explained the idea before, seeing observations in practice can be a different thing and may benefit from more explanation. It also gives reassurance that no information on individual staff members is being collected, or at least that the focus is on the process, rather than on staff.

Showing people what is being collected has the added benefit that it reduces later debate. People know that the information has been collected directly, because they have seen it being done and have often seen the timings. It also begins to throw up ideas that the staff member may want to feed into the improvement work.

10.6.3.5 Involving People

There may well be no such thing as too much involvement. The more people know about what is happening, the more they can contribute to it, and the more they know that it is based on direct observation of processes, the easier it is for people to invest in the work. The mantra of 'big eyes, big ears, small mouth' is good advice, particularly combined with 'be humble': the people using the service and the people running the service are the experts on it, and observations are a way of capturing current practice, not of catching people out.

This section was reproduced from Stark (2016) www.leanhealthservices. org, with permission.

10.6.4 Cycles and Linkages

Start by identifying the main cycles of activity. These are usually actions carried out by one person. In a higher level value stream, however, the cycle box may include a number of activities, or sub-cycles.

Write the name of the process in the box at the top, and the operator role at the bottom (Figure 10.2). You can also include the main actions if that is useful.

Once the cycles are in place, join them up with a symbol showing the nature of the flow between the cycles. The commonest symbols are shown in Figure 10.3. A clear arrow is used to show where there is continuous flow. Where there is a push process, use a striped arrow (see Figure 10.4 for an example). If there is a pull process, use a curved arrow to show that the distal process is pulling from the proximal (Rother and Shook 1999; Jackson 2013b).

10.6.4.1 Value Stream Loops

In some cases, there are groups of associated processes that usually happen close in time to one another, possibly with delays before and after this group. These groupings are often called 'Value Stream Loops.'

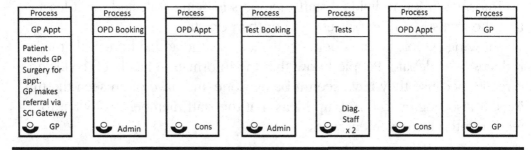

Process	Process	Process	Process	Process	Process	Process
GP Appt	OPD Booking	OPD Appt	Test Booking	Tests	OPD Appt	GP
Patient attends GP Surgery for appt. GP makes referral via SCI Gateway						
GP	Admin	Cons	Admin	Diag. Staff x 2	Cons	GP

Figure 10.2   Value stream map: main cycles.

Symbol		Meaning
Clear arrow	⇨	Continuous Flow
Striped arrow	▮▮▮▶	Pushed to the next process
Curved arrow	↻	Pulled by the next part of the system

Figure 10.3   Flow symbols used in value stream maps.

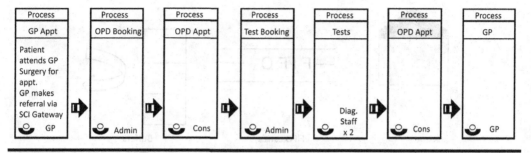

Figure 10.4 Value stream map: Flow symbols added.

Within a loop, the previously mentioned flow symbols can be used. For example, within a booking process, the referral may be received and wait in a pile to be logged. This is a push process. A batch of the referrals may then be taken by a staff member and entered on to a computer programme to log them. Having logged them, the referrals may then wait again before a second staff member takes them and allocates them an appointment. As the second staff member is not ready to take them straight away, this is another example of a push process.

When the second staff member takes the referrals, however, they may book the appointment and send a letter straight away (continuous flow). This process could be represented in detail, or shown as one cycle of activity in a larger value stream.

10.6.4.2 Linkages

Ideally, people or items move from one part of the process to the next with no wait, in continuous flow. This does not always happen, and the nature of the wait between the process can be shown in several ways.

Linkages between parts of a process can include queues, First In First Out (FIFO) lanes, buffers or supermarkets.

10.6.4.3 Queues

Queues are people, tests, paperwork and so on that are waiting (Figure 10.5). This is not a planned wait – these are numbers of items or people waiting that build up over time.

10.6.4.4 FIFO Lanes

First In First Out (FIFO) lanes are like a queue in a large post office – one long line in which the people or items waiting are dealt with in order

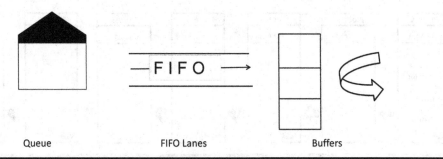

Figure 10.5   Queues, FIFO lanes and buffers.

(Figure 10.5). This is often suitable for non-urgent situations, such as routine tests. In production situations, FIFO lanes will often have a specified maximum number, and once this number is reached, the previous process stops producing (Rother and Shook 1999).

10.6.4.5 Buffers

Buffers are indicated as shown in Figure 10.5. They act as a planned supply for the next process. They are used when one patient may have to move to the head of the line based on clinical condition, there is a rate limiting constraint or two processes have a different takt time (Jackson 2013b: p 66).

A buffer differs from a queue in that there has been a conscious decision to maintain a number of items or patients at this stage. The buffer symbol is shown with a pull arrow, as the following process pulls the item from the buffer. Items, or patients, will not always be taken from the buffer in the order in which they entered it, based on patient requirements (Jackson 2013b). Buffers are discussed further in Chapter 5, 'Continuous Flow'.

The number of items in the buffer is worked out to keep the next process flowing. For example, if you have a key step that has limited capacity, you may decide that no time can be lost at that step. If an earlier part of the process sometimes runs into trouble and disrupts supply, then it can make sense to store a supply in a buffer so that the flow to the constrained stage can be maintained until the flow can be re-established.

The number of items in the buffer can be worked out by reviewing how often the supply is disrupted, and for how long. The longer term aim should be to improve the process to avoid disruption, but in the interim, creating a buffer can be an appropriate action.

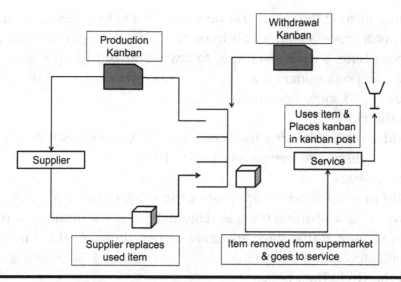

Figure 10.6 Supermarkets.

10.6.4.6 Supermarkets

Supermarkets are used for equipment or supplies. The process is shown in Figure 10.6, together with the relevant symbols (Rother and Shook 1999). In this sequence, an item is used and a withdrawal kanban goes to a storage area. The supplies indicated on the kanban are withdrawn.

The removed supplies trigger a production kanban that causes more of the supplies to be prepared or obtained. The volume of the items in the supermarket depends on restocking or manufacturing times.

A key point about the use of a supermarket is that they allow two processes to be linked. The previous process does not need to know the overall schedule. The downstream process acts as the pacemaker.

10.6.5 Developing the VSM

As a general principle, the steps are as shown subsequently. In some contexts, it may be necessary to vary the sequence, but this order is a good place to start.

1. Set Out the Cycles
    Lay out the cycles in order of sequence, as shown in Figure 10.2. Processes are drawn right to left in order of sequence, rather than drawn to reflect hospital or departmental layout (Rother and Shook 1999).

Only include the detail you need for people to understand the work. It is not a Process Map, or an Information Flow Map. Processes may be branching. It makes sense to follow an 80/20 rule approach, and to show the predominant flow. In some cases processes are such that it is necessary to show branches.

2. Add the Flow

   Add symbols showing the flow – usually continuous flow, push or pull – as discussed previously (Figure 10.4).

3. Show Queues

   Add in queues, which are part of the work in process. These are drawn in as a warning triangle (Figure 10.7). If the number of people or items waiting at that stage are known, then they are added into the box immediately below the triangle.

4. Add the Cycle Data boxes

   Add a data box in each cycle (Figure 10.8). As a minimum, these will include Cycle Time, Value Added and Non-Value Added time, and the

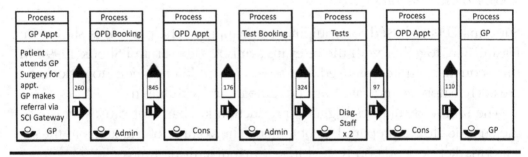

Figure 10.7 Value stream map showing queues.

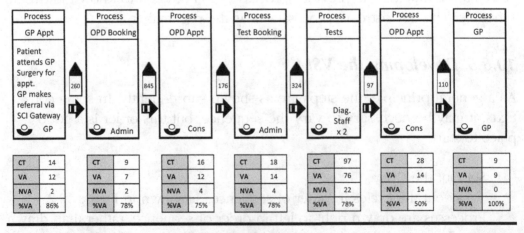

Figure 10.8 Value stream map showing data boxes.

Value Added Percentage (Jackson 2013b). Other data may be relevant for particular value streams.

Waits within a cycle are included as Non-Value Added time within that cycle. For example, a staff member may leave a consultation to look for a piece of equipment. Waits between cycles are recorded separately, but they included in the total Non-Value Added time for the value stream.

5. Add the Time Line

A crenellated line is added to show the total time line Figure 10.9). Waits between cycles can be shown on this line. The cumulative cycle time, plus the waits between cycles are added together to give the total Lead Time.

An important point about calculating waits is that you work out the entire experienced wait, not just the service opening hours (this is different from the calculation of takt time, which shows the required rate of work when a service is open for business). The experienced wait is calculated assuming 24 hours a day, seven days a week.

6. Add the Summary Statistics

A box or boxes are used to summarise the whole Value Stream, as opposed to the Cycle Data Boxes, which show the values for the cycle alone. In this example, the total cycle times are 191 minutes, of which 144 minutes was of value to the service user. The Lead Time for the whole Value Stream, however, is the waits plus the cycle times, making a total of 277,920 minutes (193 days). The value added time is the 144

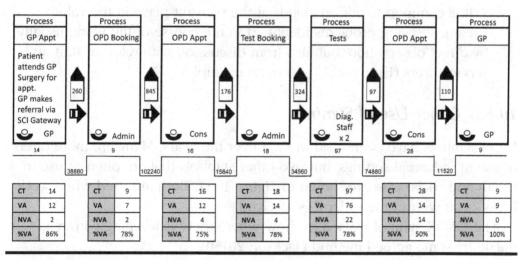

Figure 10.9   Value stream map showing time line.

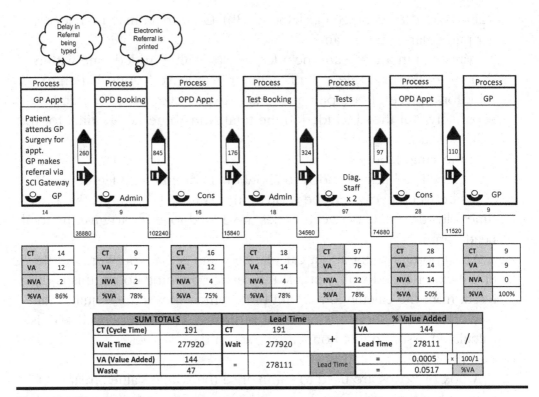

Figure 10.10 Complete value stream map.

minutes of value in the cycles, so the value added percentage is calculated from 144 value added minutes of 277,920 total minutes, a percentage of 0.05% (Figure 10.10).

7. Add in Clouds

It is common to add in clouds at the relevant place in the value stream, showing problems identified in the course of the work, usually by direct observation, but also from discussion with relevant staff and service users (Figure 10.10 shows an example).

10.6.6 Other Useful Symbols

Many symbols have been used in VSM over the years. Many are more often of use in industrial settings, but two other symbols that are often of use in health and social care are shown in Figure 10.11. Both are used when work is not dealt with in the order it is received.

The OXOX symbol is used to show where there is levelling within a queue by some agreed method (Jackson 2013b).

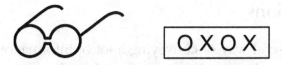

Figure 10.11   Other symbols used in value stream maps.

Spectacles are used where a person looks at a queue and adjusts it personally. This symbol is used to show individual review (Rother and Shook 1999).

Some practitioners add information flow into their VSM, using information flow symbols (Rother and Shook 1999; Jackson 2013b).

10.6.7 *Future State Maps*

Future State Maps use the same symbols as a Current State VSM. The Future State Map is developed with the relevant team to describe their improved process. In some cases, entire cycles will be removed because they add no value, or they can be incorporated into other cycles. In other cases, the main differences will be to delays between cycles.

Jackson (2013b: p 46) and Rother and Shook (1999: p 80) suggest principles for the development of Future State Maps, including

- Producing to takt time.
- Seeking continuous flow
- Where continuous flow cannot be achieved, work out how to pull from the previous process.
- Level the volume and case mix where possible.
- Use continuous improvement methods to eliminate waste, reduce batch sizes and increase the amount of the process that is in continuous flow.

Rother and Shook (1999: p 49) suggest that the first iteration of a Future State Map should 'take ... designs ... locations ... and technologies as givens, and seek to remove as quickly as possible all sources of waste not caused by these purposes.' They go on to suggest that teams should think '(with the exception of minor purchases)...what can we do with what we have?' and deal with other changes in future iterations of the value stream (Rother and Shook 1999: p 49).

10.7 Conclusions

VSM are a very useful way of conveying a lot of information in a visual way. They are not impressionistic – they are based on direct observation of processes and on real data.

VSM are not process maps: they are high-level maps that allow a whole process to be visualised. The maps should give a good impression of flow, value and waste. Using them with a team allows them to see their entire process, often for the first time. With high-level value streams, it allows staff to see how their work contributes to the overall process, and how it links to processes on either side.

Further Reading

Full references are included in the bibliography.

Learning to See by Mike Rother and John Shook is difficult to obtain, as it is out of print. If you can find a copy, it is a good introduction. It uses industrial examples, but it explains the process clearly.
Mapping Clinical Value Streams edited by Thomas Jackson, focuses on health services and is easier to obtain.

Chapter 11

Management

Hoshin does not encourage random business improvement, but rather focuses the organization on projects that move it toward its strategic direction.

Gregory Watson (2003)

11.1 Aims of the Chapter

Aims of the Chapter

1. To understand the principles of *Hoshin Kanri*
2. To be able to describe the main components of a Lean management system
3. To understand the links between strategic management and daily management

11.2 Examples

- An organisation has a 'balanced scorecard' which includes over 40 measures, which between them generate another 115 'supporting measures.' All of the measures are regarded as priorities, and all are expected to be met. There is no clear system for deciding the effort to go on different measures.

■ In one social care organisation, in response to a survey, less than 60% of staff said they knew the main priorities of the organisation. Only a third said they understood clearly how their work fitted with the strategy of the organisation.

■ An NHS Trust conducted quarterly reviews of actions from their annual plan. Managers regarded the review as a burden, and completed it as quickly as possible, often immediately before the return was due. There was rarely praise for 'good' results, but adverse results drew critical attention. Managers became adept at emphasising the positive. Vague positive statements were rarely challenged.

■ An operational unit drew up its annual plan in March, just before the beginning of the new financial year. Departments then produced their own plans, which were finalised by the end of June, three months into the financial year.

■ Departments in one organisation produced their own plans, which were then combined into one overall plan. Each department sought to optimise its own operation. There was no active consideration of whether each improvement helped with overall flow in the service.

11.3 Introduction

> Moving beyond systems to people requires a move away from the concept of organisational man/woman, to an 'individualised organisation,' which is based upon the development and recognition of people as responsible owners of their own processes.
>
> **Rosemary Butterworth (2001: p 69)**

Prioritising, linking policy to practice and engaging people who deliver services in overall aims are all major challenges for organisations. In the previous examples, there are disconnections between planning and action, between operational staff and senior managers, between departments in the same organisation, and between theory and practice.

Hoshin Kanri is a management method that seeks to bring together strategy and practice, and to balance the experience and knowledge of front-line staff with corporate requirements.

The Japanese characters in the words *Hoshin Kanri* mean – management – direction – logic – control (Norval and Wilburn 2012). Taken together, they refer to a method of developing strategic goals and turning them into action.

Hutchins (2006: p 3) translates the terms as *Ho* – Direction; *Shin* – Focus; *Kan* – Alignment and *Ri* – Reason. The meaning is similar to the translation of Norval and Wilburn.

Important organisational objectives, often called '*Hoshin*,' or 'Breakthrough' objectives are delivered through change projects directly aligned with the priorities of the organisation. Incremental change is undertaken using Daily Management, which emphasises getting the fundamentals of the organisation's service delivery right, and producing incremental improvement using Lean methods (Akao 2004).

Staff have a significant influence on the methods used to implement objectives, and in agreeing the best way of measuring improvement. The feedback between managers and staff is known as 'catchball' (Akao 2004).

While the overall direction of travel may change little, a series of overlapping improvement cycles is used to shape activity both at the *Hoshin* level, and in daily management. *Hoshin Kanri* builds layers of checks on progress into the system, at Daily Management level, and for specific projects (Hutchins 2008). These checks do not have a punitive intention, but rather are to allow quick identification of problems and the taking of rapid corrective action.

Traditional three, six and 12 monthly reviews on progress leave long periods for problems to develop, and to continue unchecked. Intermittent reviews often become only another burden for managers, and are seen as a task to be delivered, rather than an action that is linked to the day-to-day work and regulation of that work.

The purpose of more frequent review is to allow rapid problem identification and rapid reaction in a way that helps managers and staff, and which contributes to the aims of the organisation. By increasing organisational understanding of the key priorities, and of the thinking behind monitoring measures, front-line staff are in a better position to identify the significance of a change in performance for the organisation as a whole and to decide on the priority to place on improvement measures.

To a degree, the system becomes self-correcting, because staff in individual teams or units do not have to wait for managers to identify a problem or to tell them the importance of it: they already know and can take action themselves, for matters that are within their control.

How objectives and means of response are cascaded within the organisation is important, and the method aims to produce clarity on this. Objectives and actions within individual units are also considered against their anticipated impact on the whole value stream for the patient, rather than solely on how they will affect the work of the department or team alone.

Annual organisational review, led by the Chief Executive, then becomes not an audit of staff performance, but a review of the effectiveness of the planning process, of policy implementation, and of the quality improvement process (Akao 2004; Jackson 2006). In industry, these reviews are sometimes called the 'President's review,' 'President's Diagnosis' or sometimes 'Presidential Audit' (Akao 2004; Jackson 2006).

These methods are reviewed in this chapter. The detail that is useful for individual readers will vary but having a grasp of the approach is useful for understanding how Daily Management and *Hoshin* objectives can mesh to deliver large scale organisational improvement over time.

11.4 Hoshin Kanri

Corporate leaders must create a sense of community and help employees identify with the larger organisation in a way that transcends personal interests and particular responsibilities.

Sumantra Ghoshal and Christopher Bartlett (1995: p 92)

Organisations are organised typically in functional units. In health and social care, this would include services such as community teams, or in some areas, physiotherapy services and Social Work services, for example. Within hospitals, divisions can be by wards (respiratory, orthopaedic etc.) and services (Clinical Physiology, Blood Sciences etc.).

The 'Value Stream Maps' section (Chapter 10) illustrated the difference between functional arrangements of services and value streams, which usually cross several functions. Chapter 5, 'Continuous Flow,' made the point that optimising an individual function only adds value if it contributes to improving the overall service for the patient.

A common problem in translating strategic planning into action, is that how operations link to strategy may be far from clear, and strategies may not take account of operational realities. It is common to set targets, usually financial, but not to consider explicitly the means required to achieve those targets. *Hoshin Kanri* tries to improve this process.

In many organisations, most quantitative goals derive from financial requirements. Qualitative goals, by contrast, are often vague and woolly (Hutchins 2006). This allows the interpretation of qualitative goals, such as person-centred care or improved quality, to vary markedly between departments and between individuals. Hutchins (2006: p 4) comments,

'These qualitative goals mean nothing because they are too vague. This vagueness cannot compete with the clarity of the financial goals; as a consequence the qualitative goals will always be the poor relation even though their sustained non-achievement could result in dramatic...impact.'

One of the intended strengths of the *Hoshin Kanri* approach is to make clear the relative importance of different objectives, to identify how it will be achieved and to measure the degree of improvement. Shook (1997) argues that *Hoshin Kanri* moves beyond implementation of strategy to active involvement of staff in developing strategy.

Descriptions of the core elements of *Hoshin Kanri* are consistent, but there is huge variation in the detail. This is because the process of implementation of the method is organisation-specific, and different organisations develop varying approaches and emphases. This chapter attempts to steer a course through the varying descriptions. The books suggested in the 'Further Reading' section at the end of the chapter provide detail on numerous examples of the use of *Hoshin Kanri* and can be consulted for more detail, and for examples of use in different organisations.

The process seeks to follow an improvement cycle. The intention is that the system is self-adjusting, based on evidence and explicit decision-making, and captures the interest and ability of employees. Hutchins (2006) suggests that *Hoshin Kanri* describes 'what is,' which then feeds quality improvement work – the 'how to.' Quality improvement 'is the means by which to close the gap between current performance and target performance' (Hutchins 2006: p 3).

Core features of *Hoshin Kanri* are (Watson 2003; Akao 2004; Jackson 2006; Hutchins 2008; Colletti 2013; Kesterson 2015)

1. The process considers the work of the organisation as a system, rather than as isolated pieces of work.
2. There is a clear statement of the long-term vision of the organisation, usually supported by a mission statement, and often accompanied by a description of organisational values.
3. The strategies within the organisation are aligned to this vision of the future.
4. Strategies are based on an assessment of the current situation, including both internal and external pressures and demands.
5. Strategic objectives are identified by a process of reviewing and prioritising the factors affecting the ability to deliver the vision (sometimes termed 'drivers'). This includes an explicit assessment of the likely

influence and practicality of different actions. In each case, it is clear how the action is expected to affect the driver, and so how it will contribute to moving the organisation closer to its vision.

6. Strategic objectives usually cover a three to five-year timescale. Annual objectives are produced, which also require clarity on how they link to the drivers for the vision, and how they are expected to produce benefit.

7. These high-level objectives are major targets that require significant organisational effort.

8. Objectives are linked to a statement of means. They are not exhortations to better performance, with no specified method, but rather numeric targets with an expected method of delivery, and identified resources, attached.

9. Objectives are reviewed in the light of the information for the year as described previously. An interactive process, known as 'catchball' is used to give the wider organisation an opportunity to consider the objectives, and to comment on them.

10. Operational units develop policies and measures of performance for these objectives, which align with the objective and with the overall organisational vision. A further catchball process is often used to generate these measures for units and teams.

11. The vision, mission statement, strategy and objectives are clear, and are readily available to staff. Performance against objectives is measured and is shared with staff.

12. There are set review periods, including an annual Chief Executive's Review.

13. The organisation takes action to resolve identified variation from the expected performance.

14. Accountability is clear throughout the process.

11.5 History Note

The development of *Hoshin Kanri* is outlined in several textbooks (Akao 2004; Colletti 2013). The core of the system is the Plan – Do – Study – Act (PDSA) cycle, and its introduction into management systems. Akao (2004) also discusses the links with Management by Objectives, popularised by Peter Drucker.

Work on associated ideas began in Japan in the 1950s, originally inspired by W Edwards Deming. There were well-developed *Hoshin* systems by the early 1960s, for example at Komatsu. During the 1950s, Kaoru Ishikawa, whose work on problem analysis is discussed in Chapter 7, 'Error Proofing,' emphasised the links between strategy and delivery, and Yoji Akao described work on Daily Management in the mid-1960s. The best known description of the method in practice was by Bridgestone Tyres.

Companies such as Proctor & Gamble, General Electric and Hewlett Packard adopted the system in the 1980s, and the methods gradually spread (King 2013).

One of the tensions in the description of *Hoshin Kanri* has been its translation to the term 'Policy Deployment.' As several authors point out, this term is at best confusing and at worst actively misleading for people new to the topic (Colletti 2013; Kesterson 2015).

Bruce Sheridan, involved at Florida Power & Light, an early adopter in the United States, commented, 'I believe one of the translation mistakes made at that time involved the name given to Hoshin Kanri by the Japanese – "Policy Deployment." Looking back, I believe it should have been translated as "Strategy Deployment," (quoted in Kesterson 2015: p 30).

In the West, the term 'policy deployment' suggests that a policy is being passed down the company to be implemented unchanged. *Hoshin Kanri*, however, is a negotiated process where the strategic intention (the 'policy') is passed down the company, but the means of meeting the objective is negotiated and agreed at each organisational level and then reviewed frequently.

This is distinctly different from an assumption that plans are implemented unchanged, sometimes to the bitter end. *Hoshin Kanri* has problem-solving and improvement cycles at its core, and that it not obvious from the term 'policy deployment.'

11.6 The Vision

True north entails answering the following kinds of questions: who are we, what do we believe in, where are we going, and how do we get there.

Pascal Dennis (Hirano and Furuya 2006: p 269)

Colletti (2013) points out that defining terms is important in order to minimise potential for confusion. Two of the commonly used terms in *Hoshin Kanri* are 'Vision' and 'Mission Statement.'

Colletti (2013: p 10) defines these as follows:

> Vision. 'A brief description of the future state an organization wants to attain as it executes its mission over a specified period of time.'
>
> Mission Statement. 'A description of the unique value that an organization offers…representing the organization's identity and purpose.'

Organisations also commonly describe the values they will seek to display in their work. In some cases these are incorporated into the mission statement, in other instances they are described separately.

The point of these statements is that the work of the organisation should then flow from them, and be aligned to them. The vision defines 'true north' – the position against which all work should be assessed. Table 11.1 gives examples of Vision and Mission statements from several leading Lean health care organisations. When they are supported by lists of values, these are the values that the organisation wants to display in its day-to-day business, and in its work to move closer to its vision. The vision and mission statement will often remain the same for many years.

11.7 Assessment

> Many…companies have not paid enough attention to the critical aspects of strategy formulation as they have to the deployment of their strategy using hoshin kanri. This leads to an error of effectively deploying a poorly chosen strategy.
>
> **Gregory Watson (2003: p 4)**

Core principles of *Hoshin Kanri* are that it is based on a careful review of the current situation, takes careful account of service views and is followed consistently over time.

There are many different models, which have been developed to meet the needs of specific organisations, but the main stages tend to be consistent and link to PDSA cycles, as described in the 'Improvement Cycles' chapter.

Table 11.1   Examples of Vision and Mission Statement from Lean Health Care Leaders

Organisation	Vision	Mission Statement
Virginia Mason Medical Center	Our vision is to be the Quality Leader and transform healthcare – To become the Quality Leader, we must first change the way healthcare is delivered. Our aspiration is not to be the biggest, but to be the best. We will differentiate ourselves on the basis of quality.	Our mission is to improve the health and well-being of the patients we serve – Healing illness is our first priority and is what gives our people the energy for our vision. We are also committed to providing a broad range of services that improve one's sense of well-being and which prevent illness.
Thedacare	Our vision is to transform the health care industry to deliver higher value through experiments, collaboration and education that integrates the three interdependent components and spreads learning and accelerates improvement.	To redesign three interdependent components of the health care industry which will result in improved value for patients. We will accomplish this by collaborating with patients and leaders in the provider, employer, insurer and government communities to create: Transparency of Cost, Quality Risk and Consequences: Care Delivery Redesign with focus on value to the patient, and payment models that reward value.
Cincinnati Children's Hospital Medical Center	Cincinnati Children's Hospital Medical Center will be the leader in improving child health.	Cincinnati Children's will improve child health and transform delivery of care through fully integrated, globally recognised research, education and innovation. For patients from our community, the nation and the world, the care we provide today and in the future will achieve the best: • Medical and quality-of-life outcomes • Patient and family experience • Value

(Continued)

Table 11.1 (Continued)   Examples of Vision and Mission Statement from Lean Health Care Leaders

Organisation	Vision	Mission Statement
Seattle Children's Hospital Research Foundation	We believe all children have unique needs and should grow up without illness or injury. With the support of the community and through our spirit of inquiry, we will prevent, treat and eliminate paediatric disease.	We will be the best children's hospital. Our founding promise is to care for every child in our region, regardless of their family's ability to pay. We aspire to: • Provide the safest, most effective care possible. • Control and reduce the cost of providing care. • Find cures and educate clinicians and researchers. • Grow responsibly and provide access to every child who needs us

Source: Respective Organisational Websites, accessed August 2015

11.7.1 Stage 1 Assessment

> At the heart of Total Quality Management (TQM) is the PDCA cycle. This also forms the core of Hoshin Kanri, but the order is rearranged. In Hoshin Kanri one begins with the check cycle - PDCA becomes the CAPD cycle. Thus, checking the current status of company activity propels the Hoshin process.
>
> **Yoji Akao (Akao 2004)**

This stage reviews the current situation. It usually includes an environmental audit, the voice of the customer, a review of results from the previous year or other period, review of value streams and identification of likely demands (although this is sometimes incorporated into the environmental audit).

11.7.2 Environmental Audit

Environmental Audits, also known as Environmental Scanning, review the threats and opportunities in the wider environment in which the organisation works (Jackson 2006; Colletti 2013; Eaton 2014). In health and social care, this may include an increasing proportion of older people, changes to funding regimes, new treatments emerging, staffing availability and an increased need for translation services, for example. This is related to risk management.

Eaton (2013) suggests dividing this assessment into the 'Near Environment' and the 'Far Environment.' The near environment in health and social care settings refers to factors immediately affecting care delivery, such as staffing availability, current resource, required new treatments and so on.

The far environment refers to more distant possible impacts, such as legislation changes, possible therapy developments, national wage settlements and so on. Eaton (2013) suggests using a PESTLE analysis to consider the relevant categories:

- Political
- Economic
- Social
- Technological
- Legal
- Environmental

In industrial settings, Michael Porter's 'Five Forces' are often used to assess the near environment. These include threat of new entrants; bargaining power of suppliers; bargaining power of customers; threat of substitutes, and industry rivalry (Eaton 2013). Jackson (2006) suggests using the Porter Matrix which looks at Product Differentiation and Competitive Scope. These will be relevant to health and social care organisations working in a competitive environment.

11.7.2.1 Voice of the Customer

This requires a review of what information is available on the views of people who use the services. In some cases, this will include internal customers, but the overall focus is likely to be on service users, relatives and the wider community.

Services will review information on complaints and on other sources of feedback such as surveys. With a focus on quality, information on areas of strength and weakness is essential (Hutchins 2008).

11.7.2.2 Review of Performance

All organisations will want to review their performance in the previous year, or last available period. This will identify areas with increasing demand (see the subsequent discussion) and areas with quality issues or significant financial challenges. Triangulating this with the information from the Voice of the Customer can point to 'hot spots' that are likely to benefit from a greater organisational focus. In later years, this can come from information collected in the *Hoshin Kanri* process (see the 'Measurement and Review' section for further discussion).

11.7.2.3 Value Stream Review

If the organisation uses high level value streams, and it collects information on the performance across the value stream, then this information will be incorporated into the audit (Jackson 2006).

11.7.2.4 Identification of Likely Demands

If this was not incorporated into the Environmental Audit, then a separate exercise would be conducted to estimate demand based on previous experience, and on knowledge of any expected changes that may alter demand for services.

It is important not to turn this into an industry in its own right. Jackson (2006) suggests presenting the Environmental Audit on one A3 sheet, for example. The focus is on producing information that can be used, rather than lengthy reports that are weighed, skimmed and filed.

11.8 Developing the Strategic Plan

(The strategic plan describes) the most important areas of organizational effort that must be accomplished to achieve the goals of the organization.

Joseph Colletti (2013: p 10)

Once the initial assessment is complete, the organisation identifies strategic priorities. These can be developed from the attributes in the Mission Statement. The senior team identifies the drivers behind each attribute (Hutchins 2006; Colletti 2013). In identifying the drivers of a particular part of the mission statement, a Cause and Effect diagram can be used. Cause and Effect diagrams, also known as Fishbone diagrams or Ishikawa diagrams, are discussed further in the 'Identifying Causes' section of Chapter 7, 'Error Proofing.' Generally, Cause and Effect diagrams are used to show a theory of what is causing an effect, while Driver diagrams are used to show theories about what actions will result in a change.

The discipline of making a Cause and Effect diagram for each part of the mission statement helps to avoid entire categories of drivers being overlooked. The discussion required to do this helps to avoid ideas being missed, and is also useful for sharing with staff to demonstrate how the ideas in the strategic plan have been formed, and to produce a 'line of sight' from the Vision to the Mission Statement to the Strategic Plan.

For example, if part of the mission statement is to have engaged, skilled staff, then drivers identified might include knowledge, skills, creativity, involvement, pride and involvement in improvement (Hutchins 2006).

Knowing where the organisation is in relation to these aspirations is important. Indicators of performance can be identified for each of the main drivers, information on current performance identified, and where possible benchmarked against comparable organisations (Hutchins 2006). This will produce not only a measure of performance, but also a measure of comparative performance, that can be used for a 'gap analysis' to identify differences between current performance and required or expected performance or system (Kesterson 2015), or between current performance and 'best in class' (Hutchins 2006). Measurements of performance are discussed further later in the chapter.

Affinity diagrams (see the subsequent discussion for details on how to construct Affinity diagrams) can then be used to group drivers (Akao 2004; Hutchins 2008; Colletti 2013; Kesterson 2015) if desired, and so to identify work streams that include topics.

In many cases, the process produces a long list of possible areas for the organisation to work on that might result in breakthroughs. The senior team needs to prioritise the possible work streams to avoid losing focus.

This can be done using a prioritisation matrix (Hutchins 2008; Colletti 2013). The matrix used will depend on what is a good fit for the organisation. It can be as simple as mapping expected impact on the area of concern against the ease of implementation (Hutchins 2008), or it may score each possible action or groupings of action, on a range of factors of importance to the organisation, such as impact, cost, urgency, gap in performance and so on (Jackson 2006; Kesterson 2015).

History Note: Many people were involved in the development of these Quality Improvement (QI) tools, including Nayatani Yoshinobu, a Japanese academic who was President of the Society for QC Technique Development.

Others involved included, for example, staff from Mitsubishi, Nippon Paint and Sekisui Chemicals. The techniques were described in a book edited by Shigeru Mizuno published in Japanese in 1979 and in English in 1988 (Mizuno 1988). Other techniques collected together in the volume include Matrix diagrams and Systematic diagrams. One form of Systematic diagram (Mizuno 1988) appears to be the earliest appearance of what is now widely described as a Driver diagram.

11.9 Techniques: Use of Affinity Diagrams

Affinity diagrams were described by the Society for QC Technique Development in the 1970s. These diagrams are used to organise 'facts, opinions and ideas' (Mizuno 1988: p 116), and to group them into relationships that make them more useful in generating new ideas for improvement. They are often used in the course of brainstorming sessions. Affinity diagrams can be used to create and describe a theory of how something works, or what is affecting an outcome.

There are several situations in which Affinity diagrams can be useful. In practice, several of these features may apply to the same situation (adapted from Mizuno 1988):

- Facts are uncertain and hard to grasp.
- Views are uncertain and disorganised.
- Pre-existing ideas are embedded, and it is difficult to move beyond current understandings of a problem.
- A new way of thinking about a problem is needed.
- There are significant differences in view between people and common ground has not been identified.
- A new team is coming together who do not have a shared view of the problem or issue.
- Capturing ideas from both managers and front-line staff is important, including understanding the links between the different views of the situation.

The original descriptions of the process described the use of cards for each idea or fact, but sticky notes are now generally used.

The source of the facts and ideas on the notes will vary, depending on the purpose of the diagram. If using it in a brainstorming session, however, the sequence will often be

- Identify ideas by brainstorming, recording each idea on a separate sticky note.
- The ground rules in brainstorming are important: criticism is not allowed, everyone can express their thoughts and as many ideas as possible should be identified (Mizuno 1988).
- Participants then take notes and group them on a large sheet of paper or a blank wall. There is no speaking during this phase. Similar ideas are grouped. If there are ideas that seem to be separate from all others then, at this stage, they form groups of their own. Some groupings may be placed side by side in a 'supergroup.'
- Once changes have slowed or stopped, participants discuss the groups. Groups may be moved in relation to one another.
- Descriptions are created – usually one or two words – and placed above groupings.
- Arrows and lines can be used to show how the groupings link.

This process creates a shared view of the factors that influence a process. This can be used when identifying what needs to be done to support each aspect of a mission statement, for example, but the method is useful in many situations. Figure 11.1 shows an affinity diagram produced in the course of an improvement event, which could be developed into a Cause and Effect diagram if desired.

Figure 11.1   Example of affinity diagram.

11.10 Creating an Annual Plan

Developing a shorter-term plan, usually for a 12-month period, follows the same structure as the development of the longer-term strategy (say for three years). The work will review the current situation, performance over the last year, and the progress on the project plans (Figure 11.1). It will also review information on needs from customers – in the case of health and social care services, often a Government Department or other service commissioner.

There is a cascade of vision - mission statement – three-year plan – one-year plan (Jackson 2006; Colletti 2013). The three-year plan has identified key breakthrough objectives (*Hoshin* objectives) and developed project plans for how to tackle them.

The one-year plan reviews the current context, and identifies elements of the three-year plan that can now be tackled. This will include making decisions on whether any of the longer objectives now need to be amended, or whether the context has changed enough that other objectives have become more important. The process for a first annual plan and a later annual plan will be slightly different. For the first annual plan, the prioritisation and ranking of opportunities will already have been done. For a later plan, the team will review the overall priorities, combined with information on current priorities.

Once the objectives are confirmed, the projects to support them are prioritised, using a prioritisation matrix or another preferred method (see the previous section on 'Developing the Strategy' for a discussion of the use of prioritisation matrices). Figure 11.2 shows a complete system.

11.11 Techniques: Using an A3

The point of the brevity is to force synthesis of the learning acquired in the course of researching the problem or opportunity and discussing it with others. The exercise causes multiple pieces of information from different sources to be integrated into a coherent picture of the situation and recommended future action…the report must distil the…picture to only the most vital points needed for…understanding.

Durward Sobek II and Art Smalley (2008: 15–16)

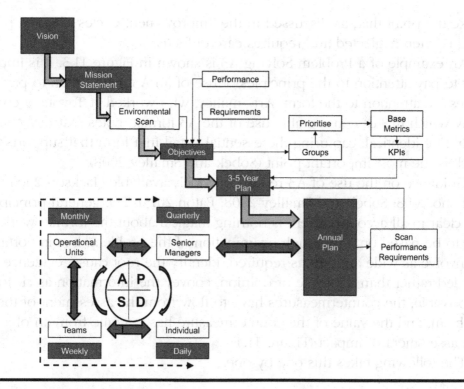

Figure 11.2   Stages of a *Hoshin* system.

A3 reports are a one-page structured report used originally at Toyota (Sobek et al. 1998), then more widely in other settings, including health care (Weber et al. 2005). The name 'A3' comes from the size of paper that is often used when printing them out.

The purpose of an A3 is to synthesise the information and make it available to others. It is both a communications tool and a way of helping to structure thinking.

Sobek and Smalley (2008) identify three main types of A3:

■ Problem-solving
■ Proposal
■ Status Report

Different variants are used by organisations, but the principles are the same. The report is based around a PDSA cycle (please see Chapter 4 'Improvement Cycles' for more information). The weighting of space devoted to different parts of the PDSA cycle is deliberately unequal: the 'Plan' part of the cycle is usually allocated the entire left-hand side of the sheet. This is to make the point that, as discussed in the 'Improvement Cycles' chapter, planning is often neglected and requires careful focus.

An example of a Problem-Solving A3 is shown in Figure 11.3. It is important to pay attention to the principles of use of an A3, rather than to pay obsessive attention to the form. Art Smalley, who worked at Toyota, a company which makes considerable use of the A3 format, notes that few A3s would be identical: capturing the essential detail in a form that supports the work is the most important point (Sobek and Smalley 2008).

Guidance on the use of A3 reports is widely available (Jackson 2006; Bicheno 2008; Sobek and Smalley 2008; Eaton 2013). The general principles are clear in all accounts: there is nothing magical about the format; work has to be based on a thorough examination of the problem; it is important to involve as wide a group as required; identify the root cause; evidence is needed rather than anecdote or opinion; convey the information as clearly as possible; the countermeasures have to flow from the assessment of the problem, and the value of the countermeasure has to come from an objective assessment of impact (Figure 11.4).

The following takes this one by one:

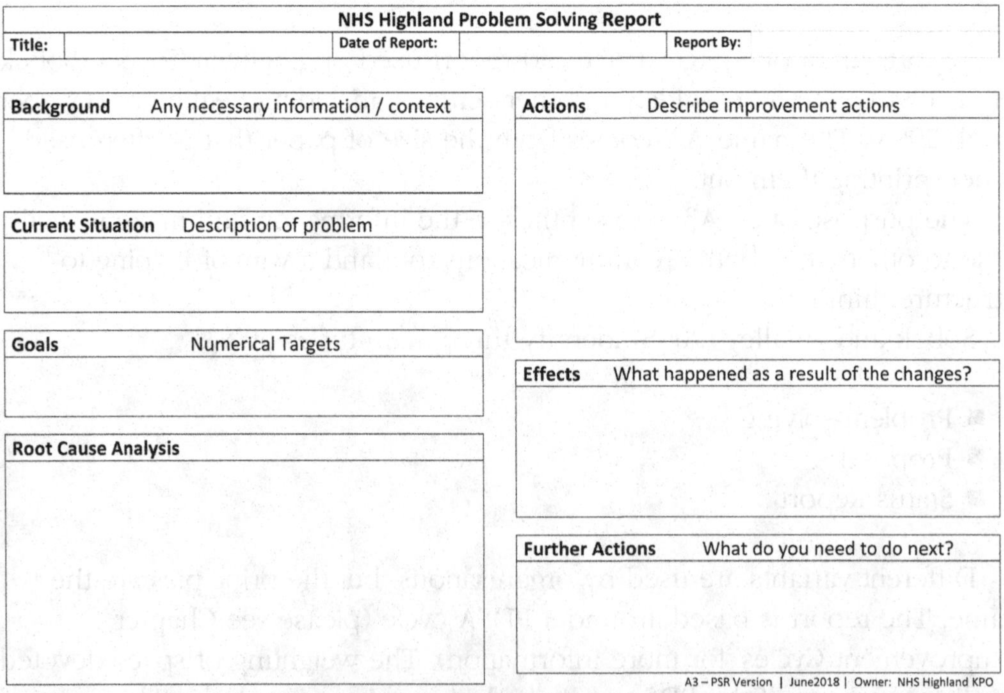

NHS Highland Problem Solving Report

Title: | Date of Report: | Report By:

Background — Any necessary information / context

Current Situation — Description of problem

Goals — Numerical Targets

Root Cause Analysis

Actions — Describe improvement actions

Effects — What happened as a result of the changes?

Further Actions — What do you need to do next?

A3 – PSR Version | June2018 | Owner: NHS Highland KPO

Figure 11.3 Example of a problem-solving A3.

NHS HIGHLAND PROBLEM SOLVING REPORT

Title: Orthopaedic Triage Process in Lorn & Islands Hospital	Date of Report: 13/07/18	Report By: Kirstin Robertson

Background

The orthopaedic service in Lorn & Islands Hospital (LIH) is provided by NHS Greater Glasgow & Clyde as an outreach (visiting service) under Service Level Agreement. The clinic is a fortnightly, provided on a rota basis by a cohort of consultants with various sub specialisms. As replicated nationally there has been an increase in referrals to the service with a corresponding rise in waiting times. It is anticipated that this trend will continue, particularly with the demographics of Argyll & Bute.

Within Argyll & Bute the physio teams have developed Advanced Practice Physiotherapist (APP) roles. The main aims are to triage orthopaedic referrals onto the appropriate service, i.e. physio, APP/MSK or orthopaedic consultant and offer a higher level conventional MSK treatment, injection therapy as well as assess and refer for MRI and other diagnostic tests. There is currently a process for this within LIH but this is subject to capacity with only a small amount of dedicated resource committed and funded for this purpose. There is no standard work around the triage process.

Current Situation

- No of patients on consultant waiting list (as at 8th January) **259 patients**
- Estimated wait for consultant appointment (as at 4th January) is **37 weeks**
- Longest Wait Snapshot (as at 8th January) **243 days**
- Number of month end patients breaching the 12 week waiting time target for previous quarter vs forecast for next quarter:

	Confirmed			Forecast		
	Oct17	Nov 17	Dec17	Jan 18	Feb 18	Mar 18
	93	112	120	118	124	130

Goals

1) Demand is outstripping capacity as outlined in the DCAQ calculations below:

- Streamlined Pathway - patients directed to the most appropriate service with only appropriate referrals being appointed directly to the orthopaedic clinic.
- All conventional treatment and diagnostics undertaken prior to consultant appointment.
- Overall reduction in the number of patients on the consultant waiting list with a corresponding reduction in waiting times.

Root Cause Analysis

1) Demand is outstripping capacity as outlined in the DCAQ calculations below:

Specialty	Actual Clinic statistics Jan16–Jun17	DCAQ Projections Jan16–Jun17				
	Average Slots per Month	Average Required Slots per Month	Optimum Capacity	Number of Clinics in 2016	Required Yearly Clinics based on Average (variance)	
Orthopaedics	250	272	341	129	140 (11)	

2) Work has been undertaken to quantify the projected number of patients at month end and who will breach the waiting time target. The forecast for the pilot period if no change were made is outlined below:

Month	Month end 12 week breaches
January 2018	118
February 2018	124
March 2018	130

There are a number of reasons why demand is outstripping capacity including:

a) Model of care is consultant focused and not fully making use of the advanced skills available within the physio team.

b) Increased referral rate and continued pressure on the orthopaedic service as replicated nationally.

c) Limitations in consultant establishment and funding to provide increased clinics in the same way without service redesign.

d) The service has previously relied on waiting list initiative clinics to provide additional capacity which is unaffordable and unsustainable.

Actions

The project will run for 11 weeks from 8th January to 23rd March 2018. In order to support this increased APP capacity has been released for the duration.

The main actions are as follows:

a) to implement a process and standard work for Advanced Practice Physiotherapist (APP) triage of Orthopaedic consultant referrals. This will include removing and redirecting referrals which would be better assessed and treated by 1) APP/physiotherapy, 2) other AHP i.e. orthotics or podiatry or 3) who do not fit with the pathway. Those referrals which require consultant appointment as either the first contact, or following APP assessment/treatment will be allocated to the correct sub specialty to streamline the patient pathway.

b) Assess patients who:
  1. are more appropriate for APP assessment and treatment
  2. may require orthopaedic intervention but require further investigation first
  3. could potentially be referred directly for surgery following APP assessment/treatment/diagnostics

Effects

The effects of the project were:

- **40% of referrals were removed** from the consultant list in the duration of the project (see also Patient Outcomes Table)
- An overall reduction in number of patients on the consultant waiting list – **reduced by 145 patients**
- The estimated wait for a consultant appointment **fell from 37 weeks to 12 weeks**
- The reported number of breaches fell to below what was forecast for the period and also to below what was reported for the previous period.

Counter Effects

- Increased waiting times for APP service, however due to the increased APP capacity the waiting time for this service is considerably less than for a consultant appointment.

Further Actions

- It was agreed that the project should continue for a further 3 month period to sustain the positive changes made. Consideration is being given to increased physio & APP resource to sustain and future proof the service model across Argyll & Bute longer term, including any reduction in orthopaedic clinics and resource transfer.
- Potential to implement revised referral pathways with most referrals into physio service initially.
- Share and spread to other localities creating standard work around the process.
- Potential for virtual and telemedicine.
- Opportunities for follow up to reduce return ratio in Orthopaedics, monitor return referrals from surgery.

A3 – PSR V1. 1st December 2016. Approved by C.Stark

Figure 11.4 Completed example of a problem-solving A3.

11.11.1 The Format Is Not the Solution

The layout of the form, with greater attention to the 'Plan' component, gives an important message. Following the format slavishly does not guarantee results, however: it is the problem identification, generation of counter-measures and objective measurement of impact that is important. Sticking perfectly to the format has little value if the underlying approach is not followed. It is easy to use an A3 to try to justify a predetermined approach. This is not the spirit of the method.

11.11.2 Involvement of Stakeholders

The group to be involved has to be wide enough to have sufficient under-standing of the problem, and to avoid uninformed judgements about other parts of the process.

It is common for people to assume that a problem in a process is related to something done by another person, team or department. This may be correct, but unless the reason why it is done is understood, there is little chance of resolving the problem.

Process observations may show that people undertaking an action that causes problems to others do it because they believe it is necessary, or it is what is wanted. In other cases, the action is required because of some aspect of the system that is not known to the other person or team.

For example, in one laboratory process, samples arrived in large batches, causing problems in level production and delays in the system. The staff who delivered the samples had believed that the laboratory staff did not like to be interrupted and preferred batch delivery. In another example, doctors at a clinic were annoyed because most return appointments were not booked by reception staff at the time the patient left the unit. The reason proved to be that most appointments were for three to six months' time, but the clinic slots were not released until the doctors' rotas were known. The doctors only agreed the rota 12 weeks in advance, so it was not possible for the receptionists to give an appointment that was further than twelve weeks away.

Involving staff from the service looking at the issue, and often from the adjacent processes, is very useful in promoting a common understanding of the problem, and in understanding why actions are taken. This makes it much easier to agree on possible countermeasures, and to reach accord on how they will be monitored, as it begins to move the problem from a perceived failure of a person, team or service to a problem in a system that needs collaboration to resolve.

11.11.3 *Identify the Root Cause*

Reaching the root cause of a problem is important. In Lean, the term '5W1H' – 5 'Whys' and 1 'How' is often used to describe the process of repeatedly asking 'Why' to unpeel the layers of the problem like the layers of an onion. Five Whys are discussed in more detail in Chapter 4, but it is useful to consider their use in the context of an A3.

Considering the root cause can be helped by processes such as constructing an affinity diagram, and developing a Cause and Effect diagram. As with work on PDSA cycles discussed previously, reaching a shared, but critical, understanding of the problem is important. Early analyses of a problem often blame individuals, or teams, rather than than considering the system issues that underpin the problem. As discussion moves away from proximal to distal causes of a problem, the underlying system issues often become more apparent. Teams and services can spend a long time focusing on symptoms rather than causes, and time taken at this stage to analyse root causes can pay dividends in saved effort.

11.11.4 *Use Evidence*

This entwines with the previous point. It is easy to jump on a possible cause, and then to pursue it until it proves ineffective. It is more useful to collect evidence on the cause of the problem early in the process.

It is easy for teams, departments and services to fall out with one another when trying to identify causes. This is less likely to occur when moving from anecdote to evidence.

Multiple causes may be suggested: which is correct? Assuming that root causes are being identified, there may well be more than one cause of a problem. Counting instances and then prioritising them for action is a more useful approach than seeing who has the loudest voice. For example, if interruptions to a nurse medication round are believed to be a problem, and to result in error, what are the main causes of interruption? Counting then using a check sheet will produce information on numbers that can be put into a Pareto chart, and then prioritised for action.

11.11.5 Convey the Information Clearly

There is a real temptation to tell people everything you know. The work on a problem is usually interesting, and it can be difficult to filter out what is important from what is merely interesting. The other side of this is the risk of being so telegraphic, for example when using bullet points, that the meaning becomes unclear.

Most authors favour handwriting an A3 report, partly to help avoid verbosity. If word processing an A3, it is tempting to use ever smaller type to fit in the whole story. This should be avoided: it is an alternative to identifying the key points and working out how to explain them to people who need to know.

Graphs and diagrams are often useful. They allow more information to be summarised quickly, and many people find images easier to interpret than lists of numbers.

11.11.6 The Countermeasures Flow from the Problem

It is useful to think about countermeasures rather than solutions. 'Solution' may imply that there is only one cause, or that the true root cause has been successfully identified. 'Countermeasures' is useful in reminding everyone involved that there may be other actions required and further analysis of the causes in due course (Sobek and Smalley 2008).

Logical leaps in problem-solving are common. Despite a good root cause analysis, there may still be no clear link between the problem identification and countermeasure.

Part of the art of problem-solving is taking people along with the work. There should be a clear line of sight between the problem identification, the analysis of the causes and the proposed countermeasures. The reason why this countermeasure was selected from the list of all possible countermeasures should be clear.

11.11.7 Objective Assessment of Impact

Each problem-solving A3 describes an experiment. The group creating the A3 have tried to identify the root cause of the problem being tackled, and have developed a countermeasure. The assessment of the problem may be correct, or can be incomplete or even wrong. It is important, therefore, that the effect of the countermeasure is not taken for granted. As described in

Chapter 4, 'Improvement Cycles,' the effect of the countermeasure has to be monitored, so that action can be taken if the anticipated improvement does not occur.

11.12 Catchball

The most powerful organisation is the one which has managed to harness the creative-thinking power of all of its employees.

David Hutchins (2006: p 3)

Catchball refers to the reiterative up, down, and horizontal communications necessary for effective determination of target and means.

Yoji Akao (2004: p 9)

11.12.1 *Management by Objectives*

'Management by Objectives' is a widely used management method which involves the cascade of objectives 'down' an organisation. It is easy to see this as synonymous with *Hoshin Kanri*, but there are important differences.

Management by Objectives, as originally envisaged by Peter Drucker (Drucker 2007), was a participatory process that involved staff. As it developed over time, it often became a process by which objectives were cascaded down a service with no discussion on appropriateness, and no explicit discussion of means. Generally, teams are expected to deliver key outputs, identified numerically, and to identify how to deliver them. The team is responsible for delivery, and failure to meet targets is generally regarded as a yes/no binary outcome which confers praise if 'yes' and blame if 'no.'

W Edwards Deming is particularly scathing on management by objectives, commenting 'Focus on outcome must be abolished, leadership put in place' (Deming 2000: p 54). He expands on this by saying, 'Internal goals set in the management of a company, without a method, are a burlesque' (Deming 2000: p 75).

By contrast, the *Hoshin Kanri* method should include involvement in the discussion of the means to achieve the target, and monitoring of achievement with a focus on identifying ways of improving delivery, rather than a yes/no answer. There is attention paid to how the objective is achieved, not only to whether it is achieved.

11.12.2 Catchball in Hoshin Kanri

The catchball phase has several distinct purposes:

- To produce improvement work that supports strategic priorities
- To link objectives with the means to carry them out
- To increase the input of people with delivery into the planning process
- To increase staff knowledge of organisational priorities
- To harness the knowledge and experience of the workforce in improving processes and delivering objectives
- To increase commitment

Methods and levels of involvement vary by organisation, and there are numerous descriptions of different arrangements (Jackson 2006; Hutchins 2008; Liker and Hoseus 2008; Colletti 2013; Kesterson 2015). In general, the process tends to be as follows:

1. Objectives are set by the senior team, based on the longer-term plan, and the means are identified following on from the project plan. This will usually include targets.
2. Senior managers discuss the means and the proposed targets, and they feed back to the senior team. The objectives are then finalised.
3. Senior managers take the objectives, means and targets to their work groups. Senior executives may attend this meeting.
4. The work groups (e.g. a community service or a Hospital) review the objectives, turn them into meaningful measures for them (process measures and performance indicators – see the 'Measurement and Review' section for further discussion) and identify means, including any resource implications.
5. The objectives, measures and means are finalised, and the Service leads take the details to smaller work groups (such as departments or clinical teams) – and so on. Liker and Hoseus (2008: p 452) describe this as 'top down direction setting and bottom up flow of information and means.'

A key feature is that the means at one level becomes the objective at the next. For example, an objective may be to increase patient satisfaction. One of the means to do this is identified as reducing waiting times (means). At the next level of catchball, reducing waiting times becomes the objective

Level	Objective	Means
1	Improve Patient Satisfaction	Decrease Out-Patient Waits
2	Decrease Out-Patient Waits	Increase rate of review of requests and appoint allocation
3	Increase rate of review of requests and appoint allocation	Means A Means B

Figure 11.5 Objective means cascade.

and the means may be, for example, by increasing the speed at which referrals are assessed and appointments allocated (means). At the following level, the objective is now to increase the speed of processing, and specific ways (means) of doing this will be identified, and so on (Figure 11.5).

11.12.3 Scaling Up

Jackson (2006) suggests that in early years of implementing *Hoshin Kanri*, a catchball phase with senior managers and the establishment of project forms (see the discussion on A3) is adequate. As the organisation becomes more used to the method, the layers of catchball can be increased. Jackson (2006: p 120) gives the example of 'Action' teams undertaking specific projects reporting to an 'Operational' team that oversees a number of linked areas of work, reporting to a 'Tactical' team which is responsible for a number of Operational Teams and which itself reports to the senior *Hoshin* team. In a developed system, each of these layers would be involved in the catchball process but clearly this would take a number of planning cycles to develop, if it was required at all.

11.12.4 Use of Data

The process should not become a 'subjective negotiation process' (Watson 2003: p 12). The catchball phase uses data to promote a negotiation on means that gradually promotes consensus and defined, agreed plans. This sometimes appears in textbooks under the Japanese term *Sureawashi*.

11.13 Measurement and Review

Hoshin Kanri is based on alignment with strategic priorities, and continuous improvement using PDSA cycles. In order for the system to correct, it is essential to know how work is progressing against objectives.

There are two types of measure that are relevant: measures of means and measures of performance against targets.

Measurement of means refers to measures of a process, like timing of an activity, such as booking appointments. Performance measures are the results of the collected processes, such as waiting times. Setting measures, often termed 'control items' (Akao 2004) in the catchball phase is easier and more useful when people understand the point of the process and the overall aim. Establishing measures at each relevant level is an essential component of the *Hoshin* process.

In the same way as the means for one level become the objectives for the next, a process measure may become the outcome measure for the next. For example, a middle manager may have booking times for appointments as a process measure, but for the person who runs the service, this may be one of their performance measures.

When prioritising, it is common to compare performance to established benchmarks, to compare current performance to it, and so to identify the gap, as an aid to prioritisation.

Referring back to the discussion of Management by Objectives, it is useful to be clear on the point of review. The reason for review is to identify that actual measures have diverged from expected measures and to take rapid corrective action. This is not an attempt to seek blame, but rather an opportunity to reassess actions to produce the required results. Liker and Hoseus (2008) distinguish between a problem-solving approach – the 'five whys' (see the 'Improvement Cycles' chapter for more details) and a person-blaming response that they call the '5 who's.' The distinction is that process measures will be reviewed daily and weekly, while performance or outcome measures are more likely to be reviewed monthly and quarterly.

Hoshin Kanri deployment promotes structured problem-solving, and the time available for review should be devoted to understanding problems and identifying countermeasures, not explaining away lack of progress, a process De Luzio calls 'Plan-Do-Check-Explain' (Kesterson 2015: p 68).

The components of a monthly review of progress are (Colletti 2013) as follows:

- Check progress against expected milestones.
- Identify any problems that have occurred.
- Use problem-solving techniques to identify causes and remedial actions.
- Modify and adjust based on the analysis.
- Record lessons learned about the *Hoshin* process.
- Update information on the project and take part in monthly review meetings.

Colletti suggests that these reports are reviewed monthly in each unit by the overall project lead who performs much the same tasks at team level, including problem-solving work at team level, identifying and agreeing on any solutions that require work across teams, and identifying problems that are out with their team's control, and taking them to the relevant leadership team for support and resolution. Liker and Hoseus (2008) and Jackson (2006) suggest very similar processes.

The main point is that review is frequent and leads to action. This action cannot simply be exhortations to 'work faster' and 'try harder,' but rather it is a measured attempt to identify any barriers and identify solutions through problem-solving.

Jackson (2006) points out that monthly reviews can fall by the wayside, particularly if things appear to be going well. Maintaining the discipline of regular review is essential and is supported by people seeing evidence of action, and of a supportive response to problems. The collected information from the reviews can also be used to inform the following year's work.

In some organisations, measures of progress on these objectives are integrated into daily meetings: Liker and Hoseus (2008) give an example of daily meetings of senior managers at a factory, lasting no longer than 20 minutes, which included both immediate problems and, where relevant, progress on breakthrough objectives.

11.14 Cross-Functional Management

Cross Functional Management: evolved to clarify the roles and responsibilities of departments relative to issues which affect all parts of an organisation. In the case of Hoshin Kanri this refers primarily to the functions of Quality, Cost, Delivery and Education, although there are others. Management of targets which relate to these functions requires an approach which crosses organisational boundaries.

Rosemary Butterworth (Butterworth 2001: p iv)

Cross-Functional Management is used by authors in two overlapping ways. The early literature (Akao 2004 pp 109–113) describes a process by which committees are responsible for a function (e.g. quality, cost control) and deliver the function across different departments. Akao describes a cascade process where responsibility for the function is allocated to each department, but a cross-functional team monitors the actions and impact.

In the process Akao describes, functional committees (e.g. on quality) produce policies, which are then incorporated into departmental plans. Akao describes a system in one organisation where the cross-functional committees then come together twice a year to describe progress and performance on all the functions that cut across departmental lines. Akao (2004) describes it as a way of integrating issues like quality and cost, and clarifying the role of each department.

The second use of the term is to describe a team responsible for delivery of a breakthrough objective (Jackson 2006; Kesterson 2015). When using the term it is important to be clear which meaning is intended.

The importance of the insight is that it can be very difficult to drive some improvements at departmental level, where there are many competing priorities from day-to-day management. A group of people taking an overview of a function may produce considerable benefits. Teams 'are cross-functional because they cross the boundaries of existing structures' (Lindborg 1997: p 2). Lindborg (1997) notes that the usual considerations in team building apply, and that senior leadership and clarity on accountability is essential, because responsibilities will fall to leaders in different parts of the organisation.

Norval and Wilburn (2012) take this a stage further and suggest that organisations identify a 'key thinker' for each large piece of work, who is a senior staff member whose task is to ensure that the work undertaken by different units produces benefit for the whole process, and not only for a department. They also suggest that they should act as 'the conscience of the group to ensure that real problems are put on the table' (Norval and Wilburn 2012: p 201).

Whether functional groups or groups focused on a particular objective
are used, the general approach of ensuring that there is alignment across
the organisation and a focus on value rather than optimisation for individual
departments is sensible and fits well with work on value streams.

11.15 Techniques: Accountability Boards

Lean processes do not sustain or improve themselves.

David Mann (2015: p 80)

Accountability is an essential part of the Lean Process. Maintaining improvements, and identifying and implementing further improvements, requires
discipline.

One way of identifying who is undertaking what action is to use an
accountability board (Mann 2015). An accountability board shows who has
agreed to undertake an action, and when the action is due. They will usually have the days of the month along a top axis, and the names of team
members on a side axis.

An agreed action is noted in the appropriate box for the agreed data,
against the name of the responsible team member, for example by using
a sticky note. If the action is completed by the due date, a green dot is
placed on the note. If the action is not complete by the due date, a red dot
is placed on the note. The action is not moved from the date on which it
was due. If an overdue action is subsequently completed, then a green dot is
added beside the red dot.

The purpose of this is not to chastise staff, but rather to keep transpar-
ency on the state of various actions. It also allows patterns to be identified.
It may be, for example, that the time required for actions is consistently
underestimated. Recurring barriers to actions may also be identified, including a lack of time for particular staff to undertake the agreed work. This is
then feedback for the allocation of future tasks, to identify underlying causes
or to review duties.

In practice, this will often be used in conjunction with a daily huddle. So,
for example, a Process Tracking chart may find that a particular factor causes
repeated delays.

A staff member will be assigned to investigate the problem further, and a
date agreed to report back. When they report back with an analysis of the

problem, they may have identified an improvement action that can be tried. The responsibility for implementing this would then be added to the chart, and so on. This also makes it easier to see progress, and it shows a direct response to the information on the Process Tracking chart.

11.16 Daily Management

> The daily management system is...defined as standardized work at all levels of management to enable a daily dialogue about the most important facts of the business. It is designed to ensure that everyone is working on the right problems.
>
> **John Toussaint (2015: p 87)**

Breakthrough objectives are all very well, but the challenge is in integrating work on breakthrough objectives into the organisation's daily work, while keeping the service functioning. Randy Kesterson (2015) interviewed managers, consultants and academics with experience of *Hoshin Kanri*. One of the recurring issues they raised was the tricky balance between business as usual and *Hoshin*, or breakthrough, objectives.

Daily Management is best considered as a way of embedding quality improvement into everyday working. Mark Eaton (2013) goes as far as using the term 'Managing for Daily Improvement.' This includes (Graban 2012; Eaton 2013; Mann 2015) the following:

- Reviewing performance on the previous shift or day.
- Identifying any problems that arose and agreeing how to resolve them, if this has not already been done. This may include a work around that is required while a root cause analysis is undertaken (Mann 2015). Accountability for actions is clear.
- Sharing any learning and any changes to standard work that happened the previous day.
- Reviewing the work required that day and agreeing any adjustments that need to be made to the usual business (e.g. because of staff absence or altered demand).

These meetings are often standing meetings, known as 'huddles.' Meetings are usually conducted beside an information board showing the current status of the service and often the expected demand for the day.

In general, as many people as possible attend. The meetings are kept short, have a clear agenda and focus on action, rather than endless discussion of problems. Attendees should come with the data they need to make decisions (Eaton 2013).

Some organisations find it useful to have huddles at different levels. For example, there might be a brief team huddle, lasting five or ten minutes. Team leaders from these huddles may attend a brief huddle with the area or department manager, and department managers may have a huddle with the General Manager or equivalent. The point of this is to produce two-way communication that captures information from the front line of service delivery and shares it quickly and effectively, both across neighbouring services where this is relevant, and with senior staff where rapid action may be required. It also aims to maintain standard work and to build improvement into the system.

Huddles should not become a mechanism for telling people whatever someone, somewhere in the organisation feels is important. Any information conveyed in a huddle should be brief and to the point.

In line with the components of Daily Management discussed previously, the characteristics of a team huddle are that it. (Barnas 2014; Mann 2015; Kenney 2015)

■ Is conducted standing up
■ Takes place in front of the visual display board, in the place the work is done or immediately adjacent to it, and within sight of it
■ Has a standard agenda, defined by the visual display Board
■ Lasts no more than 15–20 minutes

To support Daily Management, a team huddle should (Barnas 2014; Mann 2015)

■ Consider any staffing issues relevant to that day (e.g. illness absence) and required responses
■ Provide an update on any expected operational issues that day (e.g. anticipated numbers)
■ Review the information on performance from the previous day (or shift, if applicable)
■ Allocate any required actions to follow up a problem to establish the cause, or to make changes, including a review of previously agreed actions

Rother and Shook (1999) emphasise that management support should be as close to the operation as possible. The aim is to combine the maintenance of the work with identification of problems and action for improvement (Toussaint 2015). As noted previously, in some systems, the Team Leader then attends a meeting with other Team Leaders with a Supervisor. Each Team Leader takes the visual information from their own service with them. The same process is followed, but with a greater focus on actions on problems and on improvements. In some systems, a third huddle may be held with the person in charge of the overall Value Stream in which the teams work.

11.17 Techniques: Using an X-Matrix

Matrix diagrams are a common device in improvement work, as they allow the relationship between two or more factors to be shown (Mizuno 1988). The simplest form of Matrix diagram is an X-Matrix (Figure 11.6). This is often used to prioritise actions, with possible actions on the right-hand side, and relevant dimensions (e.g. impact, difficulty, etc.) on the top axis. Other uses of an X-Matrix diagram include looking at different strategies to achieve aims.

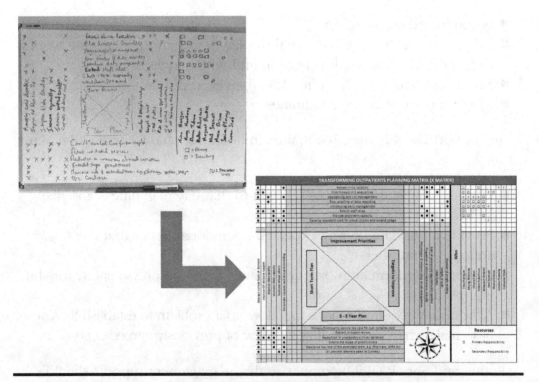

Figure 11.6   Example of an X-matrix (in development) and final version.

There are many other variations of Matrix diagrams for specific purposes, sometimes combined with other types of diagram, such as Driver diagrams. The best known use in *Hoshin Kanri*, however, is as X-diagrams.

X-Diagrams are often used to show the link between a strategy, the way the strategy will be achieved, and the results. It also includes details on which department or team will contribute to which piece of work. Formats vary widely, and the focus changes at different levels of implementation (Colletti 2013).

Jackson (2006) gives a summary of their use, noting that

- The main driver is the strategy, usually shown on the left of the diagram.
- The top of the diagram shows which tactics relate to different strategic aims.
- The right side then shows the process measures for judging progress on these tactics, and the accountability for delivery.
- The bottom of the matrix shows outcome measures that are expected to be achieved if process measures improve as planned.

Other systems use variations of this (Figure 11.6). Working clockwise, this version puts the aims in the centre, the 3–5 year plans at the bottom, the one-year priorities on the left, the projects relating to the topic at the top, the metrics at the right, and the responsible people on the far right. The general principle, of a clockwise diagram showing how actions follow from strategy, what measures are expected to happen from each intervention and who is accountable for what, are common across most descriptions.

11.18 Lean Management

Each time you implement an element of the Lean production system, implement the elements of the management system right along with it.

David Mann (2015: p 29)

It is difficult to start 'Lean management' until you have done something to stabilise processes (Mann 2015). Managers are used to firefighting, when they deal rapidly with problems, fix them enough to allow the process to continue and to meet current targets. Kim Barnas, at Thedacare in the

United States, notes how difficult it is to persuade managers to move their work to a Lean process when they are also dealing with traditional management approaches (Barnas 2014).

In a traditional management system, the focus is on retrospective attainment of targets, and managers are judged on this. This results in a 'deliver at all costs' expectation. This is understandable in a health and social care system, where staff do not want to let people down. The problem with this approach is that it tends to leave tomorrow to look after itself. It is also difficult to establish standard processes, if the approach is juggled constantly to deliver day-to-day.

One way to square this circle is to stabilise some processes, apply Lean management to them and then seek incremental improvement as managers see the benefits for themselves (Barnas 2014; Mann 2015). As processes stabilise, supervisors and managers can expect to have more time to focus on improvement.

There are four elements of a Lean Management System: Leader Standard Work, Visual Controls, a daily accountability process, and discipline (Mann 2015).

11.18.1 Leader Standard Work

In Lean, the team undertaking the work identify the 'current best way of doing the work.' In health and social care, this can relate to processes supporting care, such as the arrangements for the booking of a clinic, having the relevant staff and equipment available, booking further appointments and so on. When patient safety is involved, it may include ways of undertaking clinical activities, such as the care bundles intended to reduce Ventilator Acquired Pneumonia or infections from peripheral lines.

These actions are unlikely to be the best way of doing something for ever – standard work is the best way a team have identified of doing something for now, and should be revised in the light of experience and of new evidence.

Once a team has established standard work, however, the organisation needs to address itself to supporting the team to deliver this.

Processes are difficult to maintain. It is very easy for work to drift back to a previous way of doing things. As the team has already decided that this is not the best current way of undertaking their work, this has to be avoided. The parallel challenge is to have the information and learning to improve the process further.

A Team Leader will spend the majority of their day working on a process. The familiar litany – go to the place the work is done, look at the process, talk to the people – is the core of the Team Leader's job. The Leader watches the process underway and identifies where it varies from the expected process, generally in real time. They often demonstrate parts of the process to staff, and they coach as required. They will identify the difference between the expected and the actual, usually with the help of visual controls and this gives their team a focus for investigation and improvement.

Inevitably, some of the manager's time has to be directed to coping with and recovering from problems, but in a Lean system they catalogue problems to allow preventative action. Unlike the traditional model, management is not a day-to-day activity: as with all staff, the Team Leader has the role of both working, and improving their work and that of their team over time.

The techniques described in 'Process Tracking Charts' in the 'Visual Control' sections are used, usually combined with daily huddles and the use of Accountability Boards. In this way, the Leader captures current operation of the process for which they are responsible, identifies and prioritises variations for investigation and stimulates improvement action.

In the United States, Thedacare use *kamishabi* boards to control which processes are observed, with cards for a particular day indicating what is to be observed (Barnas 2014). A green dot is attached to the steps that are followed, and a red dot to those that are not followed. The red dots are drawn together into Pareto charts, to help direct improvement activity.

Other layers of managers play an important part in the process, as described in the 'Daily Management' section. Part of their role is to ensure that Standard Work for daily management is taking place, and also to identify where problems may require their active intervention to find solutions, for example where the problem is out of the direct control of the team. Wherever possible, the managers support the people reporting to them to identify problems and produce solutions: 'the role of Lean Leaders is to teach and encourage improvement by all, not to own it exclusively' (Mann 2015: p 72).

11.18.2 Visual Controls

(Visual controls) are, in effect, forms of just-in-time information transfer.

Kiyoshi Suzaki (1987: p 107)

Visual controls amount only to wallpaper without the discipline to insist they are taken seriously and used as a basis for action.

David Mann (2015: p 80)

The common response to health and social care problems is firefighting – efforts, sometimes very great efforts, are put into finding a way to cope and to get over the immediate problem. Despite this investment of effort, it is common for services to have difficulty describing the precise nature of the problems they are experiencing, and even greater difficulty in quantifying the relative importance of different problems. This makes it difficult to decide what issues to prioritise for improvements.

Lean is an improvement system. Visual controls allow identification of current performance compared to expected performance. This provides a method to see problems quickly and then to embark on preventative action.

Visual controls do not have to be complex. A basic assessment of actual versus expected activity and comments can get the process started. Table 11.2 shows an example of a template used to monitor discharges in a medical ward.

This then provides a note of actual issues in real time. The notes can be reviewed at the Team huddle the next day. It also allows the problems to be quantified and prioritised.

The sophistication of this can be increased over time. One way of doing this is to decrease the length of the period being observed (Mann 2015). Longer periods allow for some averaging across the period, so problems may

Table 11.2   Process Tracking Chart Used in a Medical Ward

Time Period	Number of Patients Expected to be discharged	Actual Number	Comments
9 a.m.–9.59 a.m.	2	1	Immediate Discharge Letter (IDL) not ready. Ambulance re-tasked.
10 a.m.–10.59 a.m.	2	2	
11 a.m.–11.59 a.m.	3	2	Discharge medication not ready.
12 noon–12.59 p.m.	1	2	9am patient discharged, when replacement ambulance arrived.

occur but the time recovered, hence concealing the problem. Progressively shorter periods mean that finer variations are more likely to be identified, revealing problems that can be addressed.

There is no need to develop complex IT-dependent solutions for this. Handwritten and hand-drawn data has more impact for the staff who collect it, as it is clearly their work, unedited and unaltered.

11.18.3 Daily Accountability

The accountability process has been covered earlier in this chapter, under daily management. An accountability process is essential if the system is not to revert to previous ways of working. This also allows staff to see that actions happen as a result of identified problems in processes. The system seeks a continuous cycle between identified problem – root cause analysis – PDSA cycle of improvements – revised standard work – identified problems and so on.

11.18.4 Discipline

Leader standard work, visual controls and accountability are often taken as the core of Lean Management processes. Mann (2015) identifies Discipline as the missing core element in this list.

Using Lean to deliver improvements over the long term requires regular attention to the state of the process, and of the overall system. This is discussed further subsequently, in 'Leading Lean Management.'

11.19 Leading Lean Management

The pull of previous habits is strong. Creating a system in which Lean practices are supported to happen, and to go on happening, is a core role of executives and senior managers.

Some health and social care organisations, such as Virginia Mason, expect their senior team to be fluent in all aspects of Lean and to be able to lead Lean improvement events (Kenney 2010). Other organisations do not expect all senior managers to reach this level of expertise, but do expect organisational leaders to take responsibility for the overall health of a Lean production system and to help sustain it (Mann 2015).

There is a halfway house in this. Senior managers are used to assessing the state of processes, even if they do not have a detailed technical knowledge of the area. For them to do this in a Lean system, they have to be aware of the key elements of Lean that they should expect to see.

Leaders can check the components of a Lean management system even before they have obtained a thorough knowledge of Lean, by checking that the components, described previously, are in place (Mann 2015). This needs to be undertaken regularly.

11.20 Practice Example

A General Hospital first introduced Daily Management in one ward. This ward had undertaken a Rapid Process Improvement Workshop, followed by both smaller events and continuous improvement work. Staff were familiar with the ideas, and had practical experience of applying QI methods to their own processes. They had stabilised many of their processes, and were comfortable discussing quality issues.

This ward developed a morning huddle, using the principles described in Section 11.16. Meetings were held, standing up, in front of a Production Board. As the team developed confidence in this, they began to identify QI work from their daily data, and once a week held a longer Huddle to agree, report on and discuss QI work conducted by the staff.

Over the course of several months, other wards in the same area of the hospital began to look at the results achieved on the ward, and the nurses on the pilot ward began to coach colleagues on the method. On the original ward, they found that problems occurred overnight which were not accounted for by the morning huddle. They introduced a later afternoon huddle when staff working in the evening summarised any actions from the handover from day staff, and confirmed that an escalation plan was in place for each patient, or agreed how this would be done in time. Work to be concluded before the next morning was also agreed. This improved both safety and flow, and increased staff confidence in the procedures in place. These team huddles gradually spread across clinical areas.

In the next year, the hospital developed a system of nested huddles culminating in a morning huddle bringing together information from across the hospital. This developed over many iterations, supported by a hospital-based QI coach. In the third year, the QI coach worked with clinicians and managers to develop a Hoshin system which brought together longer-term transformation projects, and work done in specific areas, with the aligned hospital metrics in a once weekly huddle that gave visibility to QI work across the hospital, and helped to identify areas where further work was required, often using information collected through the daily management structure, as well as from organisational priorities.

11.21 Conclusions

Lean methods support improvement. For improvement to be sustained, and for gains to be obtained across systems, attention to management systems is required.

At the strategic level, this usually involves a process of a clear vision of where the organisation wants to go, along with the values it wants to show. With suitable analysis, this contributes to a medium-term plan, with annual objectives falling from that. These objectives include both transformational objectives designed to change at least part of how an organisation works, together with 'business as usual' targets, or at least 'business as usual' within a culture of continuous improvement.

A process of catchball is used to refine plans and to identify objectives and means at each level of the organisation. This is then combined with regular review, built into daily management, to keep the process on track or to identify required changes.

Daily management requires maintenance of agreed standard work, visual control of processes and an accountability mechanism that supports root cause investigation, PDSA cycles and further process improvements.

The use of this daily management process is supported by leaders who review and maintain the health and integrity of the system used to support it.

Further Reading

Full references are included in the bibliography.

The best known book on lean management is Akao's *Hoshin Kanri. Policy Deployment for Successful TQM* (2004). Kesterson provides a brief summary of the concepts in *The Basics of Hoshin Kanri* (2015) in a book that also includes accounts of interviews with relevant practitioners.

Kim Barnas' book, *Beyond Heroes* (Barnas 2014) is an excellent description of introducing a daily management system in practice. David Mann's *Creating a Lean Culture* (Mann 2015) covers all levels of management system, and benefits from his considerable experience in working with a range of organisations.

Bibliography

Agency for Healthcare Research and Quality, US Department of Health and Human Services. (undated). Your guide to choosing quality healthcare: a quick look at quality. Quoted in Varkey P., Reller M.K., Resa, R.K. (2007). Basics of quality improvement in health care. *Mayo Clinic Proceedings* 82; 6: 735–739.

Akao Y. (2004). *Hoshin Kanri. Policy Deployment for Successful TQM*. Boca Raton, CRC Press.

American Society for Quality (n.d.). ASQ Quality Glossary. Available at: https://asq.org/quality-resources/quality-glossary/q (Accessed 1 December 2017).

Andersen H., Røvik K.A., Ingebrigtsen T. (2014). Lean thinking in hospitals: Is there a cure for the absence of evidence? A systematic review of reviews. *BMJ Open* 4: e003873 doi:10.1136/bmjopen-2-13-003873.

Ballé M., Régnier A. (2007). Lean as a learning system in a hospital ward. *Leadership in Health Services* 20; 1: 33–41.

Barnas K., Adams E. (2014). *Beyond Heroes. A Lean Management System for Healthcare*. Appleton, WI, Thedacare Centre for Healthcare Value.

Batalden P.B. (1992). *Building Knowledge for Improvement-an Introductory Guide to the Use of FOCUS-PDCA*. Nashville, TN, Quality Resource Group, Hospital Corporation of America.

Batalden P.B., Davidoff F. (2007). What is "quality improvement" and how can it transform healthcare? *BMJ Quality & Safety* 16: 2–3.

Beattie M., Hookway G., Perera M., Calder S., Hunter-Rowe C., van Woerden H. (2018) Improving wait time from referral to opiate replacement therapy in a drug recovery service. *BMJ Open Quality* 7: e000295. doi:10.1136/bmjoq-2017-000295 (Accessed 1 November 2018).

Berwick D. (1996). A primer on leading the improvement of systems. *BMJ* 312: 619–622.

Berwick J. (2001). Not again! *BMJ* 322; 7281: 247–248.

Berwick D.M., Godfrey A. B., Roessner J. (1990) *Curing Health Care. New Strategies for Quality Improvement*. San Francisco, Jossey-Bass Inc.

Bhamu J., Sangwan K.S. (2014). Lean manufacturing: Literature review and research issues. *International Journal of Operations & Production Management* 34: 876–940.

Bicheno J. (2008). *The Lean Toolbox for Service Systems*. Buckingham, PICSIE Books.

Black J.R., Miller D. (2008). *The Toyota Way to Healthcare Excellence*. Chicago, IL, Health Administration Press.

Boonyasai R.T., Windish D.M., Chakroborti C., Feldman L.S., Rubin H.R., Bass E.B. (2007). Effectiveness of teaching Quality improvement to clinicians—A systematic review. *Journal of the American Medical Association* 298: 1023–1036.

Bucci R.V., Musitano A. (2011). A lean six sigma journey in radiology. *Radiology Management* 33; 3: 7–33.

Burgess N., Radnor Z. (2013). Evaluating Lean in healthcare. *International Journal for Health Care Quality Assurance* 26; 3: 220–235.

Butterworth R. (2001). *Hoshin Kanri: An exploratory study at Nissan Yamato engineering Ltd*, Durham theses, Durham University. Available at Durham E-Theses Online: http://etheses.dur.ac.uk/4234/ (Accessed 27 August 2015).

Carman K.L., Paez K., Stephens J., Smeeding L., Garfinkel S., Blough C., Devers K., Hoover M., Spaulding T., Mapes D. (2014). *Improving Care Delivery Through Lean: Implementation Case Studies*. Prepared under contract HHSA290200600019. AHRQ Publication No. 13(15)–0056. Rockville, MD, Agency for Healthcare Research and Quality.

Chand D.V. (2011). Observational study using the tools of lean six sigma to improve the efficiency of the resident rounding process. *Journal of Graduate Medical Education* 3(2): 144–150.

CIPFA (2010). *Better Benchmarking for High Performance*. London, Chartered Institute of Public Finance & Accounting.

Clarke J., Davidge M., Lou J. (2009). *The How-to Guide for Measurement for Improvement*. Patient Safety First. Available at: https://eoeleadership.hee.nhs.uk/sites/default/files/Patient%20Safety%20First%20How%20To%20Guide%20measurement%20for%20improvement.pdf (Accessed 10 August 2017).

Colletti J. (2013). *Hoshin Kanri Memory Jogger. Process, Tools and Methodology in Successful Strategic Planning*. Salem, Goal/QPC.

Costa L.B.M., Filho M.G. (2016). Lean healthcare: Review classification and analysis of literature. *Production Planning and Control* 27; 10: 823–836.

Costa L.B.M., Filho M.G., Rentes A.F., Bertani T.M., Mardegan R. (2017). Lean healthcare in developing countries: Evidence from Brazilian hospitals. *International Journal of Health Planning and Management* 32; 1: e99–e120.

Crema M., Verbano C. (2015). How to combine lean and safety management in health care processes: A case from Spain. *Safety Science* 79: 63–71.

Curnock E., Ferguson J., McKay J., Bowie P. (2012). *Healthcare Improvement and Rapid PDSA Cycles of Change: A Realist Synthesis of The Literature—Final Report*. Glasgow, University of Glasgow.

Dahlgaard J.J., Pettersen J., Dahlgaard-Park S.M. (2011) Quality and lean health care: a system for assessing and improving the health of healthcare organisations. *Total Quality Management & Business Excellence* 22(6): 673–689.

D'Andreamatteo A., Ianni L., Lega F., Sargiacomo M. (2015). Lean in healthcare: A comprehensive review. *Health Policy* 119; 9: 1197–1209.

Damelo R. (2011). *The Basics of Process Mapping*. 2nd Edition. Boca Raton, CRC Press.

Damiani G.V. (2012). Stability and Standardized Work. In Obara S. and Wilburn D. (Eds) *Toyota by Toyota. Reflection from the Inside Leaders on the Techniques That Revolutionized the Industry*. Boca Raton, CRC Press.

Deming W.E. (1994). *The New Economics*. 2nd ed. Baton Rouge, SPC Press.

Deming W.E. (2000). *Out of the Crisis*. Cambridge, MA, MIT.

Department of Health (2008). *High Quality Care for all, Next Stage Review Final Report, Cm 7432*. London, Department of Health.

Department of Health and Social Care/Care Quality Commission (2017). *Adult Social Care Quality Matters*. London, Department of Health and Social Care/ Care Quality Commission.

De Souza L.B. (2009). Trends and approaches in lean healthcare. *Leadership in Health Services* 22; 2: 121–139.

Dickson E.W., Anguelov Z., Vetterick D., Eller A., Singh S. (2009). Use of lean in the Emergency Department: A case series of 4 hospitals. *Annals of Emergency Medicine* 54; 4: 504–510.

Dixon-Woods M., Bosk C.L., Aveling E.L., Goeschel C.A. (2011). *Millbank Quarterly* 89; 2: 167–205.

Donabedian A. (1966). Evaluating the quality of medical care. *Milbank Memorial Fund Quarterly* 44; Suppl 3: 166–206.

Drucker P. (2007). *The Practice of Management*. London, Routledge.

Eaton M. (2009). Lean for Practitioners. An introduction to Lean for healthcare organisations. 2nd Edition. Ecademy Press.

Eaton M. (2013). *The Lean Practitioner's Handbook*. London, Kogan Page.

Furman C., Caplan R. (2007). Applying the Toyota production system: Using a patient safety alert system to reduce error. *The Joint Commission Journal on Quality and Patient Safety* 33; 7: 376–386.

Gapp R., Fisher R., Kobayashi K. (2008). Implementing 5S within a Japanese context: An integrated management system. *Management Decision* 46; 4: 565–579.

Gayed B., Black S., Daggy J., Munshi I.A. (2013). Redesigning a joint replacement program using lean six sigma in a Veterans Affairs hospital. *JAMA Surgery* 148; 11: 1050–1056.

Goldratt E.M. (1990). *Theory of Constraints*. Great Barrington, MA, North River Press.

Ghoshal S., Bartlett C.A. (1995). Building the entrepreneurial corporation: New organisational Processes. New managerial tasks, *European Management Journal* 13; 2: 139–155.

Graban M. (2012). *Lean Hospitals: Improving Quality, Patient Safety and Employee Engagement*. 2nd Edition. Boca Raton, CRC Press.

GrabanM. (2016) *Lean Hospitals*. 3rd Edition. Routledge

Graban M. Swartz J.E. (2012). *Healthcare Kaizen: Engaging Front-Line Staff in Sustainable Continuous Improvements*. Boca Raton, CRC Press.

Grol R., Baker R., Moss F. (2002). Quality improvement research: Understanding the science of change in health care. *Quality and Safety in Health Care* 11: 110–111.

Grout J.R. (2003). Preventing medical errors by designing benign failures. *Joint Commission Journal on Quality and Safety* 29; 7: 354–362.

Grout J.R. (2006). Mistake proofing: Changing designs to reduce error. *Quality and Safety in Health Care* 15; Suppl 1): i44–i49.

Grout J.R. (2007). *Mistake-Proofing the Design of Healthcare Processes (AHRQ Pub. No. 07-0020).* Rockville, MD, Department of Health and Human Services.

Grout J.R., Toussaint J.S. (2010). Mistake-proofing healthcare: Why stopping processes may be a good start. *Business Horizons* 53: 149–156.

Hadfield D., Holmes S., Kozlowski S, Speri T. (2012). *The New Lean Healthcare Pocket Guide. Tools for the Elimination of Waste in Hospitals, Clinics and Other Healthcare Facilities.* Chelsea, MI, MCS Media.

Halling B., Wijk K. (2013). Experienced barriers to lean in Swedish manufacturing and health care. *International Journal of Lean Thinking* 4: 2 (online).

Hawthorne H.C., Masterson D.J. (2013). Lean health care. *North Carolina Medical Journal* 74; 2: 133–136.

Health Foundation (2013). *Quality Improvement Made Simple What Everyone Should Know About Health Care Quality Improvement.* London, The Health Foundation.

Healthcare Improvement Scotland (2016). *SPSP Acute Adult End of Phase Report August 2016* Edinburgh, Healthcare Improvement Scotland.

Health Quality Ontario (2013). *Measurement for Quality Improvement.* Ontario, Health Quality Ontario.

Herron C., Hicks C. (2008). The transfer of selected lean manufacturing techniques from Japanese automotive manufacturing into general manufacturing (UK) through change agents. *Robotics and Computer-Integrated Manufacturing* 24: 524–531.

Hines P., Holweg M., Rich N. (2004). Learning to evolve A review of contemporary lean thinking. *International Journal of Operations & Production Management* 24; 10: 994–1011.

Hines P., Taylor D., Walsh A. (2018) The Lean journey: have we got it wrong?, *Total Quality Management & Business Excellence*, doi:10.1080/14783363.2018.1429258 (Accessed October 2018).

Hirano H. and Black J. T. (1988). *JIT Factory Revolution. A Pictorial Guide to the Factory Design of the Future.* Cambridge MA, Productivity Press.

Hirano H. (1995). *5 Pillars of the Visual Workplace.* New York, Productivity Press.

Hirano H., Furuya M. (2006). *JIT Is Flow: Practice and Principles of Lean Manufacturing.* Vancouver, PCS Press.

Hirano H. (2009a). *JIT Implementation Manual. Volume 1: The Just-in-Time Production System.* Boca Raton, Productivity Press.

Hirano H. (2009b). *JIT Implementation Manual. Volume 2: Waste and 5S's.* Boca Raton, Productivity Press.

Hirano H. (2009c). *JIT Implementation Manual. Volume 3: Flow Manufacturing— Multi-Process Operations and Kanban.* Boca Raton, Productivity Press.

Hirano H. (2009d). *JIT Implementation Manual. Volume 4: Leveling—Changeover and Quality Assurance.* Boca Raton, Productivity Press.

Hirano H. (2009e). *JIT Implementation Manual. Volume 5: Standardized Operations—Jidoka and Maintenance/Safety.* Boca Raton, Productivity Press.

Hirano H. (2009f). *JIT Implementation Manual. Volume 6: JIT Implementation Forms and Charts.* Boca Raton, Productivity Press.

H M Government (2012). *Bringing Clarity to Quality in Care and Support.* Available at: https://www.gov.uk/government/uploads/system/uploads/attachment_data/file/136457/2900021-BCTQTLAP-2012-07-11-V3.pdf (Accessed 15 December 2017).

Ho S K.M., Cicmil S., Fung C.K. (1995).The Japanese 5-S practice and TQM training. *Training for Quality* 3; 4: 19–24.

Hutchins D. (2008). *Hoshin Kanri: The Strategic Approach to Continuous Improvement.* Farnham, Gower.

Hyland P., Mellor R., O'Mara E., Kondepudi R. (2000). A comparison of Australian firms and their use of continuous improvement tools. *The TQM Magazine* 12; 2: 117–124.

Imai M. (1986). *Kaizen. (Ky'zen) The Key to Japan's Competitive Success.* New York, Random House.

Imai M. (1997). *Gemba Kaizen. A Commonsense, Low-Cost Approach to Management.* New York, McGraw-Hill.

Inozu B., Chauncey D., Kamataris V., Mount C. (2012). *Performance Improvement for Healthcare.* New York, McGraw-Hill.

Instep UK (2009). *How to Prepare a Skills Matrix.* Somerford, Instep UK Ltd.

Institute of Healthcare Improvement (2005). *Going Lean in Health Care.* Cambridge, MA, Institute for Healthcare Improvement.

Institute of Medicine, Committee to Design a Strategy for Quality Review and Assurance in Medicare. (1990). *Medicare: A Strategy for Quality Assurance,* Volume I. Lohr K.N.(Ed.). Washington, DC, National Academies Press.

Institute of Medicine, Committee on Quality Health Care in America. (2001). *Crossing the Quality Chasm: A New Health System for the 21st Century.* Washington, DC, National Academies Press.

Institute for Healthcare Improvement. (2003). *The Breakthrough Series: IHI's Collaborative Model for Achieving Breakthrough Improvement.* IHI Innovation Series White Paper.

Institute for Healthcare Improvement (2009). *Central Line Bundle. Improvement Map.* Available at: http://app.ihi.org/imap/tool/processpdf.aspx?processGUID=e876565d-fd43-42ce-8340-8643b7e675c7 (Accessed 27 December 2017).

Investors in People (2013). *Effective Management. Management Skills Matrix.* London, Investors in People.

Ishikawa K. (1982). *Guide to Quality Control.* Tokyo, Asian Productivity Organisation.

Ishikawa K. (1985). *What is Total Quality Control? The Japanese Way.* Englewood Cliffs, NJ, Prentice Hall.

ISO 9000:2005, definition 3.1.1. Geneva, ISO.

Jackson T.L. (2006). *Hoshin Kanri for the Lean Enterprise. Developing Competitive Capabilities and Managing Profit.* Boca Raton, CRC Press.

Jackson T.L. (Ed) (2009). *5S for Healthcare*. New York, Productivity Press.

Jackson T.L. (Ed) (2012). *Standard Work for Lean Healthcare*. New York, Productivity Press.

Jackson T.L. (Ed) (2013). *Kaizen Workshops for Lean Healthcare*. New York, Productivity Press.

Jackson T.L. (Ed) (2013b). *Mapping Clinical Value Streams*. New York, Productivity Press.

Japan Human Relations Association. (1992). *Kaizen Teian 1. Developing Systems for Continuous Improvement Through Employee Suggestions*. Cambridge, MI, Productivity Press.

Japan Management Association. (1989). Kanban. *Just in Time at Toyota. Management Begins in the Workplace*. Revised Edition. Cambridge, MI, Productivity Press.

Jimmerson C., Weber D., Sobek D.K. (2005). Reducing waste and errors: Piloting lean principles at intermountain healthcare. *Joint Commission Journal on Quality and Patient Safety* 31; 5: 243–257.

Joosten T., Bongers I., Janssen R. (2009) Application of lean thinking to health care: issues and observations. *International Journal for Quality in Health Care* 21(5): 341–347.

Juran J.M. (1988). *Juran on Planning for Quality*. New York, The Free Press.

Juran J.M. (1992). *Juran of Quality by Design. The New Steps for Planning Quality into Goods and Services*. New York, The Free Press.

Juran J.M. (1995) *Managerial Breakthrough*. Revised Edition. New York, McGraw-Hill, Inc.

Juran J.M., Godfrey A.B. (1999). *Juran's Quality Handbook*. New York, McGraw-Hill.

Juran J M., Gryna F.M. (1988). *Quality Control Handbook*. New York, McGraw-Hill.

Kaplan G. (2013). Pursuing the perfect patient experience. *Frontiers of Health Service Management* 29; 3: 16–27.

Karatsu H. (1988). *TQC Wisdom of Japan. Managing for Total Quality Control*. Cambridge, MI, Productivity Press.

Kenney C. (2010). *Transforming health care: Virginia Mason Medical Center's Pursuit of the Perfect Patient Experience*. New York, Productivity Press.

Kenney C. (2015). *A Leadership Journey in Health Care: Virginia Mason's Story*. Boca Raton, CRC Press.

Kesterson R.K. (2015). *The Basics of Hoshin Kanri*. Boca Raton, CRC Press.

Kim C.S., Spahlinger D.A., Kin J.M., Billi J.E. (2006). Lean health care: What can hospitals learn from a world-class automaker? *Journal of Hospital Medicine* 1; 3: 191–199.

King's Fund (2016). *Measuring Improvement*. Available at: https://www.kingsfund.org.uk/projects/pfcc/measuring-improvement (Accessed 7 March 2016).

King B. (2013). Preface. In Colletti J. *2013 Hoshin Kanri Memory Jogger. Process, Tools and Methodology in Successful Strategic Planning*. Salem, Goal/QPC.

Kitazuka R.E., Moretti C. (2012). Jidoka In Obara S and Wilburn D (Eds) Toyota by Toyota. *Reflection from the Inside Leaders on the Techniques That Revolutionized the Industry*. Boca Raton, CRC Press.

Kohn L.T., Corrigan, J.M., Donaldson M.S. (Eds) (2000). *To Err is Human: Building a Safer Health System.* Washington, DC, National Academy Press.

Kovacevic M., Jovicic M., Djapan M., Zivanovic Macuzic I. (2016). Lean thinking in healthcare: Review of implementation results *International Journal for Quality Research* 10; 1: 219–230.

Kyte B., Locher D. (2004) *The Complete Lean Enterprise.* New York, Productivity Press.

Langley G., Kevin Nolan K., Nolan T.R. (1994). The Foundation of Improvement *Quality Progress* 81–86.

Langley G.L., Moen R., Nolan K.M., Nolan T.W., Norman C.L., Provost L.P. (2009). *The Improvement Guide: A Practical Approach to Enhancing Organizational Performance* (2nd edition). San Francisco, John Wiley & Sons.

Leatherman S., Ferris T.G., Berwick D., Omaswa F., Crisp N. (2010). The role of quality improvement in strengthening health systems in developing countries. *International Journal for Quality in Health Care* 22; 4: 237–243.

Leggat S.G., Bartram T., Stanton P., Bamber G.J., S. Sohal A.S. (2015). Have process redesign methods, such as Lean, been successful in changing care delivery in hospitals? A systematic review. *Public Money and Management* 35; 2: 161–168.

Liker J.K. (2004). *The Toyota Way. 14 Management Principles from the World's Greatest Manufacturer.* New York, McGraw-Hill.

Liker J.K., Hoseus M. (2008). *Toyota Culture. The Heart and Soul of the Toyota Way.* New York, McGraw-Hill.

Linborg H.J. (1997). *The Basics of Cross-Functional Teams.* New York, Quality Resources.

Lindsay C.F. (2016). *Lean in Healthcare: An Evaluation of Lean Implementation in NHS Lothian.* PhD Thesis, Edinburgh Napier University. Available at: https://www.napier.ac.uk/~/media/worktribe/output-455610/lean-in-healthcare-an-evaluation-of-lean-implementation-in-nhs-lothian.pdf (Accessed 1 June 2018).

Lipshutz A.K.M., Fee C., Schell H., Campbell L., Taylor J., Sharpe B.A., Nguyen J., Gropper M.A. (2008). Strategies for success: A PDSA analysis of three QI initiatives in critical care. *The Joint Commission Journal on Quality and Patient Safety* 34; 8: 435–444.

Mann, L. (2015). *Creating a Lean Culture. Tools to Sustain Lean Conversions.* Boca Raton, CRC Press.

Mannion M. (2014). Lean healthcare and quality management: The experience of ThedaCare. *Quality Management Journal* 21; 1: 7–10.

Marjoua Y., Bozic K.G. (2012). Brief history of quality movement in US healthcare. *Current Review of Musculoskeletal Medicine* 5; 4: 265–273.

Martin K., Osterling M. (2014). *Value Stream Mapping: How to Visualize work and Align Leadership for Organizational Transformation.* New York, McGraw-Hill.

Maskell B., Baggaley B., Grasso L. (2011). *Practical Lean Accounting: A Proven System for Measuring and Managing the Lean Enterprise.* Boca Raton, CRC Press.

Mazzocato P., Holden R.J., Brommels M., Aronsson H., Bäckman U., Elg M., Thor J. (2012). How does lean work in emergency care? A case study of a lean-inspired intervention at the Astrid Lindgren Children's hospital, Stockholm, Sweden. *BMC Health Services Research* 12: 28 https://doi.org/10.1186/1472-6963-12-28

Mazzocato P., Savage C., Brommels M., Aronsson, H., Thor, J. (2010) Lean thinking in healthcare: a realist review of the literature. *Quality and Safety in Health Care* 19(5): 376–382

McCann L., Hassard J.S., Granter E., Hyde P.J. (2015). Casting the lean spell: The promotion dilution and erosion of lean management in the NHS. *Human Relations* 68; 10: 1557–1577.

Mead E., Stark C., Thompson M. (2017). Creating and leading a quality improvement culture at scale. *Management in Healthcare* 2; 2: 115–124.

Merry M.D., Crago M.G. (2001). The past, present and future of health care quality urgent need for innovative, external review processes to protect patients. *The Physician Executive* Sept/Oct 30–35.

Milligan C. (2015). *Promoting Continuity of Care Through Improved Information Sharing on Discharge from an Organic Assessment Ward: Parts 1 & 2.* Unpublished Assignment for the MSc Module; Quality Improvement Projects in Health and Social Care, ADPP12. University of Stirling, School of Health Sciences.

Miller D. (2005). *Going Lean in Health Care.* Cambridge, MA, Institute for Healthcare Improvement.

Mizuno S. (1988). *Management for Quality Improvement. The Seven New QC Tools.* Cambridge, MA, Productivity Press.

Moen R.D., Nolan T.R., Provost L.P. (1991). *Improving Quality Through Planned Experimentation,* New York, McGraw-Hill.

Moen R., Norman C. (2006). Evolution of the PDCA cycle. Detroit, Associates in Process Improvement.

Moen R., Norman C. (2010). Circling back. Clearing up myths about the Deming cycle and how it keeps evolving. *Quality Progress* November: 23–28.

Moraros J., Lemstra M., Nwankwo C. (2016). Lean interventions in healthcare: Do they actually work? A systematic literature review. *International Journal for Quality in Health Care* 28; 2: 150–165.

Nadeem E., Olin S.S., Hill L.A., Hoagwood K.E., Horwitz S. (2013). Understanding the components of quality improvement collaboratives: A systematic literature review. *Milbank Quarterly.* 91: 354–394.

Nash M.A., Poliing S.R. (2008). *Mapping the Total Value Stream: A Comprehensive Guide for Production and Transactional Processes.* Boca Raton, CRC Press.

National Quality Board (2013). *Quality in the New Health System.* London, National Quality Board.

Nelson E.C., Batalden P.B., Godfrey M.M. (2007). *Quality by Design: A Clinical Microsystems Approach.* San Francisco, John Wiley & Sons.

Nelson-Peterson D.L., Leppa C.J. (2013). Creating an environment for caring using lean principles of the Virginia Mason Production System. *Journal of Nursing Administration* 37; 6: 287–94.

Nemoto M. (1987). *Total Quality Control for Management. Strategies and Techniques from Toyota and Toyoda Gosei.* Englewood Cliffs, Prentice Hall.

NHS Improvement (2014). *First steps Towards Quality Improvement. A Simple Guide for Improving Services.* Leicester, NHS Improvement.

NHS Scotland Quality Improvement Hub (2015). Model for Improvement and PDSA. http://www.qihub.scot.nhs.uk/quality-and-efficiency/2020-framework-for-quality-efficiency-and-value/improve/model-for-improvement-and-pdsa.aspx (Accessed 8 June 2015).

NHS Scotland (2017). *2020 Framework for Quality, Efficiency and Value.* Edinburgh, NHS Scotland.

Norval A., Wilburn D. (2012). Hoshin Kanri In Obara S. and Wilburn D. (Eds) *Toyota by Toyota. Reflection from the Inside Leaders on the Techniques That Revolutionized the Industry.* Boca Raton, CRC Press.

Obara S., Wilburn D. (Eds) (2012). *Toyota by Toyota. Reflections from the Inside Leaders on the Techniques that Revolutionized the Industry.* Boca Raton, CRC Press.

Ohno T. (1988). *Toyota Production System: Beyond Large Scale Production.* Boca Raton, Productivity Press.

Ohno T. (2013). *Taiichi Ohno's Workplace Management.* New York, McGraw-Hill.

Osada T. (1991). *The 5S's: Five Keys to a Total Quality Environment.* Tokyo, Asian Productivity Organisation.

Parry G. (2014). A brief history of quality improvement. *Journal of Oncology Practice* 3: 196–199.

Perla R., Reid A., Cohen S., Parry G. (2015). Health care reform and the trap of the 'iron law'. Available online at https://www.healthaffairs.org/do/10.1377/hblog 20150422.047092/full/ (Accessed 30 November 2017).

Poksinska B. (2010). The current state of Lean implementation in health care: Literature review. *Quality Management in Health Care* 19; 4: 319–329.

Powell A., Rushmer R., Davies H. (2009). *A Systematic Narrative Review of Quality Improvement Models in Health Care.* Edinburgh, NHS Quality Improvement Scotland.

Productivity Press Development Team. (1996). *5S for Operators: 5 Pillars of the Visual Workplace.* New York, Productivity Press.

Protzman C., Mayzell G., Kerpchar J. (2011). *Leveraging Lean in Healthcare: Transforming Your Enterprise into a High Quality Patient Care Delivery System.* New York, Productivity Press.

Provincial Health Services Authority (2011). *Lean 3P and Building Design: BC Children's and Women's Redevelopment Process.* British Columbia, Provincial Health Services Authority.

Quality Improvement Projects in Health and Social Care, ADPP12. University of Stirling, School of Health Sciences.

Radnor Z., Walley P., Stephens A., Bucci G. (2006). *Evaluation of the Lean Approach to Business Management and Its Use in the Public Sector.* Edinburgh, The Scottish Executive.

Radnor Z. (2011). Implementing lean in health care: Making the link between the approach readiness and sustainability. *International Journal of Industrial Engineering and Management* 2; 1: 1–12.

Radnor Z., Osborne S. (2013). Lean: A failed theory for public services. *Public Management Review* 15; 2: 265–287.

Ronge S. (2015). *Lean Transformation in Healthcare a Case Study at Skaraborgs Sjukhusgrupp*. Master of Science Thesis. Chalmers University of Technology, Sweden. Available at: http://publications.lib.chalmers.se/records/fulltext/213167/213167.pdf (Accessed 1 June 2018).

Rose M.B. (1991). *International Competition and Strategic Response in the Textile Industries Since 1870*. Abingdon, Routledge.

Rossi P.H. (1987). The iron law of evaluation and other metallic rules. *Research in Social Problems and Public Policy* 4: 3–20.

Rossi P.H. (2003). The "Iron Law of Evaluation" Reconsidered. *Presented at 2003 AAPAM Research Conference*, Washington, DC. Available online at http://www.welfareacademy.org/rossi/Rossi_Remarks_Iron_Law_Reconsidered.pdf. (Accessed 30 November 2017).

Rossie P.H., Lipsey M.W., Freeman H.E. (2004). *Evaluation: A Systematic Approach*. New York, Sage Publications.

Rother M., Shook J. (1999). *Learning to See*. Cambridge, Lean Enterprise Institute.

Rother M. (2010). *Toyota Kata. Managing People for Improvement, Adaptiveness, and Superior Results*. New York, McGraw-Hill.

Royal College of Nursing (2009). *Measuring for Quality in Health and Social Care*. London, Royal College of Nursing.

Schonberger R.J. (1987). *World Class Manufacturing Casebook. Implementing JIT and TQC*. New York, The Free Press.

Scottish Government (2010). *The Healthcare Quality Strategy for NHS Scotland*. Edinburgh, The Scottish Government.

Scottish Government (2016a). *Health and Care Experience Survey 2015/16—Vol 1 National Results*. Edinburgh, The Scottish Government.

Scottish Government (2016b). *Scottish Inpatient Experience Survey 2016—Vol 1 National Results*. Edinburgh, The Scottish Government.

Scottish Patient Safety Programme (2014). Bundle for preventing infection when inserting and maintaining a Peripheral Vascular Catheter (PVC). Version 2.0 September 2014. Available at: http://www.hps.scot.nhs.uk/resourcedocument.aspx?id=2797 (Accessed 27 December 2017).

Shah R., Ward P.T. (2003). *Lean manufacturing: Context practice bundles, and performance. Journal of Operations Management* 21; 2: 129–149.

Sheingold B.H., Hahn J.A. (2014). The history of healthcare quality: The first 100 years 1860–1960. *International Journal of Africa Nursing Sciences* 1: 18–22.

Shinbun N.K. (1995). *Visual Control Systems*. Portland, Productivity Press.

Simons P.A.M., Houben R., Vlayen A., Hellings J., Pijls-Johannesma M., Marneffe W., Vandijck D. (2015). Does lean management improve patient safety culture? An extensive evaluation of safety culture in a radiotherapy institute. *European Journal of Oncology Nursing* 19; 1: 29–37.

Shingo S. (1986). *Zero Quality Control: Source Inspection and the Poka-Yoke System*. New York, Productivity Press.

Shingo S. (1988). *Non-Stock Production: The Shingo System for Continuous Improvement.* New York, Productivity Press.

Shingo S. (2005). *A Study of the Toyota Production System.* Boca Raton, CRC Press.

Shingo S. (2007). *Kaizen and the Art of Creative Thinking.* Bellingham, Enna and PCS Press.

Shook J.Y. (1997). Bringing the Toyota production system to the United States: A personal perspective. In Liker J.K. (Ed) *Becoming Lean: Inside Stories of US Manufacturers,* Portland, OR, Productivity Press.

Sobek D.K., Liker J.K., Ward A.C. (1998). Another look at Toyota's integrated product development. *Harvard Business Review* 76; 4: 36–49.

Sobek D.K., Smalley A. (2008) *Understanding A3 Thinking: A Critical Component of Toyota's PDCA Management System.* Productivity Press

Social Care Institute for Excellence. (2010). *A Definition of Excellence for Regulated Adult Social Care Services in England.* London, Social Care Institute for Excellence.

Spath P.L. (2002). Reducing errors through work system improvements. In Spath P.L. (Ed) *Error Reduction in Health Care.* Chicago, AHA Press.

Speed A. (2013). *Skills Matrices. Concise and Easy to Use Competency Frameworks.* Purley, Management Improvements Ltd.

Speroff T., O'Connor G.T. (2004). Study designs for PDSA quality improvement research. *Quality Management in Health Care* 13; 1: 17–32.

Stark C., Gent A., Kirkland L. (2015). Improving flow in pre-operative assessment. *BMJ Quality Improvement Reports.* u201341.w1226. doi:10.1136/bmjquality. u201341.w1226.

Stark C. (2016). Conducting observations in clinical areas. https://leanhealthservices.org /2016/07/28/staff-concerns-about-observations/ (Accessed 12 December 2017).

Stark C. (2017). Looking for lean. In Graban M. (Ed) *Practicing Lean.* Amazon.

Steering Committee on Quality Improvement and Management and Committee on Practice and Ambulatory Medicine (2008). *Principles for the Development and Use of Quality Measures* (online) 121; 2. doi:10.1542/peds.2007-3281.

Stuart R. (2015). *Improving communication between the cardiology ward and the Coronary Care Unit. Unpublished BSc Practicum Assignment.* University of Stirling, School of Health Sciences.

Sugimori Y., Kusunkoi K., Cho F., Uchikawa S. (1977). Toyota production system and Kanban system: Materialization of just-in-time and respect-for-human system. *International Journal of Production Research* 15; 6: 553–564.

Suzaki K. (1987). *The New Manufacturing Challenge. Techniques for Continuous Improvement.* New York, The Free Press.

Suzaki K. (1993). *The New Shop Floor Management.* New York, The Free Press.

Tapping D., Luyster T., Shuker T. (2002) *Value Stream Mapping: Eight Steps to Planning, Mapping and Sustaining Improvements.* New York, Productivity Press.

Tarrant C., O'Donnell B., Martin G., Bion J. (2015). *Evaluation of the Scottish Patient Safety Programme Sepsis VTE Collaborative: Short Report.* Leicester, University of Leicester.

Taylor M.J., McNicholas C., Nicolay C., Darzi A., Bell D., Reed J.E. (2014). Systematic review of the application of the plan-do-study-act method to improve quality in healthcare. *BMJ Quality and Safety* 4; 23: 290–298.

Think Local Act Personal (2013) Driving up quality in adult social care. Available at: https://www.thinklocalactpersonal.org.uk/_assets/NMDF/DrivingUpQuality ASCfinal.pdf (Accessed 1 December 2017).

Ting H.H., Shojania K.G., Montori V.M., Bradley E.H. (2009). Quality Improvement: Science and action. *Circulation* 119: 1962–1974.

Toussaint J.S., Berry L.L. (2013). The promise of lean in health care. *Mayo Clinic Proceedings* 88; 1: 74–82.

Toussaint J., Adams E. (2015). *Management on the Mend: The Healthcare Executive's Guide to System Transformation.* Appleton, WI, Thedacare Center for Healthcare Value.

Toyota Motor Corporation (2012). *75 Years of Toyota. Ever Better Cars. Section 1. The Inventions and Ideas of Sakichi Toyoda.* http://www.toyota-global.com /company/history_of_toyota/75years/text/taking_on_the_automotive_business/ chapter1/section1/item4.html (Accessed 20 August 2015).

Trägårdh B., Lindberg K. (2004). Curing a meagre health care system by lean methods—translating 'chains of care' in the Swedish health care sector. *International Journal of Health Planning and Management* 19; 4: 383–398.

Trilling L., Pellet B., Delacroix S., Colella Fleury H., Marcon E. (2010). Improving care efficiency in a radiotherapy center using Lean philosophy. *IEEE Workshop on Health Care Management*, Venice, Italy. 6 p.

Tufte E.R. (2001). *The visual display of quantitative information.* Cheshire, CT, Graphics Press.

Toussaint J.S., Berry L.L. (2013) The Promise of Lean in Health Care. *Mayo Clinic Proceedings* 88(1): 74–82.

Valsangkar N.P., Eppstein A.C., Lawson R.A., Taylor A.N. (2017). Effect of lean processes on surgical wait times and efficiency in a Tertiary Care Veterans Affairs Medical Center. *JAMA Surgery* 152; 1: 42–47.

Varkey P, Reller M.K., Resa R.K. (2007). Basics of quality improvement in health care. *Mayo Clinic Proceedings* 82; 6: 735–739.

Walshe K., Freeman T. (2002). Effectiveness of quality improvement: Learning from evaluations. *Quality and Safety in Health Care* 11: 85–87.

Walshe K. (2009). Pseudoinnovation: The development and spread of healthcare quality improvement methodologies. *International Journal for Quality in Health Care* 21; 3: 153–159.

Watson G.H. (2003). *Strategy Realization Through Collaborative Action. ETM—5111.* Oklahoma City, Oklahoma State University.

Weber D., Jimmerson C., Sobek D.K. (2005). Reducing waste and errors: Piloting lean principles at intermountain healthcare. *Joint Commission Journal on Quality and Patient Safety* 31; 5: 249–257.

Wilburn D. (2012). Courage, humility, Kaizen. In Obara S. and Wilburn D. (Eds) *Toyota by Toyota. Reflection from the Inside Leaders on the Techniques That Revolutionized the Industry*. Boca Raton, CRC Press.

Womack J.P., Jones D.T. (2003). *Lean Thinking: Banish Waste And Create Wealth In Your Corporation*. New York, Simon & Schuster.

World Health Organisation (2006). *Quality of care. A Process for Making Strategic choices in Health Systems*. Geneva, World Health Organisation.

World Health Organisation (2012). *Patient Safety: Knowledge Is the Enemy of Unsafe Care*. Geneva, World Health Organisation.

Young T., Brailsford S., Connell C., Davies R., Harper P., Klein J.H. (2004). Using industrial processes to improve patient care. *BMJ* 328; 7432: 162–164.

Young F.Y.F. (2014). The use of 5S in healthcare services: A literature review. *International Journal of Business and Social Science* 5; 10: 240–248.

Index

Printed in the United States
by Baker & Taylor Publisher Services

Printed in the United States
by Baker & Taylor Publisher Services